# MYOPIA

# MYOPIA

## A MEMOIR

*For Ariel,
A very special cousin
with love,
Phyllis M Skay*

PHYLLIS M SKOY

IPBOOKS.net
International Psychoanalytic Books

Edited by NY Book Editors
nybookeditors.com

Copyright © 2017 Phyllis M Skoy and International Psychoanalytic Books (IPBooks),
30-27 33rd Street, Astoria, NY 11102
Online at: www.IPBooks.net

All rights reserved. This book may not be reproduced, transmitted, or stored in whole or in part by any means, including graphic, electronic, or mechanical without the express permission of the publisher except in the case of brief quotations embodied in critical articles and reviews.

Book design by Maureen Cutajar

ISBN: 978-0-9969996-7-0

*For my sister, Gay Lasher*

AND

*In loving memory of my parents, Jeannette and Nathan Mitnick
My beautiful niece, Rachael Lasher McKenna
and Lisa Lenard Cook*

# ALSO BY PHYLLIS M SKOY

*What Survives, a novel* (2016)

Phyllis M Skoy lives and writes in Placitas, New Mexico. She is currently retiring from a private practice in psychoanalysis and psychotherapy to live a writer's life with her husband and Australian cattle dog. Skoy is writing the prequel to her novel *What Survives*.

# ACKNOWLEDGEMENTS

I wish to express my love and gratitude to my husband, Arthur, for his never ending support and belief in me.

In loving memory of Lisa Lenard Cook for her outstanding editing.

In loving memory of Isadore Haiblum for his wise counsel on Yiddish curses.

I wish to express my gratitude to Thomas H. Ogden, M.D. for his generosity, for mentoring, for reading, for interpreting, for sharing his invaluable insights with me.

I would like to thank my sister, Gay E. Lasher, Psy.D, for her love and validation.

I would like to thank Sara Zarem, Ph.D for reading and encouraging and Asher Rosenberg, M.D. for his support and belief in me. I would also like to thank Alla and Max Zaturensky for their translation of documents from Russian to English.

## CONTENTS

1. An Awfully Hard Man to Kill . . . . . . . . . . . . . . . . . 1
2. Beyond Worlds, *Beyond Words* . . . . . . . . . . . . . . . 8
3. Dirty Jew . . . . . . . . . . . . . . . . . . . . . . . . . . . . . 25
4. I scream . . . . . . . . . . . . . . . . . . . . . . . . . . . . . . 30
5. Ruptures In Roxborough . . . . . . . . . . . . . . . . . . . 34
6. Irrevocable Bonds . . . . . . . . . . . . . . . . . . . . . . . 41
7. The House On Clinton Place . . . . . . . . . . . . . . . . 45
8. Swimming Lessons . . . . . . . . . . . . . . . . . . . . . . . 49
9. Lemon Meringue Pie in the Land of Keretaria . . . . . . 53
10. Negotiations and Reparations in the Animal Kingdom . 62
11. The Many Faces of Dora . . . . . . . . . . . . . . . . . . . 79
12. Babies and Bagels in the Convent . . . . . . . . . . . . . 88
13. Reading and Writing . . . . . . . . . . . . . . . . . . . . . 102
14. Brick Walls . . . . . . . . . . . . . . . . . . . . . . . . . . . 114
15. Music Lessons . . . . . . . . . . . . . . . . . . . . . . . . . 123
16. The Arts of Civil and Culinary Defense . . . . . . . . . . 131

| | | |
|---|---|---|
| 17. | The Television Wars | 138 |
| 18. | Moving Violations | 150 |
| 19. | Hairy Legs | 172 |
| 20. | Hiding Places | 177 |
| 21. | I Scream | 191 |
| 22. | "Mirror, Mirror on the Wall" | 205 |
| 23. | Because of Mrs. Goldblum's Garbage | 235 |
| 24. | "Suicide is Painless" | 243 |
| 25. | 353 Daley Street | 256 |
| 26. | Unveiling | 263 |
| 27. | Appendix A | 269 |

# [1]

# AN AWFULLY HARD MAN TO KILL

I've tried and tried, but I just can't kill him. I've done all he's asked of me and more, but his heart won't stop and his body won't fail. Short of putting a gun to my own father's head or sticking a knife through his belly, what can I do but feed him more potassium? And how much potassium would it take to put an end to his one remaining kidney?

I live in fear of the phone. I get calls late at night, early in the morning, at home, at work, on my cell while I'm driving to visit him. It doesn't matter if I'm with him or not, people will find me to tell me what he's been up to. If I don't answer, I'm left with lengthy messages. And people expect me to respond. He's busy making arrangements, but there's only so much he can do under the circumstances. After all, he's still alive.

He calls Bill, his realtor, several times a week. "I want you to put my house on the market."

"You're still living there," Bill replies. "What am I supposed to tell a buyer? You can have it when he dies? Oh, I don't know exactly when that will be. Sorry, no one does."

Dad begs me to put up a "for sale" sign in the front yard.

I tell him, "No one's going to buy this house on the condition that they can have it when you die."

He yells at me to hand him the phone in a tone that says: you're incompetent. You've always been incompetent and you always will be.

"I'm not a murderer," I insist. "You'll die when it's time. Meanwhile, why don't you just live?"

But who knows better than he? He believes that he's always made the right decisions, the best decisions. But now that something seems to be going terribly wrong in a lifetime of what he perceives to be accurate and calculated planning, he's pissed off at me. In the imaginary cartoon bubble I draw next to his head, I write: If Phyllis wasn't such a bloody screwup, I'd be on my way. In the bubble next to my head I write: patience.

I'm forsaking him. God's forsaking him. The fact that I'm standing by his bedside is of no importance; that he abandoned God a long time ago is of less. What it comes down to is that I have to leave because he won't die quickly enough—I am 47 years old and running a mental health outpatient clinic in another state—and that I come back a few days later isn't good enough. What sort of daughter am I anyway? I cook and feed him gargantuan feasts. I pour his wine and we toast, first to death and then to life, and still he breathes to lift his glass.

So many trips to grocery stores, butchers, gourmet grocers and vegetable stands. Sometimes when I set the bags on the same old kitchen table—the very one I've been eating at since the age of three—he can see that my eyes are puffy and red. But it's hard for his habits to change. He's too caught up in his own purpose to consider that buying all of these poisons—even though potassium can hardly be considered a poison—might be difficult for me.

He misunderstands my emotions, as he always has, and doesn't taste the tears I blend and stir into his stews and soups. I doubt he's capable of imagining me in checkout lines, reading the potassium content of each item, calculating the intake with a mathematical precision that would please him. The doctor has told him that large amounts of potassium will kill him, destroying his damaged and only remaining kidney. He'll never see my triumph transform into helpless defeat: I'm killing him with love and I'm doing a lousy job of it.

He doesn't think I'll ever get it right; so he takes matters into his own hands. The doctor said he'd help him, but the doctor has disappeared since my father went off dialysis. He needs a good death plan:

an intimate birthday with all the right foods. It shouldn't be on the scale of the celebration he had at ninety, but suited to the dignity of a dying man of ninety-one. He tells me to make the arrangements.

I call my sister. She groans. I tell her we'd better invite the neighbors from across the courtyard. My sister doesn't care much for them and she makes a growling noise by blowing air through her teeth.

On the day, we gather round to sing "Happy Birthday" and toast to a long and substantial life. "To potassium," he cries, lifting his glass in defiance of life and the Lord. He shovels down baked potatoes, tomatoes, chocolates and red wine, the enemies of his remaining kidney.

"To potassium. I don't care about the calories." These words are coming from the same father who's kept vigil over every pound lost and gained his entire life, abhorring fat. I watch him place one foot, then the other, on the broken bathroom scales. "Hmmm, ten pounds. So what? No, no, no more chocolate, I've had enough."

"Phyllis," he says, "hand me that copy of *Silas Marner*." He holds it out to the neighbor's seven-year old daughter who has joined us primarily for the food. "Here, I want you to have this. And when you finish it, read *Middlemarch*."

She thanks him and says "When you get to heaven, Dr. Mitnick, can you please ask God to send a little girl my age to live here?"

He looks away and doesn't answer. He asks me to bring his walker. "I'll have my evening shower now." He can't bear the thought that anyone will occupy these rooms, laugh, sing, play, carry on without him.

It irritates him that he's unable to plan for his absence. He twists and tosses through the night. His nightmares wake him from the intruding thoughts of others inhabiting his home, taking possession of all he's held dear, leaving lights on unnecessarily and allowing precious heat to escape through open windows.

I come into his bedroom and find him rummaging through his bedside table, reading and rereading thank-you letters he's received from me. Do I love him? Will I think of him after he's gone? My answers fail to comfort him. And when these questions nag at him mercilessly, he reaches into the drawer again and again, seeking some proof of the love he's not quite sure he deserves.

This activity makes him restless. In the middle of the night, I hear him getting out of bed in search of some relief. He's confused, and this confusion is worse to him than death itself. He wheels his walker back and forth until the cracked heels of his feet stain his stockings with blood. Again I hear the bedside table. Late into the night, I hear him searching among the odds and ends of paper clips, old photographs and thank-you notes. He opens and closes and repeats his mantra, "I'm ready, I'm ready, I'm ready." Still he doesn't die and morning comes.

I come to greet him in the morning. He shouts, "Call the mortuary, I'm a dead man." He lies there, unable to die and unable to live, stuck somewhere in between.

What horrible trick is God playing on him and why, why? He's made his funeral arrangements down to the corned beef sandwiches and salty pickles he no longer eats but wishes served to his guests after the service. He's laid out his best suit and underwear and even bathed in preparation, but still nothing has happened. The shroud—that must be it. He doesn't have the shroud.

He yells for his home attendant. "Bring me the phone. I have to call the funeral home." She hesitates.

"Give me that telephone! This is still my house." She does as she's told, but after one look, she doesn't dare to stick around. She's runs to call me on my cell phone to tell me she's quitting. She's afraid I'll escape from my father's house in New Bedford, Massachusetts to the safety of my apartment in Manhattan before she's able to reach me.

My father informs the funeral director, "It's time for you to come and get me. I'm ready."

"What are you talking about? You're not dead. I'm talking to you."

"What am I talking about? I ought to know if I'm dead or not. I'm dead, and it's time for you to come and get me. Bring the box and the shroud."

"If you were dead, we wouldn't be having this conversation."

"I'm a doctor, for crying out loud! I ought to know if I'm dead."

"But you're an ophthalmologist."

And only because Dad cannot argue this point, he replaces the phone in its cradle.

In the middle of the night, he phones his neighbor, Jack. "Take me to the hospital. I want to go back on dialysis."

"It's 2:00 in the morning." There's a pause in which Jack hopes he's reconsidering. "I'll be right over."

Jack throws on jeans and a pajama top. He lets himself in with a house key my father's given him. Jack has no idea how privileged he is. I didn't have my own key until my father was too hard of hearing to distinguish the doorbell from the television.

Jack has a glass of wine in one hand and a corked but already opened bottle in the other. My father waits for him in the living room, fully dressed, shaved and bathed, with a small suitcase sitting by his reading chair. His glasses are loosely balanced on his nose, and he holds a small book open in his lap.

"Okay," Jack seats himself on the couch. "What's going on? You want a glass?"

My father looks at the red wine he's recently regarded as the means to an end he's no longer so eager to reach. "Nope. No more of that stuff for me."

Jack sets the bottle down on the floor.

"Not even one, just for old time's sake?"

"You've got a lot more time than I do. Don't help me shorten mine."

"I thought you didn't want any more dialysis. What changed your mind?" Jack sips from his glass, undeterred by my father's abstinence.

"This." My father holds up the book in his lap, waving it to emphasize his point. "My mind was made up, and then Phyllis read this poem to me; everything changed. *The Rime of the Ancient Mariner*. It's made me want to live again."

"*The Rime of the Ancient Mariner.*"

"Yup. And I need to get over to that hospital right now."

"You're sure about this?"

"I'm sure. I haven't read this pile of books yet. I need to do that. And Coleridge...what else did he write? When you call my son-in-law to tell him I'm still alive, ask him if he can get me some more of this fellow Coleridge."

\* \* \*

It's the next evening before Jack calls. "It was Jack," my husband tells me. I wait in silence. Since my father's refused dialysis, the weakening of his kidney function has stimulated a steady secretion of poison into his bloodstream and into his brain. One of his greatest fears has come true. He's losing his mind.

But there's nothing wrong with the part of his brain that remembers the doctor telling him, "Don't worry, when the time comes, I'll help you out. When you decide you've had enough, eat lots of potassium: tomatoes, rice, red wine, potatoes. You like tomatoes, right?" My father nods, never having thought of his favorite foods as suicidal before.

"Let me make it easy for you," the doctor says. "I had this patient, lovely woman. Went on dialysis, then she decided she'd had enough. So I told her to eat plenty of tomatoes, and it was over quickly. Just like that. She went peacefully. No pain."

My father dismisses the tomatoes and moves right along to, "I'll make it easy for you," and "no pain." With all the strength he can muster, he raises himself up on his elbows and tries to lean closer to the doctor. "You'll help me out then?"

"Of course."

The doctor then whispers to my husband, "It really is an easy way to go." Has he taken several trips "over there" and discovered kidney failure to be the smoothest means of travel? In the confusion of his dementia, my father has now converted vegetables into a vial, and he knows it has to be there, somewhere.

The doctor hasn't visited my father once since he left the hospital and through several stays in the convalescent center. Since Dad stopped dialysis, the doctor's forgotten him. In his current condition, he's no longer a participating member of the "good old boy club." He's no longer Chief of Ophthalmology. He's no longer anyone but himself and my father. I can't bear to watch him search for the nonexistent vial any longer. I pick up the phone and dial the doctor. It takes a full day for him to call me back.

"How's Dad?" he asks, as if he's my brother.

"I'm having a bit of a problem with him. He says you left something in a vial for him here to help him die. Of course, I know it's not true, but he's been telling the Rabbi and all the neighbors, and some of them have been helping him look. It's upsetting. I think you need to talk to him."

A long silence ensues in which I see him conjuring courtroom scenes. He finally speaks without warmth or humor.

"I could come this afternoon around 2:00."

I smile. "That'll be just fine."

My husband snaps me back into the present, to Jack's phone call. "Jack took Dad to the hospital last night. He's back on dialysis."

"Now? He's going back on after all this time?"

I turn it around in my head. I want it to make sense. Why couldn't he have done this before the dementia set in, before I would lose him forever to those memories of events that took place long before my time? Have I ever known him? How well does one ever know another human being? Has there always been a part of him that stayed behind in those frozen places of his past where I'll never walk?

I try to imagine what his childhood was like over there, on the other side of the world. What is it like for him now to travel back there in his mind? Does he believe that the dementia is reversible? Is that why he wants to go back on dialysis? Is he hoping to return to the present?

The last time I saw him, he whispered to me that one of his aunts who'd stayed behind in the Ukraine had molested him in a barn. He'd never told anyone. But he did tell me about the size of the icicles hanging from the roofs and trees. And he did tell me about the endless potatoes he'd eaten in Russia and the first time he laid eyes on an orange in the United States. He told me how afraid he'd been, and then he laughed, as if it was all an incredible joke. He told me about the bedbugs and his hunger. And then he would say, "You just don't realize how lucky you are."

# [2]

## BEYOND WORLDS, *BEYOND WORDS*

*That row of icicles along the gutter*
*Feels like my armory of hate;*
*And you, you...you, you utter...*
*You wait!*
(Robert Frost)

Bershad, Russia, November 3, 1909
(Approximately 200 miles north of Kiev)

It's always cold in Bershad. Not the cold we know, but searing winds that burn the skin right through your mittens and clothing. My father, Nathan Mitnick, is thinking about how he will celebrate his fourth birthday tomorrow.

Often there aren't enough layers to go around, and the Mitnicks have to stuff newspapers inside their fractured boots and tattered jackets. Icicles as thick as baseball bats cling fast to the roofs and frost the windows in this village of Jews they call a *shtetl*. Zlateh and Yosef are struggling. They have a second child now, Lazarus. He will be ten months soon, and life isn't getting any easier.

Zlateh's parents disapprove of Yosef. The Schulmans never thought he was good enough for their daughter. They're certain they could have gotten the Rebbe to make a better match, but Zlateh has always had a strong will. In a time and place where people do not marry for love, Zlateh put her foot down.

"If I can't marry Yosef, I won't marry at all." This would have been a curse on the family. The Schulmans are religious and superstitious. Zlateh taunted them, singing,

> *Black cherries we bring home*
> *Red cherries are leave alone*
> *Handsome grooms we bring home*
> *Ugly ones are leave alone.*

No one can deny that Yosef was a "handsome groom." He's still the most beautiful man in Bershad. A tall, lanky but muscled man, dark skinned with black hair and blacker eyes, he looks like he might have been abandoned in the *shtetl* by a troop of gypsies instead of growing from generations of Jews.

Zlateh, on the other hand, is stocky with bullfrog eyes barricaded behind thick glasses. The villagers like to gossip and tell foolish tales. They like to say that Zlateh was much more likely to have been fathered by an invading Mongol than the meek, bearded, religious Mr. Schulman. And it's true that her dark skin, her high cheekbones and angled eyes are more Mongolian than Russian. Neither Yosef nor Zlateh has turned out as expected, and so, even if no money changes hands and no dowry is declared, even if the Schulmans sit in mourning for Zlateh, Zlateh will have her way.

Yosef's family is free-thinking and uneducated. Yosef's father likes to say, "If this is the best God can do for his chosen people, I wish he'd choose somebody else." Yosef, like his father and his father before him, is a carpenter. They are men who think with their hands, not men who study Torah. And so Yosef's family is not pleased with Zlateh. Zlateh's family thinks they are better than the Mitnicks. Zlateh is educated and not inclined to bend to her husband's will. She certainly has not bent to her parents'.

Neither the Schulmans nor the Mitnicks liked it one bit when Zlateh ran off to London to have Nathan. And then she did it again with Lazarus. No wonder they have no money. Yosef does nothing but dream and talk, talk, talk about America. This is some joke. They don't have money to eat. If Zlateh's cousins hadn't paid for her to come to London, she would have had her babies in the shtetl like everyone else. Both families wonder if Zlateh would have come back to Bershad at all if her cousins hadn't run out of money.

But in their quiet moments, before sleep or waking, both Zlateh's and Yosef's parents are uncertain. Is it right to want to hold them here? Each family has already lost one child to the pogroms, the Jew killing. No one stops it. No one cares. In 1903, just two years before Yosef's oldest son, Nathan, was born, there was Kishinev, one of the worst, and now that Nathan has been a witness, he runs to hide in the cupboard at the sound of horses or loud voices. And the war with the Japanese is making things even worse. Yosef wants to get out before he's drafted. Can anyone blame him? Jews in the Russian Army tend to disappear.

And because of this stupid war that no one in the *shtetl* wants, people are starving. The peasants are striking and demonstrating. Rumors have spread that it's the Jews' war. Yosef shakes his head in disbelief. The ignorance. The hatred. The governor does nothing, the chief of police does nothing, while the peasants rape, maim and murder innocent Jews. The police and troops stand by watching, still and silent. The "chosen people." Chosen for what?

Benny Schulman, Zlateh's brother, was a Yeshiva *buchah* (boy), quiet and respectful. He rose in the dark every day to offer morning prayers before he went off to study Talmud with the Rebbe. Yosef had never seen Benny angry. Once, he'd thrown a couple of Benny's books at him in a rage. Benny had just stood there and looked at him, not shocked or upset, but with an expression that Yosef had taken to mean that this was just another aspect of being human. Benny had picked up the books and walked away, inspecting a broken spine. When Yosef thought about it later, it was as if the spine he'd broken had been Benny's.

When Benny was murdered, he'd been on his way home from *schul* (synagogue), wearing his yarmulke, carrying his books, meditating on the Rebbe's words, like any other day. He was maybe a hundred yards from his mother's breast. The Schulmans ran outside when they heard the screams. They had stood there, helpless, while the sons of local farmers beat Benny to death. There were eight or ten of them. They cursed him, spit on him, kicked him with their boots. It had taken hours to wash the body for burial with all the blood, skin and clothing that had been tortured into one undifferentiated mass of something no longer human.

And they do not sit only with visions of Benny. Yosef knows his father never stops thinking of his other son, Yosef's brother, Yitzhak. And when Yosef sees his father looking without seeing, he knows exactly what's on his mind. Yosef feels guilty that he didn't spend more time with his brother. But first there was Nathan, then Lazarus, and Zlateh, God love her, always breathing down his neck over this or that. He still can't imagine what Yitzhak was doing in the synagogue. His father had not stepped foot in *shul* since his mother died, and that was so long ago that Yosef can barely assemble the pieces that make up her face. Now he smiles when he thinks about how much his father loved to poke fun at Yitzhak, "We'll have a Rebbe in the family after all. We know he doesn't get it from me," he'd laughed to his cronies. "Now he's growing side locks and praying. What's he praying for? That we can eat some meat with our potatoes and that the army doesn't make him go to war? Maybe my son will be a carpenter Rebbe, the next Jesus."

Yosef is unable to erase certain images from his mind. He dreams of Yitzhak, locked inside the synagogue, Cossacks on horseback guarding the doors and windows while encouraging their Christian neighbors to throw torches onto the already raging fire. He can see the hate in their faces—their cruel smiles. He can smell the burning flesh. What were Yitzhak's last thoughts? Did he wish he'd had the time to be with a woman, or did he continue to pray to his God? Yitzhak was a fool. Yosef refuses to die the same way. Yosef won't allow himself to melt away into nothing.

\* \* \*

Nathan will have a birthday tomorrow, but this is not what's on Yosef's mind. He's hurrying home from an afternoon of gambling and it's beginning to snow. He's improved his lot by a few coins, a rarity, but he's not thinking of this either. Yosef is trying to compose a letter to Dora, Zlateh's sister, who lives in New York. He wants to work it all out in his head before he asks Zlateh to write it down for him. The Schulmans thought they'd made an excellent match for her, but *Bubbe* (grandmother) Schulman screamed and ripped her clothes when Dora's new husband announced they'd be moving to America. It's been several years since they left and plenty of time, so Yosef thinks, for them to have gotten comfortable, if not rich.

It begins to snow, the wet kind that conceals pathways and leaves people bewildered just before they've frozen into statues within a quarter of a mile from home. Yosef picks up his pace and almost stumbles into his sisters' children in a huddle in front of his house. The four boys are up to something with planks of rotting wood. Yossi, the oldest, holds a box of nails.

"Uncle Yosef, guess what we're making Nathan for his birthday?"

"Come inside first. Then I'll guess. We'll all turn into blocks of ice out here." Yosef sees his nephew look at the other boys, the wood and nails, and hesitate.

"No, it's okay. Bring it inside. I'll tell Zlateh it's for Nathan. And I have something for each of you." The boys brush off the planks as best they can and follow Yosef indoors. Zlateh is quick to complain.

"*Ah rukh in zeineh kayner!*" A devil in his bones! "Look at all the snow you bring in with you. Yosef, what are you thinking? I just swept the house. "Oy, boys, take that wood back outside."

"Zlateh, look, they're making a birthday present for Nathan." Nathan, who has been hiding behind Zlateh, peeks out and smiles shyly. "Something for me?"

"Yes, and look Nathan, I have a coin for you. I have coins for all of you."

"*Ah kholeryeh oif der!*" A plague on you! "You've been gambling again! Yosef, we'll never get to America if you gamble away the little bit of money we have. You can't feed us, but you have money to gamble and give away. My mother was right." The children back up towards the door, but Yosef winks at them.

"Don't worry about getting to America. I have a way. We're going soon."

"How soon?"

"As soon as you write the letter in my head to Dora."

"And what's this letter in your head to Dora?"

"She's going to send us the money."

"*Vey iz mir*, Yosef. My father was right, too. You're nothing but a dreamer. Come on, come on," Zlateh motions to the children. "You've already made a mess, so what else?"

"We're making a sled for Nathan's birthday." Yossi is the spokesman. He's eleven and already a carpenter. His younger brother and their two cousins are still too afraid of Zlateh to come any closer to the warmth of the fireplace. Nathan sneaks another look at his cousins. No one has ever made anything just for him.

"Where's our coins, Uncle Yosef?" Yossi knows that when it comes to money, his Uncle Yosef is as forgetful as he is generous.

Yosef grins and pulls out several coins. He gives one to Yossi and one to Izzy who has just turned nine. He puts the rest back in his pocket. He looks at Nathan and says, "Your mother's right." Nathan knows better than to dispute this. Yosef tells Yossi and Izzy, "Share with your brothers." It's tough to keep promises in Bershad.

Yosef's sisters live just next door, but he goes out to tell them he has their boys. Soon it will be too dangerous even for him to be outside, and Yosef knows that he will have to feed them and let them spend the night. Well, it is Nathan's birthday. He worships Yossi. It will be a shame when he has to leave his cousins behind.

By the time Yosef returns, he has to shovel the snow from the door to open it from the outside. The boys laugh when they see him, "Snowman, Snowman," they sing. He is carrying a large bowl of potatoes from Getl, Yossi's mother. On top of that is a dark loaf of bread from his other sister, Leah.

Zlateh sees the food and wrinkles up her nose at Yosef. "What, your family thinks we can't feed their children?"

"Well, we can't feed their children." He hands her the food and she takes it. "More potatoes. I should write a book, a million ways to cook potatoes. I could make a fortune and earn the money to go to America."

Yosef laughs. "People who need to eat potatoes can't afford to buy cookbooks." He settles down by the fire to watch the boys and to give them sporadic advice. "No, Yossi, you'll need to brace that board, see, like this, or it'll all fall apart." The boys love to be with Yosef. He is full of magic tricks and games and is a playmate to them even when other adults are around. In truth, he prefers their company. He knows he is the favorite uncle.

There's no electricity in Bershad, and so with the strong winds coating the windows with snowy curtains, the room becomes dark. The only light is the fire which is shared by the boys and Zlateh, who is cooking a potato stew. When she blocks the light to stir the pot, Yosef yells to the boys to be careful, "Don't hammer your hands! You can lose fingers. You'll never be carpenters then." The boys laugh, but Nathan looks worried. By now he wants this sled more than he's ever wanted anything in his life.

The boys try to remember Zlateh's warnings to be quiet or they'll wake Lazarus, but they're excited and forget. Soon, to Nathan's delight, Lazarus is trying to walk among them. Nathan likes having him around. He's no longer the youngest and there's someone for him to teach the little of life he knows. Nathan tries to help Lazarus to walk, but he loses his temper when he falls down. It frustrates him when Lazarus won't follow his simple instructions. He grabs him by the back of the shirt and pulls him up until Lazarus screams. Zlateh thinks of Nathan as a little man and without looking to see the cause of Lazarus' distress, she hollers at Nathan to take care of his brother.

Even though he doesn't want to miss a thing, soon the smell of the stew, the cold, the dark and the flickering firelight lull Nathan to sleep. It is a childhood sleep, sound and uninterrupted. Nathan dreams that his cousins are presenting him with his birthday sled. But it's not a sled. It's a sleigh with bells drawn by four heroic white horses. The horses turn towards him. Their faces are the faces of his Uncle Yitzhak, his Uncle Benny, Yosef and Zlateh. When they turn their faces front, they are horses again, their manes so long they sweep against their tails. Nathan feels the sled rising in the silence of snow. His first flash of fear is gone. There's no cold, no sense of movement, just the buoyancy of this unearthly air.

When Nathan wakes up he is four. He's also starving. He's slept through supper and knows from experience that there's nothing left. He finds himself wrapped in a blanket with Lazarus. He wipes the sleep from his eyes and carefully unwinds himself from the blanket, wrapping the portion he's been using around his brother. He hears the hushed voices of his parents and Yossi drifting from the fireplace and cooking area. He tiptoes cautiously through the slumbering bodies of his cousins, the heat of the fire and the scent of porridge teasing him. Suddenly he remembers his birthday and the strange dream.

Yosef is poking at the wood, rousing the embers to turn to flames. Yossi is sitting cross-legged on the floor, staring into the fire. Nathan quietly sits by Yossi. Yossi doesn't acknowledge him. Zlateh comes to stir the porridge and sees Nathan. She simply says, "So, you're awake." Yosef doesn't turn around.

"Is it still snowing?" Nathan directs his question to Yossi.

"I think it's stopped," he says, as if he's been talking to Nathan all along. "It snowed all night. We couldn't open the door. We're stuck."

Nathan is disappointed that Yossi doesn't seem particularly happy to be snowed in with him on his birthday. In fact, he seems to have forgotten it entirely. It's as if Nathan fell asleep in the light and awoke in the dark. Something has changed. Nathan doesn't know what to ask.

Zlateh brings him a bowl of porridge. She offers one to Yossi but he shakes his head. "No, thank you, Aunt Zlateh."

"Eat your breakfast, boy," Yosef says sternly, his back to them.

Yossi reluctantly accepts the bowl from Zlateh. "Thank you." Nathan is not too busy eating to notice that Yossi is spooning his porridge back and forth from one side of the bowl to the other. When Nathan has finished and no one is looking, Yossi switches the bowls. Nathan grins at him gratefully. "Happy Birthday," Yossi whispers.

Nathan wants to ask to see his sled, but his father's mood imposes silence. Maybe they're waiting for everyone to wake up before they give it to him. Nathan tries to be patient. He finishes off his porridge before his cousins can wake up and take it from him. There's never enough to go around.

Izzy begins to stir and soon everyone but Lazarus is by the fire. Izzy runs over and hugs Nathan. "Happy Birthday, little cousin! Where's your sled? Yossi, where's his sled? Let's try it out."

"We can't open the door yet," Yossi says. He gets up and walks over to Yosef.

"But where is it then," Izzy insists. "Is it outside? Did you and Uncle Yosef put it outside last night after we went to bed?" Yossi doesn't answer.

Nathan can't hold himself back any longer. He sets down his bowl and runs over to his father and Yossi. "Please, Papa, can I see it? Please?"

Yossi shakes his head and walks away. Yosef finally looks at Nathan. His tone is harsh when he speaks. "Burned it... for firewood. Burned your mother's rocking chair, too. Good thing for it. We'd have frozen to death."

Nathan sits down, but he doesn't cry. What good will it do him? If he cries, his father will whip him with his belt. Even at four he has to know, he has to learn what is most important. There's nothing else to be said. Life is not about fun. It's about survival.

\* \* \*

Nathan is six years old and Yosef has been in America for a year. Zlateh and Bubbe Schulman fight all the time. When the screaming and crying frighten Laz, Nathan pulls him outside.

"Nate, why are Mama and Bubbe fighting?"

"I told you a million times why."

"Don't they like each other anymore?"

"I dunno. I wish Papa'd come home or we'd just go to America already."

"Why does Mama cry at night?"

"She misses Papa."

"I miss Papa."

"Me, too."

"How come you never cry, Nate?"

"Cause it's stupid and gets you killed."

"Crying can't get you killed."

"Yes it can. You don't remember. We had to hide and cover your mouth with a rag. You were a baby. But if the Cossacks come, or the peasants come ... they want to kill Jewish babies and you better not cry or they'll come and kill you."

Lazarus has no response for this, but after a while he asks, "Do they kill Jewish babies in America?"

"No, stupid, that's why we're going there."

"When are we going?"

"I don't know, I don't know. I don't know. Why are you always asking me so many questions? Why don't you ask *them*?" Nathan points to the hut where Bubbe can be heard clearly, and Nathan guesses that right about now she's dropped to her knees and is pulling on Zlateh's clothing.

"*Geshtikt zol ayr vayren*, he should be choked! He leaves you with two babies! What kind of man is this? How could this happen to me that my Zlateh should marry such a man? *Es zol eem drayn in de kishkis*, his guts should be twisted!"

"Mama, please stop this. Get up. Yosef will send for us when he has the money."

"*Krenken zol ayr*, a sickness should be upon him if he takes you away!"

"Mama, please. You want to wish terrible things on the father of my children?"

"Zlateh, if you go, I'll never see you again. I'll never see Nathan or Lazarus. You want your Papa should grow old without his grandsons? Why do you want to do this terrible thing to me?"

"You want my children should end up like Benny?"

"*Vey iz mir*, my poor Benny. What kind of God is this who takes all my children and grandchildren from me? You want I should die? You want to put me in the grave? Why don't you do that, Zlateh; then you can go to America?" Bubbe Schulman lies down flat on the floor, releasing her grip on Zlateh's skirt. "Okay, I'm dead. Call the Rebbe." Zlateh suppresses a giggle.

"Mama, you're not dead. You're fine." She looks down at her mother's body. She sees her old, desolate...alone. She bursts into tears.

Bubbe Schulman pulls herself up and wraps her arms around Zlateh. "I'm sorry. I'm a selfish old woman."

"No, Mama. You can come with us, you and Papa."

"You know I can't. I'm too old. But where is that no good husband of yours? *Tsezetst zol ayr vayren*, he should be smashed to little pieces." The two women sit and cry and hold each other. Zlateh wonders if her mother is right. If she leaves, will she ever see them again?

\* \* \*

It is three months later, and the day of departure has arrived. Dora has come through with the money that Yosef has been unable to dig up from the "streets paved with gold." Zlateh has one bag for the three of them. Laz grips his Zadie's sock, an item which cannot be left behind under any circumstances. Nathan has nothing but the clothes on his back and his brother's hand held firmly by his own. It's late in the evening and they are finished with their tormented goodbyes. They must move quietly in the dusk to meet the hay wagon which is going to deliver them to the German border. No one but their immediate families can even know they're leaving. Even the cousins have not been trusted. It is a matter of life and death.

Zlateh warns the boys again that they mustn't make a sound. She stands for a last look in the doorway, running her fingertips over the latch, committing it to memory before closing it for the last time. She picks up her bag with one hand and takes Nathan's with the other. He shakes it loose and tells her, "I'm big. I need to take care of Laz." Zlateh doesn't argue. She's relieved that at least she doesn't have to worry about Nathan. "Yes," she tells him. "You're the man of the family. You take good care of Laz. If he starts to cry, make sure you stuff Zadie's sock in his mouth. We can't make even one noise. If they find us, they'll kill us."

Zlateh starts to lead the boys down the road. From somewhere off in the shadows, they hear a twig snap. Zlateh drops her bag and raises her arms wide, as if this might protect her children. It is Bubbe Schulman. The children start to run to her, but Zlateh blocks the way.

"Mama," she whispers, "I told you not to do this. Why do you make it so hard?"

Bubbe Schulman grasps her daughter's skirt, "Don't leave us, Zlateh. Please don't leave us." She begins to sob.

"Mama, let go," Zlateh tries to free her skirt from her mother's clenched fingers. "You'll wake someone. Please, you have to let go." Zlateh pulls and Bubbe Schulman tugs. The hem of the skirt rips and the sound startles them. Bubbe Schulman lets go.

Zlateh picks up her bag and pulls Nathan's hand. Her whisper is hard but broken, "Come on. Bubbe will be okay." Nathan doesn't look back. He gruffly whispers to Lazarus, "Let's go. You want them to get us?"

The boys walk quickly to keep up with Zlateh. They're too frightened to remember to breathe. Now and then Lazarus trips and falls and Nathan pulls him back to his feet. He whines that he's tired, and Nathan stuffs Zadie's sock in his mouth. Only once Zlateh turns around and hisses, "You won't get a second chance. Don't make me leave you here." Zlateh's heart is on fire, extinguishing the air. Maybe she'll die, or maybe she'll make it to America, but in some well deep inside her, Zlateh knows that her mother is right. She will never see her parents again.

The wagon is where it is supposed to be. The strange little driver takes Zlateh's money in silence, counts it and scowls. "I need more money for them. Very big risk." He points a long, skinny finger with a dirty nail at Nathan and Lazarus.

Zlateh points her finger back at him, "There is no more. You take us now or give me my money back. Make up your mind."

The peasant looks at Nathan and Lazarus and then at the money in his hands. "You keep them quiet or I'll kill all three of you." He flashes a knife at Zlateh. "I'm so fast that you won't even know what's happening to you." He motions them to the wagon. Zlateh lifts the boys up first, then her bag, then herself. The peasant grimaces and says, "Remember, you're not here. Not one sound from any of you. Not one move." He covers them with the hay. As the darkness grows blacker and the air disappears, they hear him muttering, "Damn, stinking Jews."

Nathan curls up under one of Zlateh's arms, and Lazarus disappears under the other. Nathan knows it will be a long ride, and he falls asleep immediately, finally freed of his brother. Zlateh is not so fortunate. She is the defender of their fates. And even though Zlateh's put on a strong face, she is more afraid than she's ever been in her twenty-five years of life.

\* \* \*

*Nathan is riding in his sleigh. This time the sleigh is being drawn by two horses. The sleigh catches fire and Nathan tries to scream the horses into stopping. The horses turn their heads to look at him but keep racing forward. Their faces are the faces of Nathan's dead uncles, Yitzhak and Benny. Flames catch onto their manes and shoot up to swallow their eyes and ears. Nathan tries to break free, to jump, but something is preventing him. The harder he tries, the tighter he is held. The heat is stifling and Nathan can't breathe.* He twists and turns and finds himself within Zlateh's grasp, her hand held firmly over his mouth. He forces his body to relax, to let her know that the nightmare has passed. Slowly, a little at a time, Zlateh loosens her grip and removes her hand.

Nathan lies still. He's too afraid to sleep, but it's torture to be awake. He itches in so many places he can't scratch. A cramp begins to pinch and gnaw his right calf. His other leg is asleep. He closes his eyes and tries to remember the funny stories his Zadie has told him. He's had to pee for hours. He thinks of the Passover Seder and amuses himself with verses from the song his father loves about the goat. Then there are more itches and aches, a trickle down his legs, hunger, pain, fear and torment, and just when Nathan feels he can take no more or he will explode, the cart comes to a halt. There is silence and then the sound of footsteps. Hands begin to search the straw. Nathan can smell Zlateh's fear.

"Hey, you Jews still alive in there?" It is only the driver. "If you are alive, hurry up and get out of my cart. They're waiting for you."

\* \* \*

There are thirty-eight waiting for them, including the guide who will lead them over the border into Germany. Nathan and Lazarus are not the youngest. A mother is carrying her newborn in a makeshift sack tied with a knot at the back of her neck. The sack has "potatoes" written on it in large Russian letters. Her husband is carrying a tall walking stick with a small bundle tied to the top. Probably bread, maybe some cheese. Neither of them can be more than eighteen. The oldest person in the group is the guide, and he is not yet forty. As soon as he collects Zlateh's bundle of money, he herds the group into a huddle.

"You listen to me. You don't know my name. I don't know yours. You be quiet and follow close behind. Not one sound. No talking. No crying. No complaining. No stopping unless I say so. I show you the border and then you go. That's it. You make mistake, you don't listen, we all die." He points to the woods. "The toilet is over there; then we leave."

Nathan races off to relieve himself. Zlateh can tend to Laz. He's too scared to think of his brother or his mother now. Nathan wants to live. He's angry at Zlateh. Why did she bring them here? Why couldn't they just stay as they were? Why couldn't Bubbe and Zadie come—and his cousins and aunts and uncles?

When Nathan returns, the group is forming a line. The man shoves him behind Zlateh and Lazarus and warns Zlateh again, "You keep them quiet." Zlateh nods vacantly, exhausted, beyond thought. Even the one bag is now too heavy.

Displaced and confused, they disappear into the woods without a murmur or complaint. It is too dark now for Nathan to see more than a few feet in front of him, and so he follows Zlateh's thick socks and swollen shoes in a hypnotic motion that soon comes close to sleep. In this trance of his own making, Nathan does not feel cold or hunger, fear or time. There is just the one foot pushing its way in front of the other.

They stop once or twice to rest. Zlateh gives them some bread and water and a small piece of cheese. Nathan will not be able to remember whether there really was cheese or he only wished it so. In

Nathan's memory, there is only the dark and the one foot moving in front of the other.

Just as slivers of dawn begin to finally break through and light the tops of trees, at the hour when the border guards are due to change their shift, the leader with no name signals them to stop.

"We're here. You've got to go now while the guards are changing. Stay low and quiet. If they see you or even hear you, they'll shoot. Go!" The line moves forward obediently, not hesitating to say thank you or to see their guide vanish as quickly as he first appeared.

Slowly, deliberately, they cross the border. And now that they are here, they have no idea what to do. They sit together, still quiet and huddled, until the young mother bares her breast to feed her baby.

"The baby's been so good," she says. "Avraham only had to quiet her once. She started to cough."

The man she's called Avraham says nothing. He stares straight ahead as if his wife is talking about another baby, another husband. She turns away to offer her breast, but there is no response. She screams and rocks the infant who will not suck now or ever.

"Why is she screaming," Nathan asks Zlateh. Aren't we safe now?"

"I don't know if we'll ever be safe. The baby is dead. Poor woman. He must've smothered it to keep her quiet. What kind of life is this? *Ah klug tsu meineh sonim*, a curse on my enemies!" Zlateh pushes Lazarus onto Nathan's lap and goes over to the sobbing woman. Avraham does not move and Zlateh cannot part the mother from her dead child.

"Come on, Sweetheart, give her to me. I'll carry her."

"No!" The woman cries with a sound that is not human. "She'll wake up and she'll be hungry. You can't have her. You can't feed her. Let me be."

The woman sits and rocks and the man stands completely still while the group scatters into Germany. Nathan hopes his mother is wrong. She should not have said that the baby is dead. He hopes the baby will wake up, will open its tiny mouth and request the nipple again. He's angry with her for saying it even if it is true. Some things should not be spoken.

Germany is freedom, and as if waking from a deep sleep, in ones, twos and threes, they make their way silently into her protection.

Since no one has said hello, there is no need to say good-bye. When Nathan looks back, the nameless woman is still sitting, trying to rock life back into her dead child. There is no one else to be seen.

* * *

Somehow Sophie, Nathan and Larry make it across to Germany. As all of these Russian shtetl stories do, the facts vary. They stay together in one small room while Sophie secures the necessary papers to get on the boat to New Jersey. Before she leaves the two boys alone in the room, her instructions to Nathan are very clear. "Don't wander off. Take care of your brother. Don't leave this room, and don't make any noise."

My father is six. His brother is almost five. They've been quiet for I don't know how long. They've been good for I don't know how long. They wait. Larry begs; he pleads. And then they do what boys will do. They wander. They get lost. They get hungry and steal some fruit. Finally, they are stopped by a German policeman who asks them where their parents and their papers are. They are unable to answer his question. They are without parents and papers. They don't speak German. The policeman takes them into custody.

My father relates this tale with a twinkle of humor, the lighter side of a pretty scary tale. In this compartment of his mind, he recognizes that children will be children, even if they are on the run from persecution and death. This brief interlude lasts only a minute, as he thinks of his mother and her frantic search for them. I try to picture a younger Sophie, her thick glasses and heavy frame, tired, hungry and dirty from their harrowing journey, imagining that she has gone through all of this only to lose both of her children just when they are so close. She doesn't know if she will ever see them or her husband again. New Jersey is worlds away, and how can she ever face Louis without their children. I see her frantically running up one street and down another, asking in her broken German if anyone has seen two little boys.

One of the guards in the jail feels sorry for the two little boys and goes searching for their mother. Somehow, the story goes, he finds her, brings her to the jail. A little like Cinderella minus the prince, the slipper and most definitely, the happily ever after ending. How the boys are released to her when she has no papers, my father says he doesn't know. Maybe the guard just turns them over to her. Maybe she is able to get the papers while they are being held at the jail. The mechanics of all of this are really unimportant to me. What interests me is how removed my father seems to be from his own story. Yes, boys will be boys, but what is the price? What was it for him then, and now, what is it for me? Is it just another shtetl story when there have been so many? Certainly it's not for my father, and so I must believe, it's not for me.

# [3]

# DIRTY JEW

"Dirty Jew, dirty Jew, I can lick the pants off you!"

"C'mon Nate. It's the 'talians." Larry is seven. He can run and he knows how to fight. But there are five boys in this gang. And they're bigger than his nine-year old brother, even if he can box and has a strong right hook. He pulls on the sleeve of Nathan's jacket. Nathan takes a quick glance over one shoulder, decides that in this case flight is more advisable than fight, and smacks his brother on the shoulder.

"Let's go!"

They duck down an alley, passing the fruit stand where Larry normally grabs an apple when Nathan isn't looking. They fly past the kosher market where Sophie sends Nathan to buy meat on the rare occasions when Louis is working. The Italian boys know these streets as well as they do or better. In point of historical fact, they got here first. This was all theirs before the Russian Jews who didn't go to New York's Lower East Side overflowed into South Philly. They're hard to outwit and even harder to outrun.

Nathan directs Larry, "Over here," and ducks behind Mort the Tailor's dusty shop. Larry doesn't hear him and runs around the corner, straight into the gang of Italians. "Gotcha, ya little Jew bastard! Wattsamatta? Your big brotha run away an' leave ya?" He grabs Larry's jacket with both hands and shakes him until his book bag falls to the ground, scattering its contents into the stagnant water accumulated in the gutter. Larry's fear turns to anger. He's going to get a much worse beating from Louis for allowing this to happen to his school supplies.

The bully is standing so close to him that it's nothing for Larry to quickly punch him in the face, bloodying his nose and causing him to lose his grip on Larry's jacket. But not before he rips the pocket, leaving it hanging by only a few threads.

The gang charges and Nathan jumps in from behind. He and Larry are a team. They have to stick together. In the old country, there were so many cousins, aunts and uncles, grandparents. In this new world, they have only each other.

Everyone hits; everyone gets hit. Eventually they tire. The Italians run off and leave Nathan and Larry to recover what they can of Larry's school bag. His English grammar is soggy and torn. The papers are all wet, but they manage to find most of the pencils. Only now does Larry start to cry.

"Nate, I'm gonna catch it. I'm really gonna catch it. Look at this!" He holds the dangling pocket in his hand and begins to wail.

Nathan looks at Larry and thinks. His father will beat the living daylights out of them both. It'll hurt much worse than the Italians because he'll use his belt on them, one at a time, and he won't care whose fault it was or who started it. The ripped jacket is new, at least it's new to Larry, and it was in relatively good shape. Nathan will be beaten for not taking better care of his brother, and Larry will be beaten for not taking better care of his things.

Nathan grabs Larry by the arm. "C'mon. I'm gonna see what we can do." Larry's wailing is reduced to the sniffling of hope. He lifts his soggy book bag over his free arm and allows Nathan to pull him along. Nathan pauses in front of the tailor's. He's never spoken to Mort before. All he knows about Mort is that he too has escaped from Russia, and even though his shop is so cluttered and dusty that it looks like he's had it for a hundred years, he arrived in South Philly only a few months before Nathan's family. Larry pulls away from his grasp, "Nate, we don't have no money."

"No," Nathan the teacher replies, "we don't have *any* money."

"Yeah, that. Let's go!"

Nathan hesitates but knows that at this point he has little to lose. He is used to being in charge and he tells Larry, "Wait here."

A very squeaky door lets Mort know when anyone enters his shop. He is almost always in the back, stitching and eating, eating and stitching. Now he gathers his overstuffed frame from the antiquated sewing machine chair and reluctantly sets his second pastrami sandwich of the hour back onto its greasy paper wrap. He slowly ambles out to see who is disturbing his lunch. He's disappointed to see Nathan, a child who clearly has no money. He spreads his large frame over a streaked glass counter, leans as far forward as it will allow and asks in heavily accented English, "Whaddya want, kid?" Nathan, who has known real fear, is not afraid. The worst that can happen, he'll get tossed out.

"It's my brother. He's waiting outside. We got in a fight."

"Does he look as bad as you?" Nathan's eye is beginning to turn slightly purple with hints of orange.

"Worse. Much worse. But not as bad as he'll be once my father sees his jacket."

"Whaddya mean?" Mort knows. He's been there before but not with this kid. He wiggles his tongue between two front lower teeth, trying to coax out a stray piece of pastrami. It's wedged in pretty deep. He pushes harder, sucks in his breath and tries again. No luck. Nathan senses that a whimpering Larry might tweak Mort's sensibilities.

"Wait, I'll show ya." He backs out the door. Larry is busy trying to convince a stray dog into petting distance. Not wasting any time with explanation, Nathan pulls Larry into the shop. Before Larry can object, Nathan holds up the dangling pocket.

"I see whatcha mean," Mort sighs. If he helps them, they'll just keep coming back. And he won't get any work from this one. The kids won't tell their parents, and it doesn't look like they could afford a tailor anyway. They're greener than he is and probably stitch up their own clothes. But he's got a boy Nate's age back in Russia he's trying to get over here, and he knows the Philly streets are tough. And business is slow. "Ya gonna get into anoder fight, and then you'll be back wantin' me to fix ya up for notin' agin."

"I promise I won't." Nathan raises his right hand solemnly.

"Yeah, well, just in case ya break da promise, it ain't gonna woik wid me. Only da one time."

He points a sausage shaped finger at Larry who quickly removes his jacket. His face is streaked with tears but at least he is temporarily out of danger. He hands the jacket over to Mort. The boys watch his large frame disappear into the back room.

"Hope he doesn't take too long," Nathan worries. "Then we'll catch it for being late from school." There are so many ways to "catch it." Sometimes there doesn't even have to be a reason.

Nathan and Larry wait quietly. They're out of steam from the fight and tired from the worry. There are no chairs in the small shop, and they sit cross-legged, side by side on the floor, propped up against their book bags. Larry's is wet and smells musty. He begins to sob quietly, having nothing to divert his attention from the damaged grammar book and the certain knowledge that it is bound to bring about more pain and suffering. Nathan waves his hand at him.

"Shuddup. You want him to think you're a crybaby?"

Larry sniffles a few more times but stops. He is quiet until Mort finally emerges from the back, waving the jacket proudly.

"Like new. Just like new. You don't do better if ya go to one of da big shops." He holds the garment open for Larry and helps him back into it. The pocket is back in place with no sign of the tear.

"Tell him thank you," Nathan coaches Larry.

"Thank you, mister." Larry rushes for the door. He has other things on his mind.

"Thanks a lot, mister," Nathan leans on his toes over the counter to shake Mort's hand. Mort is a bit taken aback by the boy's manners, not knowing quite what to make of this miniature adult, but he reaches out and takes it. He's surprised by the strength of the handshake.

"Ya welcome. Now no more fights, ya heah?" The door bangs shut on his words.

The brothers run the rest of the way home. By the time they get to Daly Street, they are breathing hard. Sophie is leaning out of the front room window, waiting for them. She gestures to no one in particular,

"Late again. Why do I tell them anything, it's like I am talking to the wall." She shakes her fist and shouts into the street, "Gay in drerd," "drop dead." This is nothing she doesn't suggest to her family members several times a day. The neighbors are used to it. But it's still enough to arouse the mild curiosity of those who are perched on stoops and in windows close enough to take in the scene. Sophie is aware that she is center stage and mutters under her breath, "Dumkop, mish zikh nisht arayn," "dumbbell, stay out of this." It is unclear whether she is referring to the neighbors or Louis who now frames the window behind her. Nathan and Larry hesitate nervously in the street. Louis leans in front of Sophie and commands in Yiddish, "Get in here, now!" The boys hurry inside and shut the door behind them. It is up to those who have been left so unceremoniously outside in the cold to ponder which will be the more painful, Sophie's tongue or Louis's switch.

# [4]

# I SCREAM

*I scream*
*You scream*
*We all scream*
*For Ice Cream*
(The Courtship)

My mother and father are in their early thirties. The Great Depression is in full swing. Hitler is yelling crazy things and waving his arms about. Here in Philadelphia, folks aren't really sure what to make of him. And at the moment, there are more immediate concerns. The sky is falling. People are leaping to their deaths from tall buildings. Banks are failing. There are soup lines. Who would have thought this could happen in America?

Miraculously, everyday life goes on. Jeannette and Nathan are courting. When he can beg or borrow trolley fare, he takes the long ride to the other side of the tracks, Roxborough. Jeannette lives there with her father, stepmother, a younger brother and a younger sister in a large stone fortress high on a hill.

Nathan Mitnick is a handsome man. He has the good fortune to resemble his father. He's healthy and strong with a tanned, muscled body from summers of lifeguarding in Atlantic City. Jeannette is fat. Not merely plump, obese. She has the misfortune to resemble her mother. In a worn photograph, they stand together on the beach: Nathan, not tall but dark and lean in a well-fitted swim suit, his arm around Jeannette, short, white and fleshy in an oversized skirted suit that is meant to hide her flaws but fails miserably.

Chance brings this unlikely pair together. Nathan's friend David and Jeannette's friend Anne throw a party. Nathan is introduced to Jeannette. She's shy but intelligent. He's shy but ambitious. Neither can believe their good fortune.

Nathan has no money so they walk in Wissahickon Park. It's a Sunday afternoon in early summer. The park is green and in full bloom. The sun is warm and strong. Nathan talks and Jeannette listens. She's content just to look at him. He's delighted to have such a rapt audience. His brothers and sisters tell him he's full of bull. Jeannette hangs on every word. These patterns are established in the early days of their courtship.

Nathan doesn't talk about the past. He's committed to the future. In the fall he'll go back to night school and his laborer's job at the Philadelphia Inquirer. But it's summer now. He is vigorous, even enthusiastic, from long days of swimming and working out with the other lifeguards at the shore. Everything is possible. Nathan dreams aloud. He'll finish college, and then become an engineer or maybe even a medical doctor. He believes in working for himself. No boss standing over him, thank you very much. No, he doesn't need anyone checking up on him, telling him how to do his job. Jeannette is transfixed. She's seized by unaccustomed passion. She invites him to dinner. He accepts.

Jeannette woos Nathan in the way she knows best: food. She bakes. Her stepmother, Rose, cooks. Nathan shows up every Sunday, walks with Jeannette in the park, and takes her back to the stone mansion where he has now become a regular at Sunday dinner. He's in awe of their abundant life. He watches wide-eyed as Jeannette turns real butter into chocolate cakes. He can't help but stare the first time he sees Jeannette's father devour a whole loaf of bread with his meal. Rose gestures at assorted platters and bowls, "Eat, eat. Help yourself, eat, please. You're so thin." Nathan digs in. Jeannette sits back and smiles. This is bliss.

But bliss is brief. There's always some nasty pricking, some insy tinsy nagging and tugging at the insides, an inner alert to imperfection. That is, of course, if the object of one's desire is mortal.

Now it's late summer. The park is heavy with wet heat and the pungent odor of dying flowers. Nathan drinks this in and describes it in poetic detail to Jeannette.

"There's death all around us, making way for new life. Nature is glorious. It gets rid of all the unnecessary garbage, cleans up and starts over. Just look at how it's done. Nature is pretty darn smart." He hesitates, shifts course.

"I wish my brothers were smart. I tell them, you have to go to school, like me. You can get out of South Philly. You want to spend the rest of your lives here? What for? There's nothing here. You want to live like Mom and Pop? Marry some shlump and end up in a hovel with a brood of children?" Nathan shakes his head. Jeannette is quiet. She likes it better when he's romantic and sticks to nature. She's only met his family a couple of times, but she likes them and privately thinks he ought to lighten up. She smiles thinking of his sister, Rosie. She's always telling him to stop being such a prude. Nathan misinterprets the smile as encouragement.

"Ever since my father died, I've felt responsible for them. My mother told me I had to help her bring them up. So I worked hard to put food on the table. It hasn't been easy. There I was just starting out in college and I come home one day to see there's a black ribbon hanging on the door." Jeannette is hearing this story for the first time.

"What do you mean? What happened?"

"That's how I found out my father was dead. I left in the morning, and when I came home there it was. He'd been sick for so long. I didn't know he was dying." Tears come into his eyes. Jeannette rests her hand on his.

"But those two never listen. Larry isn't so bad. He's smart, but he just doesn't think. Bobby's a schlemiel. And Rosie. She comes to me and asks me should she get married. What am I going to tell her? She dropped out of school. She won't do any better. Such a pretty girl. So I ask her if he treats her well and if she loves him. She says yes, so..." he shrugs, purses his lips and does a gesture that looks like he's throwing in the towel. "I don't know if my father could have done any better."

"Rosie's a sweet girl. And Sammy seems like a nice man." Jeannette feels defensive of the spirited sister who teases her and more importantly, teases Nathan.

"Yes," Nathan sighs. "She's a good girl. She helps my mother with Ruthie. I can't believe they had another baby when my father was sick and out of work." He shakes his head again. These people might be his relatives, but their thinking is beyond him. No sense whatsoever.

"I think it's romantic," Jeannette grins and pokes him playfully.

"There was nothing romantic about it, believe you me." If he's glimpsed any flirtation between his parents, he's managed to cordon it off to some remote area of his brain. All he can see now is the fighting, Sophie's endless complaining and belittling of Louis. He'd been embarrassed and shocked when he finally realized she was pregnant.

Jeannette sees his discomfort and leaves it alone. She's sad for a moment, thinking of her baby sister, Kathie. Now that was romantic. She's sure that her father and mother loved each other very much. But it killed her mother. The day Kathie entered the world, Kate left. Jeannette is lost in these thoughts when she hears the jingle of the ice cream cart. She brightens instantly.

"Oh, look Nathan. Ice cream. It's so hot. I'm going to get one."

Nathan nods but doesn't smile. He only has enough money to ride the trolley car back to South Philly. Does Jeannette know this? She must. She doesn't expect him to pay. And yet, she doesn't offer him one.

They walk along, side by side, Jeannette contentedly licking her ice cream, Nathan waiting and hoping for her to offer him a bite. He will not ask. Her face softens with the comfort of the cool ice. His hardens with what he interprets as her selfishness. When he thinks of how he's being wronged, he fights back tears.

He watches Jeannette pop the last bit of ice cream and the tip of the cone into her mouth. It's not possible that she has not even offered him a bite. He's too overwhelmed by this flaw to even mention it. He never tells her how he feels. They go back to Roxborough, their Sunday dinner and court until they marry.

# [5]

# RUPTURES IN ROXBOROUGH

Jeannette works as a mapmaker at Curtis Publishing in downtown Philadelphia, although she has graduated first in math from the University of Pennsylvania. Curtis Publishing does not hire young married women. They have a tendency to become pregnant. So no one can know that Nathan and Jeannette are married. They are assumed to be living in sin right under Jeannette's father's roof.

Abraham Berg, Jeannette's father, also comes from Russia. But even in Russia, he is able to rise far above the Mitnicks in stature. Abe's father is a highly valued tailor who is allowed to travel to places where Jews are restricted from living or traveling under the Czar. When Abe is seventeen years of age, he and his father immigrate to the United States.

As an adult, Abe establishes a successful clothing factory. He brings over and marries his first cousin, Kate, a common thing to do in those days, and they have four children, Jeannette being the oldest, then Beatrice, Benjamin and Kathie. Kate is in her early forties when Kathie is born, and she dies in childbirth. Abe's sister and brother-in-law beg to take the baby, Kathie, off his hands until he remarries. Abe doesn't want Jeannette or Beatrice to have to feel responsible for their baby sister and so he agrees. But when he marries Rose a couple of years later, his sister keeps stalling when it comes to giving Kathie back.

Rose is perfectly willing to raise Kathie and Abe continues to ask his sister for her return, but he doesn't insist. This is never resolved, and so Kathie grows up in the home of her Aunt Ruth and Uncle Al and their two children, Beatrice and Charles.

When Jeannette and Nathan move into my grandfather's home, newly married and in their early thirties, they take over the upstairs apartment. It's complete in that it has its own kitchen and bath, living room and two small bedrooms, but it is the attic and can only be accessed by a ladder that has to be lowered down onto the second floor of the house.

It's March of 1943, and it is wartime. Jeannette and Nathan and their two year-old daughter, Gay, are still living with Abe and Rose. So are Jeannette's brother, Ben, and sister, Bea. Kathie is 17 and comes and goes, furious at her father for never reclaiming her. She's a pretty girl with flaming red hair who loves to dance and ice skate. Abe is ridden with guilt when it comes to Kathie, and so he alternates between attempts to be stern and out and out spoiling. Ben works with his father in the factory. Bea is a Marine and works as a court stenographer. For entertainment, Jeannette, Bea and Kathie all play the piano and sing. This is something they enjoy doing together at the grand piano in their father's large house on Fleming Street.

Nathan has given up the study of engineering. He now travels from Philadelphia to and from school in Kansas City to study medicine. Why should he have a boss when he can work for himself? The only thing that worries this future is the fact that he cannot memorize his anatomy. He sits in the attic in Philadelphia with the offending book in his lap, wishing he were anywhere else. He is here visiting his family after some months away. Gay does not recognize him and cries when he tries to kiss her.

On this particular day, Jeannette is off at work and Gay is downstairs in the kitchen with Aunt Rose. Grandpop is married to Aunt Rose and Gay knows to address her as such, even though she is in every other way possible Gay's grandmother.

Now Nathan imagines himself sitting in front of a large mahogany desk in a cushioned rolling chair. His patients sit on the other side of this enforced separation, decorated with classical textbooks lined up in front and held together by two weighty brass bookends in the forms of the ancient mariner. On one side of the bookends is a human skull. On the other side, and at the end of his desk, is a skeleton dangling from a metal perch. He pictures himself in a stylish silk and woolen suit, a crisp white shirt and an elegant silk striped tie. His shoes are expensive and polished Italian brown leather. In reality, Nathan is dressed in boxer shorts and Abe's old bathrobe. A pair of worn athletic socks keeps his feet warm.

Nathan is unhappy at this moment. Yesterday evening, he had a quarrel with Jeannette. He was trying to study, and Jeannette and Bea were playing the piano and singing songs he didn't recognize. Music is not something he has any time for anyway. He had to march downstairs and yell at them to be quiet. Bea just smiled and said, "Sorry, Nathan, but this is my house, too." Jeannette had not said a word in his defense, but she stopped playing and came upstairs. Bea went right on playing. Jeannette said she had every right. That was how it started.

Time has a way of getting away from him up in this attic. He yearns for his freedom from family, from study, and for a place of his own. This desire distracts him from his purpose. These damned bones are the primary obstacles he sees to his success, like prison bars holding him back. The whiff of something baking drifts into his nose from downstairs. He realizes that Rose must be baking with Gay. Of course, Gay is too young to bake but not to lick bowls.

What would any of them do without Rose? She is the only person he feels safe around in this house. He doesn't feel that she judges him. Even Jeannette seems sometimes aligned with her siblings who make sarcastic comments about Nathan's ongoing studies. He slams the anatomy book shut at the clavicle. He rests his head on it and falls asleep.

Jeannette walks in the door at 5:30. She's taken the streetcar from Curtis Publishing (who didn't let her go even when she became pregnant with Gay and they discovered she'd lied about not being married) to Roxborough, where she's stopped off several blocks before Fleming Street to the grocer to pick up some things for Gay and

Nathan. Rose cooks for everyone, but Gay needs to have her juice and milk upstairs, and Nathan has to have his tea. She also picks up a fresh loaf of bread for her father's dinner. Since the war is on and everything is rationed, even the fuel to heat the house, Jeannette uses Gay's ration book for her purchases.

Jeannette greets Rose who tells her that Gay is still napping in her grandparents' bed upstairs. As far as she knows, Nathan is on the third floor studying. Jeannette leaves the bread with Rose and makes her way up the long staircase to the second floor and then up the ladder to their apartment. By this time, she is out of breath. She enters the open kitchen to find Nathan still sleeping with his head on Gray's Anatomy. She drops her bags down onto the table close to him. His head jerks off the book and up into the air. "Did you just get home?" he asks.

"Did you have a nice nap?" she retorts, setting her pocketbook next to the groceries and taking off her coat. She throws the coat across a chair and begins to unpack the purchases into the small icebox. He recognizes her tone as one of irritation.

"I didn't mean to nap," he explains. "Memorizing these bones is so boring, I fell asleep. I can't seem to make it stay in my head."

Jeannette shuts the icebox door firmly. She takes her pocketbook off the table and sets it hard on the chair where she's thrown her coat. She pulls out another chair and sits across the table from Nathan. "Well, you better figure out how to make it stick in your head," she says, crossing her arms and plunking them down in front of her. "We can't live here forever, you know. My father and I aren't going to support us while you sit here and fall asleep because it's 'boring.' Are you planning to flunk this class a second time?"

"I'm trying not to, Jeannette." Nathan pushes the Gray's Anatomy away from him.

"I think you're just going to have to try a little harder or Gay will be graduating from high school before you pass the Boards." She gets up and picks her coat up from the chair and walks over to a coat rack that stands near the stairway and hangs it so violently that it falls to the floor. As she bends down to retrieve it, Nathan picks up the Gray's and throws it across the room. It lands on its opened spine, a bunch of pages crushed beneath it.

"That's it, Nathan. Kill the book. That'll help us a lot. Well, I'm going to tell you something," she says, throwing her coat back up on the rack. She turns to him, her face still red from the cold outside and now from the heat firing up from within, "If you don't pass this class this very time, you're going to work with Ben in my father's factory. I've had enough!"

Nathan gets up and stomps loudly to his fallen book. "I don't need more pressure than I have already. I could use a little support," he snarls as he rescues the Gray's and tries to smooth down the bent pages.

"A little support," Jeannette faces off. "We live in my father's house and eat his food without paying a cent. I'm working full-time at Curtis drawing maps. In my spare time, along with taking care of a two year-old, I'm transposing foreign knitting patterns for *The Ladies Home Journal*. You wanted to change from engineering to medicine, and I supported that, even though my father thought it was about time you finished something and went to work. Just how much support do you need?"

Nathan doesn't know quite how to respond, so he refuses to come down to dinner. He allows himself some time for pouting before he returns to his studies, but he does eat the tray of food Jeannette carries up the flight of stairs and ladder so that he shouldn't go hungry. He's so angry that the food churns inside him, causing his stomach to make noises of complaint. He holds in the tears of frustration. His daughter doesn't know who he is, and he knows this kind of mood in Jeannette. There will be no sex. Tomorrow he'll take the train back to Kansas City, and he can't be sure when he'll see them again.

\* \* \*

The war seems never-ending, even though The Bergs hardly have the worst of it. Nathan's sister Rosie has told him that the family in Russia no longer answers her letters. The Mitnicks are quite concerned by the interruption of this communication. It's the only way they have of knowing if their relatives are all right. The rumors are unimaginable.

By June of 1943, Jeannette manages to squirrel away enough money to take the train to Kansas City. She takes a leave of three months from her job at Curtis. She explains to them that Gay is having a terrible time adjusting since Nathan left, even though Gay is actually a happy little girl, who loves her Aunt Rose and Grandpop and all of her aunts and uncles. She's a precocious child with pretty blond curls and enormous brown eyes. Everyone adores her.

The journey by train is dreadful. Soldiers pack the cars from one end to the other, shouting to one another and singing war songs. There are no seats when Jeannette boards, so she sits on her suitcase with Gay on her lap. Cigarette smoke fills the car and it's difficult to breathe. After only a few hours, Gay is sick with fever and diarrhea and screaming and crying at the top of her lungs. The toilets are filthy.

A sympathetic young fellow in army uniform gives Jeanette his seat. He takes her place on her luggage, as much as to guard it as to have a place to land. Jeannette is running back and forth to the toilet with Gay. Gay is sick for the entire two and a half days it takes for them to arrive in Kansas City. When Gay wakes up that morning, her fever has broken but she is weak. When Nathan comes to greet her with open arms, she runs back to Jeannette screaming, "Mommy, Mommy!"

\* \* \*

It is August of 1944. Nathan is finished with medical school and is working at Newark Eye and Ear on his specialization. He has managed to pass anatomy and move on. Jeannette and Gay go to Newark every other weekend to stay at the hospital and visit with him. Gay loves to ride these trains because the conductors give her coloring books and crayons to keep her occupied. The coloring books are filled with different sorts of trains. These are what Gay looks forward to the most about these trips, other than the cone-shaped paper cups next to the drinking fountain near the toilets. She is three and a half and has to be very careful with these flimsy cups because they collapse so easily.

But when they travel for these weekends in Newark, the train is the only fun. Gay is bored and Mommy and Daddy argue. Space is cramped because they stay with Daddy in the hospital, and the food is not at all like Aunt Rose's. Hospital food is bland and made for people who've just had surgery. There's no one for Gay to play with and no aunts to take her to the movies. Sometimes Mommy and Daddy forget she's there. Daddy talks about wanting to fight in the war, and Mommy reminds him that he has a family to support. They go for walks, but mostly they watch Daddy draw eye procedures on napkins and golf balls.

Over the next few years, all recorded history ceases. Mommy stops writing in Gay's baby book. Only the stories Gay and I hear much later, along with pictures and letters we discover after our parents' deaths, can lead us shakily into a time of our own memory. There is a photograph of Nathan in Philadelphia, standing in front of a sign that reads, "Nathan Mitnick, Doctor of Osteopathy." We find this in his office while going through his papers.

"He was an osteopath?" I ask my sister. "I can't believe that. He had as much respect for osteopaths as he did for chiropractors. None."

"This must have been the practice he had in Philadelphia before we moved to New Bedford. He couldn't get it going."

"Look at this letter he wrote to his friend," I hand her a letter I've pulled out of a drawer that speaks of an easier road to obtaining a medical degree and a license along with a steady stream of referrals my father promises he will be able to get in New Bedford. My father suggests to his friend that he consider coming to New Bedford as well.

In the next photograph we see of our mother, she is standing in our tiny apartment in the north end of New Bedford. She has a frown on her face and is pregnant with me. My sister is standing next to her. She doesn't look happy either. There are no records to fill in how we arrived here. We call them "the missing years."

We discover another photo of the outside of this first apartment. This sign hangs next to the entrance and reads, "Dr. Nathan Mitnick, M.D." This is the only designation we've ever seen. The conclusion that we come to is that Nathan was ashamed of being an osteopath and equally of the failure of his practice in Philadelphia. So he erased them in our history. I think this is too bad. In my mind, he's always gone from pauper to prince, and so I had expected that I should be able to do the same.

# [6]

# IRREVOCABLE BONDS

I'm a wet bundle on my sister's eight year-old lap. My diaper is soaked and my face is covered with mucus and tears. I can smell her fear and feel her terror spill over against me. Does she know that I'm a time bomb? I know it, even though I've only just burst from my mother's womb. My recent arrival seems to have ruptured her brain.

My father never comes near me or touches me. From the beginning, my timing is off. My birth is an aneurism, a bloody explosion. And now my mother's just like me. A bundle. She can't walk or talk or eat or do anything on her own. In truth, with just two weeks of life under my belt, I can do more. I can cry and wave my infant arms and legs. My 42 year-old mother just lies there.

The room is dark where we sit like one. I cry for my bottle and a dry diaper, but my sister is too terrified to move. I scream and rage for her as well. Finally, I stop, as it's of no use. We're stuck here together, joined to my mother in a coma of our own.

Our home is a two-room apartment. One room is my father's medical office and is off limits to everyone but his patients. He's still new in town, and so they're very few. The second room functions as a kitchen, a small eating area and two tiny partitions for sleeping. My bed, for the time being, is my mother's bureau drawer.

No one knows we're here. The shades are pulled tight to protect against prying eyes. My father's afraid of strangers. While my mother could still speak, my father forbade her to talk to any of the neighbors. They're outsiders and must never know what goes on inside. Even the daylight isn't allowed in. My father's insistent in this. It seems unlikely that we'll move from this chair for many hours.

I have no language. There's no way for me to understand all the noises my father's making. I can't know that he's yelling to my sister, "Gay, your mother's dying. Stay here, don't move, take care of your sister!" I begin to wail only when he bangs the door on his way out. My sister hopes she might have overheard him telephone someone to come, but she has no idea now that he's gone if this is real or imaginary. The hospital is in Boston, an hour away, and we're a five-hour drive from the nearest relative. No one will be here soon. But all of this is beyond me.

Gay's never held a baby until now. She has no idea what to do with me. Her tummy is still sore and my squirming in her lap only aggravates the wound. It could be coincidence that her appendix exploded within days of my mother's "accident," but it does seem that we've all detonated together. Only my father appears intact.

My sister feels my wetness leak onto her skirt and knows that I must be changed. She's known it for some time now, but she's been hoping she can avoid it. It's not that she's frightened by the mess, the smells or my disgusting diaper. She's frightened of somehow killing me or of dying herself. If she moves from this position, anything might happen, and she's not sure it's worth the risk. She slides one foot forward and when nothing terrible happens, she pushes herself up from the chair, swinging me in her skirt like a hammock.

I love the ride, so I protest when she plunks me down on the kitchen table. The trance is broken. We are two. She looks from me to the pile of clean diapers on the other side of the room and picks me up again. Together we make our way to the diapers. Gay grabs a towel from a stack of clean laundry, throws it over the pile and rests me on top, unpinning my dirty diaper before she realizes that the garbage is on the other side of the room and she has no wet cloth to clean me. She's not sure what to use or how to do it anyway. She takes in a deep breath, rolls the used diaper into a ball and slides the fresh one under me. It's 1949. There are no Wipes or Pampers with Velcro.

Gay picks up a large safety pin and prays she won't stick me. She tries to remember how the thing was pinned when she took it off, but she has no idea. So she folds it this way and that, deciding each time that it's too thick to pin. This rolling about is a new game for me. I don't cooperate by holding still, but soon I pick up her anxiety and tire of it. I begin to whimper.

She manages to close both safety pins and lifts me off the laundry pile. The diaper sinks to my knees. I kick my feet and the diaper with delight, but Gay just studies me. She lays me back down and systematically starts all over again. Life is already dictating what is to become her pragmatic approach to most things. There is a way, and damn it, she'll just have to find it.

I slip in and out of consciousness. Here and there, her fingers fumble against me until she's satisfied. Sometime during my sleep, she's warmed a bottle for me. I wake to find a nipple pressed against my lips. It's just the right temperature. She must have tried it out herself. She's had no one to observe.

Gay's easier with me now. She strokes my head and baby-soft skin while she hums a tune our mother used to sing. In this way, we sit and comfort each other. It's the birth of our relationship.

We're interrupted by angry voices. A wild Rose with thick, prickly thorns and the slightly broken stem she drags behind her: my father's sister and her husband.

"Who the hell does my idiot brother think he is?" she asks of no one in particular, raising her hands, beseeching the Almighty to explain it to her. "How could he have gone off and left an eight year-old child with a two week-old baby? My brother the doctor! He thinks he's so smart." She turns to my sister. "Let me tell you something about my brother. He thinks he's better than us. But who does he call every time there's an emergency? His no-good sister, that's who. Well, here we are. How's your poor mother, sweetie?"

Gay stares at her. My uncle steals me from Gay's arms and waltzes around the room in circles.

My aunt looks from my uncle to my sister and then back to my uncle again.

"Well, never mind," she says. "Sammy, give me that baby before you drop her and we've got two people with smashed brains." She covers her mouth. "I'm sorry, honey," she says to my sister, as my uncle places me in her arms. "Hi, sweetie pie. I'm your Aunt Rosie. And I'm going to take good care of you."

"I want her back. Give her to me." Gay holds out both arms.

"Sweetie, you've been sitting with her for hours. Don't you want a rest? She's fine. See?"

But I learn quickly how to be in synch with my only ally. I begin to screech with every ounce of strength in my fourteen-day-old body. We're in this together. Our only reliable world is each other. My tiny fist socks Aunt Rosie in the eye. As she turns her head, a baby foot collides with her ear. My face is turning red and all four limbs are flailing. She practically throws me back to my sister. I snuggle against Gay's chest, instantly quiet. Rosie stalks to the tiny kitchen where she and Sammy busy themselves with food. Gay checks my diaper and sits back down with me in her arms. I snuggle into her body and instantly fall asleep, tired out from my brief but wearying tantrum.

"I'm making my famous potato salad," Aunt Rosie shouts to Gay.

"I hate your potato salad," Gay whispers in my ear. But I must have been soundly asleep because I grew up loving my Aunt Rosie's potato salad. I'm quite sure I would've hated it, too, if I had only heard.

# [7]

# THE HOUSE ON CLINTON PLACE

In my earliest memory, I'm crying and throwing up in my bedroom on Clinton Place. Throwing up hurts a lot. Mommy is in my bedroom with me, holding a bucket next to the opened side of my crib and is comforting me with soft words. "It's okay, honey. Don't cry. There, there." I sniffle and throw up some more. It's a reddish-brown color.

Mommy looks down and inspects it. "It's not blood, Sweetie, it's tomato sauce. I don't think you can eat that yet. This is the second time it's upset your stomach."

I stop throwing up and lean back onto my pillow. Mommy wipes my mouth with a wet washcloth. It's warm, and I like how it feels. She bends over to pick up the bucket, but her hand freezes in mid air. Then she lurches towards me, knocking over the bucket and spilling its contents onto the floor. She has a monster grimace on her face, and she keeps lurching towards me. I scream and scream. Daddy comes running and carries Mommy away.

In my next earliest memory, I'm also in my crib in the bedroom at Clinton Place. I am just over three years old when we move there from the apartment on Dartmouth Street, and it's the only home I can remember. I'm supposed to be having a nap. I can't sleep and I want out of my crib. I throw my plastic lamb and shout and cry. When I stop to catch my breath, I hear Gay talking to Mommy. "She doesn't want to sleep," my sister says.

"But it's her nap time," my mother replies.

"She's too old for a crib and doesn't need a nap," my sister argues. I start to cry again to support my sister's point of view.

"Well, then you go get her and watch her," Mommy shouts at Gay. "I have a headache. I think I need to lie down."

I hear a crash. Gay calls Daddy out from his office. Mommy's lurched and made another monster face. Gay calls it a seizure when she comes to rescue me. "Mommy's had a seizure," she tells me. I don't know what that is, but I do know it's connected to the scary Mommy who appears so suddenly from the nice, sleepy Mommy who reads to me in bed.

It's 1952, and Daddy is serving his time in the military. He never got to fight in WWII, and he's fiercely patriotic. This county is giving him a chance, and he wants to fight in Korea to prove himself. He is also weary of Mommy's seizures and operations. He'd rather fight the war in Korea than deal with an angry 11 year-old and a tantrum-producing three year-old.

My sister no longer has a functioning mother. Sometimes my mother doesn't even remember who my sister is or that she has a toddler, me. My 11 year-old sister runs the household. She terrorizes the help my father hires, frustrating them until they quit.

My mother has been on Phenobarbital. It has kept her confused, more forgetful than her short-term memory loss can be held accountable, and still she is having seizures. The doctor is trying Dilantin, but breakthrough seizures occur as he attempts to regulate dosages. She is depressed and sleeps a lot. She has enormous mood swings. She's had several operations on her brain in the three years I've been around. Her hair begins to grow and her head is shaved again. Wigs are expensive, and so my mother wears a scarf wrapped around her head to hide scars and baldness. She is frightened. She's no longer the wife who told her husband what he could do if he didn't pass anatomy. She doesn't even remember saying it.

On the day that my mother and I are scheduled to return home after my birth, she falls from the edge of her hospital bed, completely dressed, while waiting for my father to come to take us home. She has what we always refer to as "the accident," an aneurism that comes very close to taking her life. For the first five years of my life, and off and on for the rest of her life, she struggles with the brain she's been left. We are forever bound in the explosion of my birth and her brain. At the time of my birth, my mother is 42 years old.

My father flies back and forth from New Bedford to Washington in his friend's small plane to fulfill his military service in the Pentagon. He's a Captain, the level automatically given to physicians. My father is handsome in his army uniform. He examines famous eyes, those of General Marshall and President Eisenhower. He's written letters to apply for duty in Korea, but my mother's sister, Bea, has thrown a javelin into his plan. She's written her own letter, containing a vivid description of the state of the Mitnick household and my mother's condition. My father's been denied active duty overseas, for which he will hold his sister-in-law responsible for the rest of his life.

It seems that there is enough bad weather between New Bedford and Washington, D.C. to make my mother almost wish my father had gone to Korea. She sits by the radio with my sister, taking in the latest weather reports and fearing the worst. Her nerves are as sharp as the sound of fingernails dragged across a chalkboard. And my father is no help. He reports all his near misses of plane disasters with sheer delight.

"Gosh, Jeannette," he reports, blustering in the door with a wide grin on his face, "You could've lost me this time." My mother looks bewildered. She is focusing on the words, "lost me." Gay is shaking with fear. I'm excited that Daddy is reporting something he thinks is fun.

My father continues, oblivious to any of our reactions, or that Gay and I are even there. "We'd just taken off and were barely out of D.C. when the rain started pelting down, hard as hail on the roof of the plane. Lightening was flashing and the thunder was crashing so loud that Jim couldn't hear anything on his radio. Next thing we knew, the plane was upside down. Upside down! What is wrong with you, Jeannette?"

My mother is in tears. She has finally connected the words "lost me" to their meaning. Gay starts to cry with her. I don't have any idea why this story my father is delivering with so much enthusiasm is making them cry. "You could've been killed," my mother sobs, "then where would we all be?"

My mother is so helpless. How could my father die? I'm not sure what to make of this. My mother says and does lots of things my sister tells me we're not supposed to pay any attention to, and my father certainly doesn't pay attention to them. But when I hear he is flying back to D.C. the next week, I pretend I'm in the plane with him when I go to sleep. My mother doesn't believe in God, so I pray for all of us, but only in my room when I'm alone. My sister would make fun of me. She doesn't believe in God either.

Then whenever my father is at home, he yells at my mother and tells her she's stupid. She cries and goes to bed. Once when this occurs, I go to climb into bed with her. She shouts at me, "What are you doing?" She grabs a hairbrush from her dresser and starts to beat me with it. Gay comes running in and can't get her to stop. Gay hurries to get my father, and he wrestles the hairbrush from her hand. I'm so scared. No one tells me that my mother is on heavy drugs and can't help herself. And why would they? I wouldn't be able to understand that she doesn't always know who I am or why I'm there. I go to bed not knowing what I've done wrong. This is one of many times that this will be the case.

# [8]

## SWIMMING LESSONS

It's summer and hotter than hell in San Antonio, Texas. The only place hotter is Tijuana, Mexico, where we've driven several times on Daddy's brief breaks from his army training. I'm three years old, and I'm not doing particularly well in Texas, but then again, none of us is.

There is a pool in the motel where we live for only a few months while Daddy learns how to be a soldier. He wants to go and fight for our country. He tells Mommy he's going to go to Korea, and she's scared. She still has lots of trouble managing on her own and falls down a lot. Daddy plans to be away for a long time, so he decides it's time that I learn how to swim.

All I've known of swimming is the edge of the ocean, where water meets sand and my toddler feet are safely anchored between them. Mommy is always nearby, measuring this distance and moving me back as the tide inches in. Somewhere on the other edge of the ocean, where water meets sky, my father appears and disappears. My mother measures this distance as well. She warns my father not to go out too far, but he never listens.

I'm not one of those children who like being tossed about in water, lifted up in the air and suddenly dunked without warning. This frustrates Daddy, and because I scream and demand to be returned to safety, he dumps me in the sand at Mommy's feet. He looks with envy at more contented children, and I look with envy at their gentler fathers. It's become a tenuous truce.

The swimming pool now looms between us. The wet tile and concrete feel slippery and dangerous. There's no way to wrap my toes around this stuff. Daddy struts the length of the diving board, leaps into the air and disappears into the watery blackness. I back up quickly to the lounge chair where my sister ignores him. Mommy is hiding inside, out of the sun. I don't know what will happen, but I'm so frightened that I want Daddy to forget I'm there. I curl up beside my sister, and she begins to read aloud whatever it is that she's reading. And even in the comfort of this, there is a churning in my stomach.

"PHYYYLlis!" This is a call from which there is no escape. I move closer to Gay.

"PHYYYLlis, GET OVER HERE NOW!"

"You're being paged," my sister informs me, rolling her eyes, an eleven year-old cynic. I know that she has no power to save me, but I still wish that she would.

"NOWWWW!" I tear myself from Gay, the lounge and safety and move reluctantly to my fate. I look back and move forward until I am standing about two feet from the edge. Daddy is prancing about in the water like some large Walt Disney cartoon, showing me—showing off—how easy it is for humans to be fish.

Daddy grins, treads water and beckons, "Just jump. I'm right here to catch you."

I back up. I have no desire to experience the black time between the jump and the catch. Something passes through me like the slow motion chase of a nightmare.

"Come on," Daddy coaxes. "Just jump in, right here, next to me," he waves water at me and dunks an index finger to indicate the spot. "I won't let you drown." And now I wonder, certainly not for the first time, if that is true. When I make no move, Daddy grows impatient.

"The quicker you get in, the easier it will be. There's nothing to be afraid of. Look at me." It is of no solace to look at my father. He already knows how to swim. I tremble in a morning chill that does not exist.

"Phyllis, I'm waiting."

"I don't want to, Daddy."

"What do you mean, you don't want to! You have to. You're going to jump into this pool and swim. There's no question about what you want."

"But Daddy, I don't know how to swim."

"This is how you learn."

"It isn't how I learned," my sister unexpectedly volunteers.

"Nobody asked you. Do you want to teach her?"

"Yes, please, Daddy. Let Gay teach me."

"Phyllis, this is the last time I'm going to tell you, JUMP IN THIS POOL NOW!"

I back up another foot.

"I don't want to have to come out there and get you. Don't make me have to come out and get you."

"I can't, Daddy."

"DON'T ever say you can't. You CAN. Just do it."

But my feet are welded to the concrete and I truly cannot move. Even as I watch my father yelling in disgust and frustration, climbing up the ladder and out of the pool, I am frozen. Even when he is so close that he's dripping on me.

"For the last time—are you going to jump or am I going to have to throw you in?"

I'm three years old and have not yet learned what to do in the face of a choice between unacceptable options. But I do not intend to do this of my own will. My father, long out of patience, lifts me over his head and tosses me into the deepest end of the pool.

If my father has warned me not to breathe underwater, I have no recollection of this in my panic. This is everything I've feared it would be.

I'm a tiny child and the pool is eight feet deep. It is a long way down to the bottom and an even longer way back up to the top. I have no air to start with and as quickly as I'm immersed, I breathe in deeply. The swallowing and choking is unbearable. I breathe in again, desperate for air where there is none. A fire explodes in my chest, and then, everything stops.

\* \* \*

I'm flapping like the freshly caught fish I've seen on the wharf in the New Bedford harbor. My father is pressing my chest into the concrete, exorcising water from my eyes, my nose, my mouth and every pore of my body.

"She's breathing. You see how it's done." My father instructs my sister in his best lifeguard voice, but I think I detect some relief there as well. As soon as my vision clears and I begin to move about, my father shakes his finger at me and lectures,

"I told you not to breathe."

# [9]

# LEMON MERINGUE PIE IN THE LAND OF KERETARIA

I am four.

    I love to help Mommy bake. I sit on a stool beside her, sneaking bits from big and little bowls.

    Mommy forgets a lot; so it takes her a long time to do things. Daddy yells at her for this but tells me I have to understand. I don't mind. I like being with her. Except when she gets mad. Mostly she gets mad at herself. When she knits, she rips and rips, and then she knits it back again. She says it used to be easy. That was before I was born; before she had to take her medicine. Once Mommy got mad at me and hit me too hard with her hairbrush. I don't know why. Gay got so scared, she told Mommy she was going to call the police. Mommy stopped, just like that, like Gay'd woken her up from a bad dream. Sometimes she cries. She doesn't know why she's sad. Daddy says it's because of the accident, when her brain was bleeding. I don't know how a brain could bleed. It's inside your head. I want to ask.

    Lemon meringue pie is my favorite. Mommy's is better than Lillian's Bakery where we buy our challah for dinner on Friday nights. I like going there with Mommy. Lillian knows how much I like the brownies with the thick chocolate icing, not the plain ones. She always has one waiting for me. The bakery smells best on Fridays because Lillian bakes the challis fresh. But I tell Mommy I think her pies are better than Lillian's. It's true and it makes her smile.

There's not much for me to do. I talk and talk and talk. I lick the bowls, spoons and spatulas, which is why I'm there in the first place. I ask her to tell me again about her brother, Ben.

"Mommy, tell me about you and Uncle Ben, when you played outside and didn't get your white dress dirty."

"We didn't play; we read. But you're right about the white dress. I used to sit out on the steps with your Uncle Ben—he was a quiet little boy—he'd just sit there—and read for hours. My mother was so proud of me. I never got that dress dirty."

"Are you proud of me, Mommy?"

"Of course I am. Why do you ask?"

"I get dirty."

"You sure do. That's why you don't have a white dress."

"I'd get it dirty."

"You would."

"Would you be mad at me?"

"I might."

"Mommy, Mommy, tell me about the boy, the bad boy who pulled the eyes out of your dolls."

"That was Cousin Charles. He wasn't really a bad boy."

"If he wasn't bad, why did he pull the eyes out of your dolls?"

"I don't know. He was mischievous, curious like you. I would cry; then he'd promise not to do it again. But then he'd come back in a week and pull out more eyes. Eventually, none of my dolls had eyes."

"Your dolls were blind."

"I guess they were."

"Daddy could've fixed them."

"Maybe." Mommy looks sad; then she smiles. She remembers these stories well which is why it's hard for me to understand how she forgets where she's left her apron or why she's gone upstairs.

"Cousin Charles is the one who sends you the Love dresses on your birthday."

"Did I ever meet Cousin Charles?"

"No, I don't think so. He lives in Chicago now. His company makes those dresses." She is breaking eggs. She puts the white parts in a big bowl and the yellow parts in a smaller bowl.

"Why are you doing that, Mommy?"

"Doing what?"

"Putting the white parts there and the yellow parts there."

"If you don't take the yellow parts out, the white parts won't get stiff when you beat them."

"Why not?"

"They're too thick and heavy."

"I like the yellow parts best."

"You like the lemon part best."

"I do. I do."

Mommy puts the mixer in the bowl. She holds it with one hand and turns the handle with the other. I watch her, tucking my feet under me on the kitchen stool.

I love to watch the eggs get stiff. Mommy lets me take a fork and play at making hills in them. This is fun but what I wait for is the thick stuff she makes with the lemon juice. I love to run a finger through it and slowly lick it off. It's sweet and sticky and still tastes like lemon. She grates the outsides of the lemons into this so it will be what she calls "tart." I have never tasted anything better. It's like a happy dream.

"I wish I was Handy Mandy."

"Why do you wish that?"

"If I was Handy Mandy, I'd have seven arms. I could make the lemon part, beat those eggs and make the dough. I could do all that, Mommy, at the same time. And you could be Nox the Royal Ox. I'd brush your hair for you, just like Handy Mandy brushes Nox's hair. We'd live in Oz and have adventures. Mommy, can we read about Handy Mandy again?"

"Why don't you get the book. You read to me and I'll help you with the big words."

I race from the sweet smells, the warm kitchen, up the cold back stairs to my room and into my book closet. I grab *Handy Mandy In Oz* from the shelf and run back down the stairs before Mommy can forget why I left and ask me how she can possibly read with me when she is busy making lemon meringue pie.

Mommy is rolling the dough. She smiles at me and says, "Just in time." She takes the pancake of dough and lifts it off the wax paper onto the glass baking dish. It flops over the sides. Mommy cuts that part off. She always rolls a little ball for me to eat. When we make fruit pies, there's more dough, and we make long, skinny snakes that Mommy crisscrosses over the fruit. But this is not that kind of pie.

"Here you go." She hands me my little ball of dough.

"Thank you, Mommy."

I climb back up on the stool, with my book and my dough. I set the book in my lap and pop the dough into my mouth.

"Mmmmm, Mommy. It's so good. What makes it taste so good?"

"Butter."

"Like Handy Mandy's naughty goat, What-a-butter. I wish I had a goat. I bet Grandpop would let me have a goat. Or at least a dog."

"Phyllis, you know how your father feels about animals."

"Mommy, I'll tell you the story and read my favorite parts."

"Good, honey." Mommy starts to wash dirty dishes. I move my stool closer so she can hear, even though I know I've already lost her attention. If I leave her for even a minute, she can be different by the time I get back.

"Handy Mandy had seven arms with seven hands. One hand was iron for taking pots off the stove; one was leather for cleaning the house; one was made of wood for cooking and working in the garden; two were rubber for washing the dishes; two were white for braiding her hair. She lived on a mountain with lots of goats. One of them was What-a butter. What-a-butter was naughty and ran away. Mandy went looking for What-a butter." I open the book.

"'What-a-butter, I say WHAT-A-BUTTER—come down here this instant.'"

Daddy sticks his head in the door. "I'm warning you, Phyllis, keep your voice down." He shuts the door hard behind him.

I try to whisper.

"You know what happens next, Mommy?" Mommy looks from the sink to the office door.

"Please tell me."

"The rock Handy Mandy is standing on is shot straight up in the air by water, just like the elephants do it in the zoo. Swooooosh!" I try to show Mommy what I mean, but my book falls with a big bang on the floor. She's not looking anyway.

Daddy's head appears again. "What's going on in here?"

"Sorry, Daddy. I dropped my book."

He's gone. Mommy is busy washing, washing. I think she could use Mandy's rubber hands.

"Mommy, please listen. This is the part where Handy Mandy meets Nox and she finds out about the wicked king and the nice little boy king who's been stolen."

Mommy pulls her hands out of the soapy water and shakes them over the sink. "I'm listening." She dries them on a dishtowel.

Mommy goes back to the mixing bowl. I don't know if her arm got tired or she forgot what she was doing.

Daddy opens the door. "Jeannette, boil these instruments."

Mommy sets down the mixer and takes a handful of Daddy's instruments from him. Before he shuts the door, he tells me, "Keep your voice down."

"Phyllis, please get me Daddy's pot." I know which pot is Daddy's. Mommy burned it and it's bumpy on the bottom. She forgot it on the stove. Now they use it to boil Daddy's instruments. They have to be clean before he cuts people's eyes."

Mommy drops the instruments into the pot, puts water in the pot, and sets it on the stove. She turns the fire up high. She goes back to the sink and washes her hands before she starts mixing the eggs again. This happens all the time.

I whisper to Mommy, "Daddy can be the mean king."

"That's not nice, Phyllis."

"Or the bad wizard who turns people into potted plants."

Mommy has that look on her face that she gets when she's lost or not sure what she's doing. She looks around the room and remembers that she's forgotten to set the timer for the instruments.

"Fifteen minutes," she tells herself. She sets the little timer. "Fifteen minutes."

Our kitchen is not pretty. The stove is old and has brown stains. The refrigerator is rounded and small and smells of old freezer ice. The linoleum on the floor never looks clean, no matter how hard Gay and I scrub it. The walls are an icky yellow and green; but still it's the coziest place in the house. Daddy likes the house just the way it is. Mommy doesn't say anything about it, even though the kitchen is her territory. The kitchen, ugly as it is, is where I most like to be with Mommy. It's where she bakes her pies.

Mommy makes her pies from scratch. She never uses anything from cans or mixes. She always makes her own crusts. They smell like I imagine heaven. Just on the other side of the door, there are awful smells, blood and alcohol and nasty eye medicines that come in tubes and dark brown bottles with rubber droppers. That is where Daddy does his work. Mommy tells me, "Shhh." She draws her finger to her lips, "Daddy's working."

I don't know why I have to be so quiet. I can hear Daddy talking to his patients. I live here, too. My friend Jeanie's mother never tells us we have to be quiet and there are three doctors working in their house. We chase each other up and down the three long flights of back stairs even though the doctors' offices are just on the other side. I know they must hear our feet and maybe our voices, "I'll beat you." "No, me, me!"

Daddy says that Jeanie's Daddy is a very tough man, but I never see that when I play over there. He is always nice to me. He never tells us to go play somewhere else or to shut up. My father never says bad things about him, so I guess he must like him. He doesn't like Jeanie at all. He says she's bad because she's adopted. It's not her parents' fault. It's because of those parents who left her that she pulls my hair and scratches my face when she's mad. I tell Daddy I pull her hair and scratch her face back and I'm not even adopted, am I? Daddy laughs and says I'm not, but sometimes I wish I was. I pretend I am.

The eggs are almost stiff. Mommy offers me the mixer, "Be careful." I try to do it just the way she does. Sometimes my hand slips and I spill a little.

Daddy sticks his head into the kitchen again.

"How're the instruments coming, Jeannette?"

Mommy looks up from the lemon filling she's stirring on the stove, right next to the boiling instruments.

"They're fine."

"How many more minutes?"

"Ten."

"Did you start them when I asked you?"

"Yes, but I forgot to put the timer on."

Daddy shakes his head and disappears into the other room. I giggle, "Don't worry, Mommy, I won't let you be potted."

I play with the egg whites. Mommy stirs. The bell goes off. Daddy's head pops back in.

"Let me know when they're ready, Jeannette." Mommy looks around.

"Oh, I don't know where I was. Here, Phyllis. Be very careful. It's hot. Put cold water in the pot to cool it off." She hands me the pot of lemon filling she's been stirring, making sure that my hands are tight around the potholders.

I walk step by step to the sink. I don't want to spill a single drop of this lemon filling. I'm happy but scared that Mommy trusts me to carry it. It smells so good but it's heavy. It's many steps from the stove to the sink and I hope I can lift it when I get there.

Oh, good. Here I am at the sink and I haven't spilled a drop. I lift the pan slowly and inch by inch lower it into the sink.

"I did it, Mommy. It's in the sink."

"Good. Now add the cold water."

"How much, Mommy?"

"Just enough to cool it off."

I don't know how much that is. I look at Mommy. She's using something I don't know the name of to pick the hot instruments out of the pot and lay them on a tray.

Handy Mandy would just go ahead with it and not bother her mother anymore. I run the cold water until it's icy cold. I turn it down to a trickle and just cover the top of the filling.

"Mommy, come see. Is this good?"

Mommy puts the last instrument on the tray and walks over to the sink. She grabs me and shakes me and begins to scream.

"What have you done? You've ruined it! How could you do this? How could you be so stupid?"

"What did I do, Mommy?" I'm too afraid to cry yet.

Mommy doesn't answer. She keeps shaking me and shouting, "It's ruined. I can't believe it's ruined."

Daddy comes running in, shutting the office door behind him.

"Jeannette, what the heck is going on in here?"

Mommy's face is red. She doesn't stop shaking me.

"Look what she did. *Just look what she did.* It's completely ruined. *You're a mean little girl.*"

Daddy frees me from Mommy and looks into the sink.

"What happened, Phyllis?" Now I burst into tears. Daddy is different. He isn't yelling at me. His voice is soft and kind.

"Mommy asked me—she asked me to put water in it. She said just enough to cool it off. I did what she said, Daddy. I did what she said."

"I told you to put the pot in water, not the water in the pot. You ruined my pie."

"No, Mommy. I wouldn't ever ruin your pie. I love your pies. Please, Mommy. I didn't."

Daddy gives me a quick hug. "Go to your room until I call you. It's okay. It's not your fault."

"But Mommy's mad at me."

"Phyllis, go to your room. I need to talk to Mommy."

I leave the kitchen and leave the door open just enough so that I can spy on their conversation from the bottom of the back stairs. I'm ready to run if I hear footsteps or the door.

Mommy's voice is still angry but I can't understand the words. I sneak a little closer. I can hear Daddy.

"But Jeannette, she's only four. She just did what you told her to do. Why would she want to ruin the pie? She loves your pies."

Mommy is crying. "I know, I know. She's only four."

I quietly climb the stairs and go to my room. I lie down on my bed. I'm sorry I listened. I'm ashamed of myself. I made Mommy angry. I made her cry. And I called Daddy the mean king and the bad wizard. I get up and shut my bedroom door. I'm not leaving here again. I'm going to stay in here forever until I starve to death. I think of the pie and burst into tears. I cry until my head hurts and I can't breathe. Then I fall asleep.

*There's fire all around me. Smoke; smoke that won't let me breathe. Mommy and Daddy are standing still as statues. No—no, like candles. Two waxy candles, just like the ones Mommy lights on Friday nights. I can't reach them. They're melting away. I'm losing them. Their faces are dripping into nothing right in front of me. I try to scream but nothing comes out. I start to choke. No air. No scream.*

"Phyllis, wake up." I feel Mommy's hand shaking my shoulder. "Were you having a bad dream?"

"Yes, Mommy. It was very scary. How did you know?"

"You were moving around and moaning in your sleep."

"I couldn't scream. I tried."

Mommy is sitting on my bed. She turns around so she can cuddle me.

"Do you feel better now?"

"Are you still mad at me, Mommy?"

"No. I'm upset that the pie was ruined, but I'm not mad at you."

"Mommy, do you think I'm mean?"

"No, but you are difficult."

"Daddy said I'm only four."

"I know."

I roll away from her and pretend to fall back to sleep. I don't understand. I think to myself that the Kingdom of Clinton Place is much more confusing than the Kingdom of Keretaria. In the Kingdom of Keretaria, the bad king is always the bad king and the good queen is always the good queen. It's not so easy to know what's what in the Kingdom of Clinton Place.

# [10]

## NEGOTIATIONS AND REPARATIONS IN THE ANIMAL KINGDOM

My father's sisters are nothing like my mother's. And my father's sisters are nothing like each other. Aunt Rosie is plump with shapely legs that we are told were once beautiful. Prominent cheekbones and a slight slant of eye are her only physical similarities to my grandmother. Their kinship is also evident in their collective capacity to curse up a terrible storm in Yiddish, but only Aunt Rosie can translate every expletive into perfect English. And while Bubbe always curses with the same even expression, Aunt Rosie bursts into smiles at the very pleasure of it. I can visualize her as a child, sticking out her tongue at my father and crying, "Nyeh, nyeh, nyeh, nyeh, nyeh!" Her razor-sharp tongue can slice and deflate him in an instant.

Aunt Rosie and Daddy fight ruthlessly. As a child, I sit rebelliously in Aunt Rosie's corner. After all, I am often as not the impetus as well as excuse for their battles. She is one of the few who dares to defend me, and this engenders some degree of loyalty. Later on, I take less pleasure in my father's defeat and understand why he is reluctant to make these obligatory visits. The long deadly drives to Philadelphia are filled with protestations of undying love for his family. The even deadlier drives back to New Bedford bear little resemblance and certainly none of the nostalgia.

The drive to Philadelphia goes something like this:

"You know, Jeannette, Rosie's been a good sister. I remember when she gave me her last dollar so that I could ride the trolley to see you." My mother doesn't respond. It's a straight monologue we hear on every trip, and my sister and I sit quietly in the back, knowing better than to say anything. "And Ruthie's taken care of my mother all these years. I tell you, it can't be easy living with my mother. I wouldn't want to have to do it. So I give her money (this is for our benefit, so that we won't find him a complete scoundrel) to help with things. Ruthie's Sam doesn't make much money, certainly not as much as I do anyway. And they've got so many boys." We are always confused as to how many boys there are or their names. "I feel for all of them," my father sighs.

The drive back home to New Bedford goes something like this:

"I don't like my family much, but I do love them. My sister never learns (when he refers to 'my sister,' my father inevitably means Rosie). She says the stupidest things. They're all ignorant. That's what happens with no education." This last remark is an unwarranted threat to me and to my sister. My sister has skipped a year of school, and I'm in a gifted program. "You don't want to end up like them," my father goes on, "and their kids aren't too swift either." My mother leans over and whispers something to my father. "It's okay, Jeannette, I'm sure they know anyway." My sister must know it anyway, as she's indifferent to my boisterous aunts. I don't know it anyway, and I think they're the best aunts any girl could have.

Aunt Ruthie is the baby of the family and nineteen years younger than my father. When I look at a picture of her in her early twenties, I'm astonished by her beauty. With dark eyes and lush black hair framed in a hat I would've thought much too stylish for her to have afforded, she's trim and seductive. I want to place Humphrey Bogart in her background instead of my Uncle Sam. Rosie's husband is always "Sammy," and Ruthie's is always "Sam," thus the husbands are never confused, at least in name. Sam speaks even less than Sammy, if one can believe that possible. But he lives with Bubbe which explains a lot.

Ruthie is the last daughter and taking care of Bubbe is her life's work. Her husband and long line of sons all live under Bubbe's roof and tongue. Ruthie is religious and long suffering. A variety of ailments plague her until she, like Bubbe, can do nothing but sit in a chair. It's many years before I learn that she takes psychiatric medication for what was then known as manic depression.

My father's brothers are nothing like each other and certainly nothing like him. Although all three Mitnick men are undeniably handsome, my grandfather was clearly the "looker" in the family. Uncle Larry is now gray and gruff, and I'm a bit afraid of him. He smells like his auto parts store and scratches my face with his rough beard when he kisses me. But I adore Uncle Bobby. Everyone does. I love to hear his stories, how he would barely escape my father's deadly grasp following one of his youthful escapades. Out Bobby would go, through a window in the darkness of night, leaving my father behind him furiously holding onto all that remained of a torn shirt.

How Daddy seems to have envied the free-and-easy life his three youngest siblings led as children. How different to have been born in the United States, where flight meant merely avoiding the punishment of an angry brother or father's hand and not murder at the hands of hateful strangers. Daddy praises Uncle Larry for his intelligence and his unbeatable game of chess, but his eyes light up with admiration whenever he talks about Bobby, his fun-loving baby brother.

Daddy rewrites the chapters of his life. When the facts are consistent, the characters often change from angels to demons and from devils to saints. And when the characters are consistent, the facts are subject to poetic license. There is the "how during the depression your Aunt Rosie gave me the money to take the trolley to visit your mother in Roxborough AND even gave me the money to buy her flowers" story. In one version, Aunt Rosie is a benevolent and loving sister who selflessly relinquishes her matinee money —sometimes it is her makeup or magazine money—sometimes her last dollar—to give her less fortunate brother the opportunity to court the woman she hopes to make her future sister-in-law. In a less favorable variation, he has to beg Aunt Rosie for the trolley money and she only gives him enough fare for a one-way ticket. "How did she think I was going to get home?" he asks of no one in particular.

We arrive in Philadelphia primed for the generosity and graciousness of Aunt Rosie. The clan is gathered to receive us. Bubbe is in her wheelchair, sputtering and cursing, blind and crippled from diabetes and completely unaware of our arrival. Aunt Ruthie is too busy attending to Bubbe to acknowledge us. The cousins are all lined up, waiting for something, and the uncles are hiding in another room, probably trying to sneak a cigarette out of my grandmother's range of smell. Aunt Rosie is at the door. She flings it open with such a flourish that we momentarily mistake this for something other than what it is.

"Goddammit, Nathan," she hollers, "do you have to pull up here in that big fat-assed car of yours? The neighbors don't care about your money and neither do we!" She throws smiling side-glances in our direction. She is confident the children of Nathan will embrace her. And we do, with some reluctance. After all, she is our aunt. But who is she anyway? Who are any of these people? The charmed creatures of the drive to Philly or the demons of the drive back?

Uncle Sammy is quiet but laughs a lot. Whenever my aunt barks a command at him, he gives her one of his winning smiles and responds, "Yes, Dear." My mother is in awe of this relationship, but I don't appreciate this until many years later. Now I am six and have a different agenda. I'm also painfully shy and terrified of most of my father's family. They are loud and often louder in Yiddish. I tug on my mother's dress.

"When can I see the alligators and snakes?" I have been asking this question about every ten miles of the trip, interrupting my father's monologue and contributing to his anxiety and annoyance.

"Ask your Uncle Sammy," my mother replies. She has no idea that I cannot ask anything of a man who owns alligators and snakes and is also married to a woman like my Aunt Rosie.

"Please ask him for me," I plead in a whisper.

"What do you want, honey?" Aunt Rosie's voice modulates from corner street hawker to Maria Callas in seconds. I'm too afraid to answer. I've already been warned about pestering them.

"C'mon honey, tell your Aunt Rosie what you want."

Now the eyes of the entire Mitnick clan are on me. I'm confused. My sister and I have been taught never to say what we want. Furthermore, we've learned all too painfully the irrelevance of actually doing so.

"She's such a good child," Aunt Rosie remarks to blind Bubbe, who has no idea she's being addressed. "Don't be afraid, dear. Your Daddy's not going to get angry with you now. Your Aunt Rosie's here to protect you. Tell Aunt Rosie what you want."

My mother, hearing the "nyeh, nyeh" quality in Aunt Rosie's voice, finally intervenes.

"I think she wants to see the alligators and snakes."

Bubbe begins cursing again, as if she has just been reminded of their existence, or possibly it is the existence of my Uncle Sammy that distresses her. Perhaps it is unnerving to suddenly have her oldest son in her living room with his two strange children and his polite wife who hardly seems Jewish. Aunt Ruthie quiets her momentarily, "It's okay, Mama, I'm getting you the bed pan."

The bedpan is alien and dark, like Bubbe, whose large skirt cloaks it in mystery. I try never to see the bedpan. I turn away when I hear its name evoked or summoned, and I'm never sure, but I think it might be the source of the faint but stale odor I always smell in this house. Bubbe is repugnant to me and I feel shame, shame for her, shame for me, shame for my father, whose feelings of revulsion have been passed along. But since I am unaware of my inheritance, I feel only guilt at my nausea.

"Sammy, take the girls down to see your pets."

My sister protests, something rare for her. "That's okay, Aunt Rosie. I don't want to go."

"You don't have to," Sammy says. "C'mon Phyllis, I'll take you down. But I only have one snake now."

"Any alligators?"

"We'll see what we can do," Sammy smiles. He's pleased that I'm interested. The reptiles reside two blocks away in Rosie and Sammy's basement, providing us both with a temporary escape from Bubbe and Aunt Rosie's firing squad. For the moment, we're safe.

Aunt Rosie and Uncle Sammy are carnies. When I finally learn that the alligators and snakes are not "pets" but part of Uncle Sammy's carnival routine, I'm old enough to be intrigued by more than the reptiles themselves. Now it is enough for me to allow Uncle Sammy to wind the snake around my arm. I love to feel the coolness of its skin and touch the intricate patterns of color woven into its hide.

Uncle Sammy doesn't talk much. In fact, he says more to the snake than I've ever heard him say to anyone. I don't mind this at all. He's a welcome relief from the overheated and overcrowded living room filled with Bubbe and Yiddish and unfamiliar family members. They hug me too tightly and give me soft, wet kisses. Then I feel sick to my stomach and say no when Aunt Ruthie unsuccessfully tries to feed me. She's always offended by this and accuses my father. "What, my cooking isn't good enough for her? Look at my boys, every one of them loves my cooking. Don't you?" I'm never sure which are her boys or how many of them she actually has, but from somewhere there is always a chorus of "I love your food, Ma."

I feel safe and at home with Uncle Sammy and I'm never confused about which children belong to him and Aunt Rosie. "Pudgie," whose real name is Louis, is two years older than my sister. I'm not sure why they call him "Pudgie," but he is named for my grandfather whom he does not resemble even remotely. He is the spitting image of his father. "Pudg," as he is also called, is friendly and funny and oblivious to everything negative around him. He pats my father on the back, as no one else will dare, and says, "Hey, Uncle Nate, How ya doing?" My father adores him. Gay tolerates him. This places him in a special category since she won't admit she likes anyone in the family. Pudgie's younger brother Philip is two years older than I am, my namesake and my hero. He's handsome and always in trouble and in fear for his life. His mother is his main assailant and persecutor. Close behind her and waiting in line are teachers, principals and only slightly later on, mothers of neighborhood girls. Pudgie is his protector, just as Gay is mine. In my early teens, I fantasize that Philip is not really my cousin. Once we discover this, we fall madly in love. I'm smart enough to realize that I am alone in this reverie, and fortunately, I never reveal it.

Bubbe's daughters have produced only sons, and her sons have produced only daughters. Her sons' wives are quiet and polite like my mother. They bear no resemblance to Bubbe whatsoever. I often can't remember which aunt goes with which uncle. Uncle Larry has two daughters. They are both beautiful. Judy is arrogant and exotic. Susan walks in her shadow. Uncle Bobby's two daughters are rarely there. One is in and out of the hospital with what is whispered to be schizophrenia. The other is depressed. Since I don't see them very often, I get them mixed up as well.

Uncle Sammy and I linger over his entourage of snake and alligators. The basement is cool and quiet. Then we hear the sudden invasion of loud footsteps in high heels. The basement door is jerked open and my aunt's voice vibrates down the stairwell.

"Sammy, what on earth have you two been doing down there? Bubbe wants to see her and Ruthie hasn't fed her a thing. Wouldn't you like to have some of your Aunt Ruthie's chicken soup? She thinks hers is better than mine. Can you imagine that?"

"We're coming, dear." Uncle Sammy carefully removes the snake from my arm and tenderly lowers it back into its nest. We both know it's useless to argue. She'll stand up there and persevere until she's satisfied by the sound of our footsteps that we are in compliance. She's waiting by the door, hands on hips, with the look of a mission successfully completed.

I trail slightly behind them until Aunt Rosie grabs one of my hands and Uncle Sammy, following her lead, grabs the other. There is something very special about the way this feels, and I wish we could just go on walking. I pretend they're my real parents. I imagine what it would be like for Gay and me each to have our own older brother. I picture myself waking up every morning to help Uncle Sammy feed the snake. I envision myself playing with my cousins and knowing all their names. I picture the crowded dinner table with not enough chairs, aunts searching for additional forks and spoons, the lively shouting and cursing of my father's childhood home in Philadelphia. I hear the Yiddish and the English, with smatterings of Russian and German. I see myself running the two blocks to knock on the familiar door of an aunt, asking for an egg or a cup of noodles, or even some advice or comfort. I suddenly feel sad and alone.

Aunt Rosie is still talking about Aunt Ruthie's chicken soup. She compares ingredient by ingredient the superiority of her own. Ruthie uses too much salt. Her carrots are not cut as nicely. The broth never tastes quite right. Does Sammy notice the fatty taste? Sammy makes a grunt that Rosie chooses to interpret as agreement. Even with my limited childish capacity, I understand that my uncle adores her.

Back at Bubbe's the cousins are all seated on the stairs. Bubbe is regal in her chair, a shawl draped around her shoulders. Aunt Ruthie waves a large spoon with one hand and a dishtowel with the other. "Bubbe is ready for you to say hello," she announces. 'Then we'll have some chicken soup."

The queen is prepared to receive her court. This routine is as repugnant as it is familiar. One by one we approach Bubbe, tell her who we are because Bubbe can no longer see anything but black and gray shadows, and then kiss her on the cheek. My sister and I lag behind our cousins. They're used to this. They don't even seem to mind. Now it's Gay's turn, and I'm left alone to watch. My cousins are all jammed around the table, ready to eat. My sister doesn't break stride. Confidently and properly she states her name, leans over quickly to deliver the required peck on the cheek and races for the table before Bubbe can make any further demands of her through our Aunt Ruthie in Yiddish.

I look around me, but in fact, there is no one left. Bubbe scares me. My father is afraid of her, and it seems to me that everyone but Aunt Rosie is afraid of him, so where does that leave me? Aunt Ruthie stays behind Bubbe to translate, but I don't view her as any kind of protection. I know that Bubbe barks orders at her all day long, even though I can't understand a word she's saying. Aunt Ruthie runs from room to room, attempting to satisfy her long enough to get a bit of rest. But we never see her achieve this during our brief visits.

"Come on," Aunt Ruthie encourages me. "Kiss your Bubbe so we can all eat dinner."

I don't think of her as "my" Bubbe. I don't even think of her as my father's mother. This fat, smelly, angry stranger who is not happy to see me is my grandmother, and it's my duty to kiss her. I'm keeping Aunt Ruthie from eating dinner. Mommy reminds me of this from the table. There's so much noise that I'm almost unable to hear her. I begin to tiptoe toward Bubbe. I close my eyes to a slit so that I can avoid looking into her unseeing cloudy white gaze. I approach from the side because it seems safer. I whisper, "I'm Phyllis," and I quickly light a kiss on her cheek, backing away a couple of steps immediately after. She says something unintelligible to my aunt. I recognize my Hebrew name and "daughter of Nathan" in my aunt's reply. Bubbe has no idea who I am, but she continues in Yiddish. "She wants to know if you're behaving yourself." I nod my head vigorously up and down, even though, if I am to believe my father, this is a downright lie and Bubbe can't possibly see what I'm doing. Aunt Ruthie says something in Yiddish to her and then interprets for me, "Yes, she's a good girl and she studies very hard." I can see that my aunt is free with her translation. Bubbe now makes a motion with her hand. I'm dismissed and forgotten. She has moved on to the soup.

By the time I join my cousins at the table, I'm not hungry. I watch them closely, hoping that this will help me to learn how to better negotiate this environment. My sister announces, "I won't have any soup." Aunt Ruthie retaliates, "So Gay, do you have a boy friend yet?" My sister's confided to me all the terrible things she will do if Aunt Ruthie asks her that question just one more time. I sneak a glance at her expression out of the corner of my eye and make her laugh. We wink at each other.

Immediately I feel a tug of guilt. My sister is as dismissive of Dad's family as he would like to be, but I so desperately want to belong. Somewhere. This family is too noisy and overwhelming. And I am always afraid of what Grandpop (Mommy's father) will do if I'm unable to finish all the food on my plate. Daddy's warned me about this. He's also said more than once, "A word to the wise, you're noisy and irritating. Your grandfather doesn't like noisy and irritating children." Tears well up in my eyes. Aunt Ruthie sees this but has her own interpretation.

"Ah, look at that. It's the onions. Does the same thing to me, too, especially when I'm cutting them. Well, that means it's good chicken soup."

Aunt Rosie can't resist. "If it's such good chicken soup, what's the kid crying for?" As usual, she manages to get the last word.

\* \* \*

We never sleep in South Philly. We always make the trip to Roxborough to stay with Grandpop, my other Aunt Rose and Tuffy and Cookie. Often Alec, Aunt Rose's brother is there as well.

Aunt Rose is Grandpop's second wife. He married her after his first wife, my mother's real mother, died giving birth to my Aunt Kathie. My grandmother was the same age when she died as my mother was when she developed a brain aneurysm while giving birth to me. Cookie is Aunt Rose's dog, and Grandpop and I share Tuffy.

Aunt Rose is anything but a "wicked stepmother." I desperately want to call her "Grandma," but I'm too afraid of offending the memory of my dead grandmother. Aunt Rose is touchable and reachable, unlike the alien being I call Bubbe. Rose is also from Russia, but she seems to have escaped more than the country. She's free of the chronic fear that we'll all be reduced to starvation momentarily. Her kitchen is always filled with the most delightful odors of Russian and Jewish delicacies and the essence of nutmeg, cinnamon, vanilla and butter baking in the oven. With Aunt Rose, we can eat or not. Food is neither pushed on us nor taken away.

Tuffy always greets us at the door in Roxborough. He's small, mostly mutt and part Boston Bull Terrier, but big enough to bowl me over with his enthusiasm. Pinning me under all four paws, his tongue licks my face furiously. Grandpop observes and admonishes, "Well, Tuffy, who will you sleep with tonight, you fickle dog?" I have no idea that he is playing with me. If, in fact, my father is right and I am a noisy and irritating child to him, then he must be angry with me for stealing his favorite companion. But it's always Tuffy who makes the final decision. Once he hears the first sounds of Grandpop's snores, he leaves his bed and jumps onto mine, usually positioning his compact little body half on my head and half on the pillow. Mommy worries that I'll be suffocated.

Sometimes I forget that Grandpop isn't supposed to like me. He lifts me onto his lap and tells me stories about life in Russia. He smells of the cherry tobacco he smokes. It lingers in the sweaters he always wears. His fables are filled with icicles and snowstorms, but his lap is safe and warm.

Grandpop spends hours in his workshop. He's made my sister a giant dollhouse, complete with miniature wooden handcrafted furniture. I live for the day he'll make me one, but he dies soon after I'm ten. He doesn't spend one day in bed, never sick in his life and determined not to be. So he picks the hottest and most humid day of a Philadelphia summer to paint the house and have a stroke. Mommy tells me proudly that her father has died with a perfect set of teeth, not a single cavity. I wonder if it has anything to do with the fact that he found the dentist to be a waste of time and money, and so he never visited one in his life.

Grandpop is not at all like our South Philly relatives. He rarely speaks, but when he does, we all listen. My father likes to say that he "carries a big stick." He eats ham and bacon and never goes to shul. He never fasts on Yom Kipper being strong in the belief that one should only starve from necessity. There is only room for one god in this home, and Grandpop clearly writes all the commandments. Not even my father challenges his absolute authority.

There are two commandments that I never see broken. One is the rule about the amount of food on the plate. Everyone fills his own plate from gigantic serving platters that my Aunt Rose keeps filled throughout the meal. The only warning I receive is a quiet reminder from my mother. "And it has been written that whatever you put on your plate, you must eat. No one leaves the table until their plate is clean." If an overindulgent parent fills your plate, or Aunt Rose momentarily forgets herself and spoons food into an opening left by the food you're currently chewing, you cannot, of course, be held responsible. If, on the other hand, you've done it on your own, you could find yourself sitting there until breakfast. In that case, the plate is covered and served to you at the next meal. Grandpop is firm that one ought to learn the difference early in life between hunger and greed.

The second commandment pertains only to Grandpop. "And it has been written that I, Lord and Master of this house, will be served my own loaf of bread with each meal. Not just any loaf will do. It will be

Russian, soft and thick and black on the inside and crusty, topped with seeds and white flour on the outside." And so it has come to pass that Grandpop always has his own, while the rest of us dine on an assortment for the table. No one ever goes without bread. No one ever leaves the table hungry.

Grandpop's house has been a refuge for most of his family and his family's families at some point in their lives. The elegant old stone dwelling is lined with sweet-smelling honeysuckle bushes and guarded by two stone lions at one stair landing and two stone dogs at another. It's rumored that hidden passageways once provided an escape route for slaves running north. Now it provides escape for unemployed and indigent relatives, as well as adventurous grandchildren.

My sister was born in this house. She lived here for the first four and a half years of her life. It's home to her. She's never quite forgiven my father for returning from his medical residency in Kansas City and whisking the family away to poverty in Massachusetts. She barely remembered him and disliked the changes he made. Nor can she forgive my mother for letting it happen. I look at photos of her as a child in my grandfather's house. She's grinning and playful, full of joy and the world around her. In photos taken after the move, my birth, and my mother's illness, my sister looks old, serious. I'm asked, "Is that your mother?"

My sister knows the Roxborough family. They are what once was her happy childhood. I've never been exposed to either family for longer than a weekend, and so they're all alien to me. This is not true of Tuffy. He's uncomplicated in his love. He's devoted to me, and I to him.

I'm so small in this huge house. I could disappear down a tunnel and no one would notice. They're all so busy with each other. I'm the outsider. My mother leaves me to whisper in Aunt Rose's kitchen. My sister ignores me for Myra, a cousin who is close to her own age. My grandfather likes to be with his wood in his workshop. My father is not one whose company I ever seek.

Tuffy and I chase each other in and out the many doors of the dining room. I dash under the enormous wooden table and Tuffy follows on my heels, barking ecstatically. Under chairs, in and out of doors, back under the table again, he bounces just behind. Oh, such devotion. Such loyalty. Such power I wield over this innocent being, a power I certainly cannot lay claim to have over any other living creature.

And so with the cruel innocence of childhood, I tease and test him. I slam the door on his exuberant chase, excited by his whines and cries as confirmation of his love. I'm not satisfied with only one round of this game. The look of shock and disappointment and the whimpers from behind that door give me a thrill I can't begin to explain. The continuous banging, barking and whining attract my grandfather.

"What are you doing?" he asks.

"I'm playing a game with Tuffy," I giggle. I have no sense of wrong-doing, and my grandfather somehow recognizes this.

"Let's go in here for a minute and talk about this." He beckons to me gently. He calls softly to Tuffy. Tuffy is panting and cautious now, but he bolts quickly into the dining room behind us. My grandfather puts two chairs together closely, and motions me to sit.

"I have something very important to tell you," he says. He calls Tuffy to come between us. He pats him gently, and Tuffy plops at his feet, tuckered out from all the running and chasing and frustration.

"You see this dog?"

"Yes, Grandpop. I see him."

"You see how much he loves you? You know how much he loves you?"

"Yes, Grandpop."

"You love him, too?"

"Oh, yes, I love him more than anything in the whole world!"

"Then why do you want to hurt his feelings?"

This is a new concept for me. If you love someone, you don't want to hurt their feelings? It doesn't exactly match too closely with my experience of the world so far.

"I don't ever want to hurt Tuffy, Grandpop," I jump down from my chair and wrap my arms around him. "I'm sorry, Tuffy. I'll never do that to you again. I promise."

Grandpop lights his pipe. He's not finished. "Never tease an animal," he stresses. "They love us so much, and they're so innocent."

And what about children? I'm too young to ask. Or is it only animals who should receive this considered treatment? My grandfather's words stay with me. I never again mistreat Tuffy or any other animal. And Tuffy never abuses my love. People are an entirely different story. The lesson is not easy.

\* \* \*

Just four years later, after Grandpop puts himself to rest painting the house, Tuffy is despondent. Long after the *shiva,* Tuffy still won't touch his food. Aunt Rose is worried. The only time Tuffy comes to life at all is when we visit. He responds to me alone and manages to nibble half-heartedly in my presence. Aunt Rose asks my father if we can take Tuffy home with us.

"By no means will I have an animal in the house!" He goes on to point out my lack of responsibility. "Who'll feed him? Who'll walk him? And who's going to clean up after him?" Since I cannot possibly be depended on to do so, it will inevitably fall on my parents. And don't forget the veterinary bills.

I beg and I plead. I promise, threaten, cry, slam doors and stomp my feet. I sleep with Tuffy and join him in starvation, if only briefly. I threaten to run away with Tuffy. I'll get a job. I'll devote my life to his care. I whisper to him that we'll somehow manage to get him home to New Bedford. But in the end, I'm forced into a tearful good-bye. Tuffy is not allowed to accompany us home, in spite of all my efforts. I refuse to speak to my parents during the entire drive back. In retrospect, this is probably more of a gift to them than a punishment. My father generously offers me a turtle, but I haven't yet recovered from my father's rude disposal of the last one in just one flush of the toilet. The implications of this offer are ridiculous to me even at the age of ten. How can he think that some turtle could possibly take the place of my grandfather's favorite companion? Later I hear about Tuffy from my mother. He dies of grief within months of Grandpop's death.

It's many years before I can forgive my father for this decision. It's Thanksgiving and I refuse to come home unless I can bring my English

Cocker. Troubles is an abused dog I've inherited through adoption. He's too traumatized already for me to consider changing his name, even if it is undeserved. He proves himself to be loving and loyal and anything but "trouble."

My father hems and haws. His lifetime rule has always been: No Animals. However, this is not on a permanent basis, I remind him. He weakens when I give him this technical out, as his desire to see me outweighs his rigidity, a definite but impermanent sign of his aging.

Troubles is housebroken. He's a good dog with only two shortcomings. Leftover Chinese food must never be thrown in the garbage. He will kill and destroy for this. His only other passion is me. He follows happily at my heels but is distraught whenever I leave. Once the door closes behind me, he howls mournfully for a painful thirty to sixty seconds and refuses to budge from the threshold until my return. But for these minor infractions, and an occasional attempt to eat little children, he's the perfect dog.

My parents are impressed. Since I'm now an independent adult and they don't have to be afraid of additional responsibility, they can't praise Troubles enough. "What a sweet dog he is," my mother pats his head admiringly. "You're a good boy," my father tells him. Troubles is oblivious to the honor being bestowed upon him by a man who has never before spoken directly to a dog.

Troubles quickly inspires their confidence and gains free access to the house. After my father proudly shows me the new heating system he's had installed in the basement, we both forget that Troubles is down there exploring. We've just settled into conversation in the living room when we hear a scratching and whining at the door. I quickly jump up to let him in, and I remember Tuffy.

"Remember that time Grandpop caught me teasing Tuffy?" I ask my father.

"No, I don't remember that. I don't remember you ever teasing Tuffy."

"Well, I did. And I felt horrible about it afterwards when Grandpop stopped me and told me what I was doing. I promised Tuffy I would never do it again, and I never did."

"I don't think I ever knew about that," my father says.

"He never told you?"

"No. I don't think he ever did. I guess he figured he'd punished you enough."

"I didn't feel punished. He taught me something I just didn't realize. I felt pretty awful about it, but I knew he knew that. And he must have felt sure I'd never do it again after I promised Tuffy. He knew how much I loved that dog."

"Yes. Your mother used to be afraid that Tuffy would smother you at night. He loved to sleep on your head."

I smile. "Yes, I remember that. And I felt so bad when he died. Dad, why was it so important to you that we not have a dog in the house?"

My father sighs. He looks softly at Troubles and I can see his regret. "He was old, Phyllis. We were afraid that you were too young to accept the responsibility."

I'm quiet. These are mere repetitions of words that feel artificial and meaningless. My father shifts uncomfortably in his chair. "There's more to it than that," he says.

"Tell me," I say. "I want to know."

"He's a sweet dog," my father points to Troubles, "and maybe you would've learned to be responsible. I don't know. But where I come from, we couldn't even feed the family, never mind a pet. Keeping animals in the house meant poverty, like living with the pigs. No, it was just something inconceivable to me. For Grandpop it was different. But my father? My father couldn't even feed his own children. We knew better to even think of such a thing. We had to fight each other for food. Whoever got up late in the morning didn't eat. I had to go to work to help feed my family, not to feed a dog."

I know that I heard all of this as a child, but I hear it now as an adult. My heart goes out to him. I smile at him. "I'm glad we can share Troubles now," I tell him.

"He's a really good dog," he acknowledges.

Several hours later, I see my father climbing up from the basement with a small package of newspaper.

"What's that?" I ask him.

"We forgot to turn off the light. When I went back down, I found something Troubles left behind." I can't believe it, but he's smiling.

"I'm sorry, Dad. Thank you. You should have left it for me. I guess he got confused. The basement floor is concrete, so he must have thought it was okay. I'll take care of it, Dad." I reach for the package.

"No," he says, "I don't mind. I wasn't even going to tell you." he looks down at Troubles, inevitably at my heels and says, "You're a good boy, Troubles." Troubles cooperatively nuzzles his leg. This feels a lot like reparation.

# [11]

# THE MANY FACES OF DORA

My father is a firm believer in "the Lord helps those who help themselves." He has an assortment of tales at his fingertips to illustrate this philosophy and to support his position. These parables often don't show him in the best light which he somehow fails to recognize. Whatever positive feelings he might have toward the benefactors in his life are complicated by the one time they've let him down. In his peculiar habit of rewriting history, his bitterness over one incident will shift to an incredible generosity of spirit for another, or vice versa. I am confused about my relatives. I have no idea what to make of them.

Take Aunt Dora, for example. In truth, she is my great aunt, Bubbe Sophie's sister. I remember her when I am five and she is still rolling strudel across her cracked linoleum kitchen table. Her days of marching for the International Ladies Garment Workers Union are a fairy tale for me and a fading memory for her. My father claims that Aunt Dora is one of the founding members, but we never establish that as fact.

I have several photos of Aunt Dora. One portrays the woman who might have founded and led the ILGWU. She is a young woman in Russia, perhaps in her twenties. She is outfitted (most likely by the photographer, as was the common practice in those days) like a czarina. The bodice of her velvet gown is covered with intricately woven lace that extends high on her neck. The tight velvet sleeves flare into lacy fans at the wrists. She is wearing a heavy locket around her neck. Dora looks as if she'd been born to this style of clothing, although she could have afforded none of it.

The Dora I remember was photographed in the 1930's, a good fifteen to twenty years before my birth. She hasn't really changed that much by the time I am five. Even in this pose, she looks like a woman who could take on the world and emerge, if not victorious, at least smiling.

Once a month, early on Sunday morning, we drive to the Dorchester section of Boston to visit Aunt Dora. Her second husband, Uncle Morris, is a tall, skeletal man with a reportedly ferocious temper and more than a tiny taste for vodka. They live in an old tenement building on a grungy street in the heart of what Daddy refers to as "the slum." He takes a backward, panicky glance at the car before we enter the small sunless vestibule that leads to their third-story walk-up. "Hope the hubcaps are still here when we get back," he worries aloud, but it's more than likely he's afraid he'll never see the whole car again.

Daddy pushes the bell and we wait in silence for the buzzer to open the door. When he hears the familiar low-pitched grinding sound, he shoves with all his body weight. The door creaks and moans in agony. Finally inside, we march single file up the rickety, dust-covered stairs. This climb is frequently but not always accompanied by my father's warning that we, too, could end up like this if we don't get a good education and marry someone "decent." It's not hard to figure out that Uncle Morris doesn't fit into this category.

Aunt Dora always greets us as though we are long lost relations from Mother Russia. She throws her arms around my mother, then my father, proclaiming her joy in a mixture of Yiddish and sighs that only my father can begin to understand. "Ohhhhh, mine kinderlach, my beautiful children, come in, come in." She presses both of us to her, one against each breast, releasing us only to measure our height and weight and to insure that all of our organs are intact.

In contrast to the surroundings, the afternoon meal is always a feast. Aunt Dora prepares everything herself, even the breads and pickles. No matter how many dishes she places on her table, Daddy invariably notices the absence of some delicacy that Aunt Dora once prepared for him.

"Aunt Dora, remember that herring salad you made with all the onions and horseradish sauce?" Dora pushes her heavy arthritic body slowly from the table and pries open the door of what she and Daddy still refer to as "the icebox." After several moments of hard scrutiny, she reaches into its mysterious contents and retrieves the herring dish (or whatever else that's missing) from among many stacked containers and packages. Ignoring Daddy's protests, "Sit down, sit down, I'm sorry I even mentioned it," she is at his side, "Take, take, why do you think I make it?" One thing is certain. We know she hasn't made it for Uncle Morris.

Uncle Morris never sits with us at the table. We're convinced that he never eats. He slinks around, popping up and scaring us without any intention of humor. Casting an eerie shadow between the kitchen and the living room, like an apparition from Auschwitz, he studies us intently, as if he is preparing to later paint the scene on canvas. Sometimes he simply puts on his hat and coat and announces to Aunt Dora that he is "going out." I always feel relieved to see him go until I see Aunt Dora's expression. Then I feel ashamed. I hear Mommy and Daddy whisper that he can be mean after "he's had a few."

Aunt Dora is everything her sister, Sophie, is not. She's warm and generous and loves us all passionately. Most of this I take in through osmosis, as she frequently forgets that we understand little of her Yiddish. She lapses into long passages that are lost in Daddy's loose translations. He forgets we're there at all until she wants us to answer her questions. She starts in English, digressing into Yiddish mid-sentence, interrupting herself from time to time to ask if my sister and I are following. Our glazed expressions always disappoint her. "The children should know Yiddish." Mommy fakes it.

Sometimes Aunt Dora and Daddy speak in Yiddish on purpose, and all we can make out are the names of relatives being discussed. We know instinctively that these are the moments we ought to strain for any recognizable phrases that might shed light into the deep, dark recesses of our family closet.

Leaving Aunt Dora's is a ritual. One by one we prepare for the hour-long car ride with a trip to the bathroom. I secure the door firmly with a chair just in case Uncle Morris happens to be lurking about. Somehow during this time, Aunt Dora manages to wrap up all the leftover food in a large package for us to take home.

Aunt Dora insists, sometimes in Yiddish, sometimes in English, "Take it, take it. I make it special for you."

Daddy always says in English, "We can't take all of that. You'll eat it later."

"No, I'm never going to eat it later." This is always followed by a long string of Yiddish. Daddy says something in Yiddish and they both laugh. Mommy smiles and says nothing.

I ask, "Can't we take the strudel?"

Aunt Dora laughs and says something to Mommy in Yiddish. Mommy has no idea what she's saying. Gay smiles and says nothing. She knows we're going to leave with the food.

But Daddy always asks pointlessly, "What about Uncle Morris?"

Dora utters a string of Yiddish. This time no one smiles. She adds in English to Mommy, "You don't take it, I have to throw it out." This always works like a charm, since Mommy doesn't believe in throwing food away. It usually takes all four of us to carry the food packages to the car. My father lingers a moment on the stairs with Aunt Dora. Dollar bills are pressed back and forth, first from my father to Aunt Dora and then back again until they're wrinkled from the intensity of the exchange. I'm never quite sure where they end up. This is always accompanied by a several rounds of "yes you musts," and "no I can'ts."

If Daddy's in a good mood, as soon as we're in the car, he'll ask, "Anyone want to stop for pickled tomatoes?" This means we'll have deli for dinner, since we never leave this heavenly smelling place without pastrami and corned beef, thick rolls and Jewish rye. If he's cranky and tired, Dora's leftovers will do. And they're never not good enough to have twice in one day.

\* \* \*

Once Gay is off to college, we spend more weekends in Philadelphia and fewer in Boston. But now when we visit Aunt Dora, Uncle Morris asks me if I'd like to watch television with him. There is a small black and white set in their bedroom. We sit on the bed together. Uncle Morris has surprisingly good taste. We watch productions of Hamlet, Macbeth, Othello, Romeo and Juliet. We see The Hunchback of Notre Dame and Jane Eyre. He tunes into ballet and opera and ancient history programs. We watch classics and comedies; we laugh and we cry together. Uncle Morris and I become television friends, but I still think he's creepy. As soon as a movie or program ends, Uncle Morris gets up without a word and turns off the set. He's back to slinking about or grabs his hat and leaves. I don't remember him ever saying good-bye.

Aunt Dora has a gold-colored comb and brush set from Russia that sits on an engraved mirror on her dresser in the bedroom. I tell Uncle Morris how pretty it is and he says he thinks that Aunt Dora will probably let me use it if I ask her nicely. I see some of Aunt Dora's hairs in the brush and so I tell him, "That's okay; I don't think Mommy would like it."

Now that I'm older, I don't always go to Boston with Mommy and Daddy. We have our own television set and I like to stay home by myself. I'm still a bit afraid of Uncle Morris, and Aunt Dora doesn't see too well anymore. Sometimes her dishes are dirty. Mommy says I shouldn't say anything because it will hurt her feelings. The bathroom smells like boiled cabbage. I make excuses and don't go for a few months.

So I'm surprised when I get a package in the mail from Uncle Morris. I feel guilty that I haven't been there.

"He must miss you," Mommy tells me, "but he never says. Aunt Dora asks for you."

"It looks like it's from him. I wonder what it is."

"Well, let's open it."

It's in brown paper and covered with layers of scotch tape. It's addressed to "little Phyllis Mitnick" with our address and "from Uncle Morris" in the return address.

"That weird Uncle Morris," I laugh to Mommy. "He still thinks of me as a little kid." Mommy hands me the scissors and I cut through the paper and tape. I dump out the contents on the kitchen table. It's my Aunt Dora's comb and brush set, filled with hair and thick with dust and dirt.

"Yuck. Mommy, that's disgusting. Is Uncle Morris angry at me?"

"I don't think so. You're right. Uncle Morris is weird."

"What should I do?"

"I'm not sure. Give it to me and I'll take care of it."

"But maybe I should send him a thank-you note. I don't want to hurt his feelings. Do you think Aunt Dora knows about this? She might not even know he sent it." I hand over the offending package to Mommy. "Ick. That really is disgusting."

"I'll talk to Daddy."

"Mommy, is Uncle Morris crazy?"

"He's getting old. I think he has some problems."

"If you tell Daddy, maybe he won't let me see Uncle Morris anymore. Do we have to tell him?"

"Let me think about it."

"Let's just throw it away and not say anything." Mommy considers this.

"I bet Uncle Morris won't even remember he sent it to me. It's so filthy, I bet Aunt Dora threw it out and Uncle Morris took it out of the garbage."

"Okay," Mommy wraps the comb and brush set back up in the brown paper.

"We won't tell anybody?"

"We won't tell. I'm sure he meant well."

The comb and brush set is not mentioned again.

\* \* \*

I'm in college and both Aunt Dora and Uncle Morris have passed away. Dad talks about Dora as if she is two people. In fact, in Dad's various monologues, Dora seems incredibly like his sister, Rosie, either angel of mercy or heartless she-devil.

When I was a child and Dad talked about his family escaping from Russia, the fact that the numbers didn't add up never crossed my mind. But after hearing and reading many Jewish escape tales, I begin to ask more pointed questions. These were people who lived on potatoes and bread. Where did the money come from? It was hardly likely that Sophie had any jewelry to sell. In fact, it seemed unlikely that she owned any jewelry or valuables. According to the fantasy of legends, clever Jews always managed to hide some diamond somewhere, and it takes my sister to bring me back to reality. "Diamonds, ha, that's a good one. I don't think so." So once again I confront my father. I lure him into my confidence with the promise that I will one day write the story of his escape. He likes the idea.

"No," he sighs, "there definitely weren't any diamonds. I don't know."

"Well, Dad, they had to have gotten the money from somewhere. Did they do something illegal? Did they steal it?"

"No, no. Nobody in my family ever did anything dishonest." He is indignant.

"Well then how did they get the money?"

"Aunt Dora sent it."

"Aunt Dora?"

"Yes, she came over first. Later she sent money to my mother. My father needed to get out of there before he was drafted, and my parents thought he'd get a job. But he couldn't get work, you know. It wasn't easy for him. He didn't speak any English." I think of Dad cursing out his Portuguese patients who "refuse to learn English," but I don't say anything. "In the end, he had to ask Dora."

"Where did Aunt Dora get all that money?"

"I don't know. It wasn't so much in those days, but it certainly was way more than we could ever hope to get. Dora worked in the garment industry."

"But still, Dad, she must have had to work very hard to pay for all of you and to support your father while he was looking for work."

"Well, my father stayed with some far-removed cousins in New Jersey. That's where we all lived when we first came over. There were so many of us sleeping in one room. Then we moved into the house on Daly Street."

"But how did they buy a house? Did Dora help pay for that, too?"

He shrugs. He is uncomfortable with acknowledging how much his aunt helped his family. This is especially true since he has been telling us for years about how when he told her he'd been accepted to MIT, she didn't offer to help him to pay the tuition. Now I wonder if this didn't have more to do with two bad marriages and the resulting change in her financial circumstances than indifference to his situation.

"You know, that's how they did things back then. One member of the family would come first and help the others to come. Yes, she must have worked very hard to help us." It's clear that he hasn't said this aloud in a very long time, if he's ever said it.

"But what happened to the rest of the family? Didn't they want to come?"

"I don't know," my father says. "I guess they knew what they had over there. My grandfather was too old to change his life. My uncle was dead; you know the story, killed in a pogrom. The other sisters, well, they stayed with their mother and father." He places his hands together as if this explains everything.

It is still a number of years before I read the letter from my Aunt Rosie where she describes her mother's parting from her own mother. She is chasing Sophie down the road, pulling and tearing at her clothing, crying and screaming, cursing Louis for taking her daughter away.

"They never saw their families again?"

"No." My father sits back in his chair.

I sit back in my chair, too. I cannot imagine making such a choice.

"Did they write?"

"Oh, yes. There were letters back and forth."

"Well, what happened to them? Why don't you write to them anymore? You still write to our cousins in England and Argentina."

He is quiet. Finally he says, "During the war, the letters stopped coming."

"And no one ever heard from them again? No one found out for certain what happened to them?"

"No. I guess it was too difficult. Letters came back saying, no such person at this address. "Then after the war"—he stumbles, "Russia was never very good to Jews. We assumed they'd all been killed or they would have written."

"So in a sense, Aunt Dora really saved your lives."

"Yes. I never really thought about it that way, but you're right. She did."

And why would he have ever thought about it that way? He was five years old. He could not have realized he was being given a second chance. He never chose it.

# [12]

# BABIES AND BAGELS IN THE CONVENT

In terrible dreams I see Mommy and Daddy's faces melting, swallowed by fire and flames, right before my eyes. I wake up soaked with salty tears and sweat. I imagine I am also melting. Mommy hears my cries and rushes to comfort me. She rocks me against her, and I am reassured for this moment that her body is solid. She takes me by the hand to the bathroom to wash away my fears. The universe is again in its proper place. The wash cloth is soothing and cool. Mommy asks if I am ready to go back to sleep now. I am only four years old and still afraid, but my eyes droop heavy with sleep. She takes my hand and we step together out of the bathroom. Violently her hand jerks mine in a convulsive grip. Her face is distorted and transforms into the melting mother of my nightmares. I scream out in fear. I have created her. Daddy is there. He rushes away the melting mommy nightmare. I am left alone, shaking and sobbing in terror. I crouch on the floor, waiting. When Daddy finally returns, I cringe from him. I am so afraid that he will punish me for hurting her. "I'm sorry, Daddy." He grabs hold of my hand, pulling me along. "Back to bed," he says. I'm too afraid to ask, and he offers no explanation. Alone in my bed, I wonder if it has all been part of the same dream from which I have never really awakened.

\* \* \*

I've read my mother's attempt to write about her illness. It's painful. She seems to be missing her own experience. This is often how she slips away from me. When I look at our photographs together, I can't always remember her presence, a sense of her being there. I feel instead an empty crevice, an absence.

And so, I imagine my mother sitting on the edge of her hospital bed. She's packed and waiting for my father to come and take her home. She's finally given birth to me, the sister my sister has so desperately wanted. She leans over and her world funnels into a deep, devastating blackness.

My mother opens her eyes to a blinding flashbulb whiteness. The room is empty. She's alone. Her hands reach up to ward off the pain in her head and she discovers that she's wrapped in a turban of bandages. She has no memory of her life. She doesn't know who she is, but she wonders if she might not be a character from a film stuck in the part of her brain that hasn't been struck by lightning. She is alive in The Snake Pit. She's paralyzed with terror that she doesn't know she's insane and has been committed against her wishes to a mental institution. Slowly she wills herself from the bed. She must escape. Everything is white and fuzzy, as if she is moving in a dusty fog. In the slow motion of dreams, she makes her way to the door and somehow manages to open it. There is a long corridor and then an exit sign to a staircase. The stairs wind on and on, down into the belly of the snake, a descent into hell. My mother screams and screams. It's a good forty-five minutes before the hospital attendants find her. It's a good forty-five years before I fully understand what has happened.

*  *  *

I am a child with the heart of an adventurer. It's a hot and steamy summer day. We live far enough from the ocean to be clear of angry hurricane waters and too far to feel cooling breezes. I'm bored and lonely. I've had enough of sitting on the front porch. I wander down the street, past the safety borders I've been instructed not to pass. I hear shouting and laughing and splashing water. I do the ultimate forbidden and cross the street. I follow the sounds until I see a large swimming pool filled with children. Waving and shouting, too, I run up to the edge. Hands and voices reach out to encourage me. The temptation is more than I can bear, so I break away and breathless from excitement, run home to my mother. It's only mid-afternoon, but the table has been set for dinner. My mother is sitting with her back to me, her head buried in a crossword puzzle book hanging over the edges of her dinner plate. She's careful not to disturb the silverware. She doesn't seem to hear the banging of the back door screen behind me and continues to move her pencil across the page.

"Mommy, Mommy, the children asked me to swim with them, okay? Can I?" She turns her pencil over in an exasperated motion to erase what she's just written. "It's more than seven letters," she complains.

"Can I? Please?" I persist, believing that she's heard my request but doesn't want to answer me.

"You can ask your father." The pencil is now between her teeth, and her eyes are fixed on the seven-letter dilemma.

"But they want me to swim with them now! Daddy's in the office. They're just over there (I point but she's not watching) and their mommies are there. Please Mommy can I go? They want me to come!"

There is tension in my voice that demands an answer. My mother hears and feels this without her eyes ever leaving her book. I see her deliberating, when in fact, she has no awareness of me. There's an irritating blockage, a clogging in her brain, something annoying that's keeping her from discovering those seven letters. To make it stop she says, "Yes, yes. Fine."

I run out without changing into my suit, letting the screen door bang closed again. I'm out of breath when I reach the pool. There's a pain in my chest but I don't care. I don't want to miss a second. I don't know if I even take off my shoes, but yes, I must have. I can feel the lukewarm water swirling around my feet. There's a huge blue and green striped ball being tossed around and the excited confusion of kicking legs and waving arms and water splashed in my face. I have no idea that I don't belong and no one seems to notice. Do I catch the ball and toss it back? Maybe. My vision is blurred with water and time.

A hand grabs hold of my sopping wet tee shirt and wrenches me from bliss. I am in the air, suspended, looking directly into my father's fear and rage. What have I done? I'm at a loss. And all that my very young memory retains of the short trip home is a sense of bewilderment.

I'm roughly deposited in the kitchen where my mother still sits with the crossword puzzle book. She looks at my father, then at me, but she says nothing. My father wags his finger in front of me.

"How could you just go off like that without asking permission? Do you have any idea where you were? Do you know what that place is?"

"I asked Mommy if I could go! I asked Mommy! You said I could go, didn't you, Mommy?"

My mother looks up. Now we have her attention. She closes the book. "But Phyllis, you never asked me if you could go."

"You liar!" I'm screaming at my mother. I stomp a wet foot hard against the kitchen linoleum.

"How dare you talk to your mother that way!" My father's face is distorted with anger. "Go to your room this minute, and don't come out until you're ready to apologize."

I run from the room shouting, "I'm never coming out! I hate her! She's a liar!" My mother has betrayed me. I'm convinced she's done this on purpose, and I can't imagine why. It's with him that I can expect this weird unpredictability, not with her.

Then I wonder if she's afraid. For some reason, Daddy thinks this place where he found me is a very bad place. Mommy doesn't want to admit she said I could go because she's afraid Daddy will be mad at her. But I don't really care. This is no excuse to allow a four year-old to take the fall.

I hate her, and I will never trust her again. I creep from my room to the top of the back stairs, where I can eavesdrop on my parents' conversation in the kitchen below. My father is ranting and raving.

"She is crazy going to a place like that!" Does he mean me? My mother mumbles something I can't make out.

"I know she's your sister, but that's what I feel. She belongs in the nut house."

Have I been swimming at a "nut house?" Why did my mother lie? Their voices are too low now, and so I tiptoe a little farther down the stairs. As hard as I strain, I still can't make out their words. Suddenly the kitchen door opens and my father yells for me to come down. I pretend not to hear him as I sneak back up the stairs and into my room, quietly shutting the door behind me. The second time he yells, I open the door.

"Phyllis, come down here. I want to speak with you." There is a different quality to his voice. It is almost apologetic, and because this is alien to my father, it's frightening.

I climb down the stairs slowly. I've been betrayed. I think I can never love her or depend on her in quite the same way again. I'm too little to understand what I'm feeling. I don't have the words or the experience.

Daddy's waiting for me at the kitchen door. Mommy's still at the kitchen table, but now her head is slightly bowed and she doesn't look at me. She's staring past the book to some undefined spot beyond the table. Daddy waves me past her and into his office. Now I'm nervous. To be called into his office implies a very serious offense. He asks me to be seated as politely and carefully as if I were an ambassador to his country.

"This is very difficult for me," he says. I do not respond.

"You're very young, and I don't know if you can understand what I'm going to tell you." Since I have no way of reassuring him that I will understand, I continue to regard him a bit suspiciously. My father is uncomfortable speaking to children, and he either proceeds as if he were speaking to an adult or in some fabricated fashion he has gleaned from movies or television. Somehow I now feel privileged. He is not yelling at me, and I have gained access to the inner sanctum. At the same time, I feel afraid. There is some mystery here that I am not sure I want solved.

He begins to speak and within a few seconds, he's lost me. I already know my mother had "an accident." I know that's why she sometimes "falls down." But I'm getting angry and frustrated now. He's explaining right and left functions of the brain. I'm four and I'm getting a medical school lecture. I think I ought to understand what he's saying. I tune him out. I stare at the Van Gogh self portrait print on the wall. When I tune back in, he's talking about her loss of short-term memory function. I remember thinking he made this up to protect her; that it isn't possible for her to have forgotten. It is just an easy way to get out of a tough spot. She's betrayed me, and that's that.

Next comes the statement I dread the most. "She was never like that until you came along."

And how did I just "come along" anyway? There are certainly mysteries about my arrival. My sister wanted me so my parents decided to give me to her. Although my father rails against making idiotic mistakes, this is clearly one he and my mother discussed and made anyway. My birth seems to have gotten the Mitnicks kicked out of their Garden of Eden. I imagine myself spurting forth with such a force of evil that my mother's weakened brain has exploded into zillions of irretrievable sections of matter. I'm the serpent who's altered their lives, some kind of beast to be held back before I can cause more trouble. It would be ludicrous to believe that these actual thoughts could go through my head at the age of four, but I know I felt like a monster.

My father explains that I have been playing in a nursery for Catholic children. Those sweet, friendly ladies in the funny hats and robes are nuns. I'm a Jewish girl, and he'd like me to stay away from there. He has his reasons; when I'm older I might understand them, but for now that ought to be enough. Yes, he concedes, my mother probably did give me permission (he doesn't actually admit I've been telling the truth), but she didn't realize where I was going and has forgotten that she ever said it was okay.

"Why is it wrong for me to play with the Catholic children?" I want reasons.

"I know it seems hard on you now, but it can lead to other things."

"What other things?" There are more evil sins I can commit without my knowledge. I feel more afraid of these. How can I recognize dangers when I don't even know what they are?

"Why do you always have to talk back to me? Why don't you just accept what I tell you? You always have to answer back with everything! You're going to have trouble all your life if you don't learn to listen. Larry and I never talked back to my father. If we did, whack across the face! And Bobby—well, I had to beat the crap out of Bobby. Why don't you see that I know what's best for you? Do you want to end up like your Aunt Kathie? She always knows better than everybody else and look at her, she's completely crazy."

And so Catholicism, asking "why," and my Aunt Kathie's mental state become intrinsically bound by some mysterious force which both attracts and terrifies me. I stand in front of Catholic Churches for hours, mesmerized by the darkness and stained glass, imagining the inside of the confessional and longing to experience these forbidden and thus unknowable things. I envy my Catholic friend. Sometimes I wait for her outside her church, desperately hoping she'll ask me in. And when she finally does, I freeze with shame that my longing has been so visible and fear that some member of the Temple might pass by and witness my tenuous principles and conflicts of faith. I haven't found a Jewish equivalent for "Hail Marys," and I'm not convinced that my once-a-year Yom Kippur request for forgiveness can possibly compare with all of these ongoing confessions, even if I am able to make it all the way through the fast. After all, it's just one day. I worry about being struck by lightning.

Since it's difficult for me to know on which accounts lightning could strike, I test both my father and God. Dad's messages are confusing, and the Lord is not speaking to me directly. The temptation to test beckons from the Mount. It also presents itself to me in the form of invitations from the large Polish Catholic family down the block.

The Janowskis have their own bully/ scapegoat set of teenage twins, and a child my age, tormentors and tormented. Their dog regularly bites the mailman and anyone else foolish enough to climb the steps to their doorbell without at least one member of the family in tow. This small creature, inappropriately named "Lady," is in part responsible for any religious fervor I may have. In order not to have to walk around the entire block to make my way to school, I pray from the moment I close our front door until I round the bend from Clinton Place to Clinton Street. Whenever I go over there to play, it's never without calling first and requesting "dog assistance."

I'm seven years old when I'm invited to the Janowskis for lunch during Passover. There's been an ongoing debate in our house as to which foods should or should not be eaten during Pesach. Whenever Daddy wants to criticize the purchase or cost of a particular food item he doesn't think is necessary, he insists that Mommy identify the "Kosher for Passover" label. When it doesn't suit him, or the "Kosher for Passover" labeling means twice the price for the same food, Daddy swings far to the left. "This is no longer religion," he shouts, "it's capitalism!" It's hard to know where Marx and God meet, if they do, or when one or both might be inclined to strike Mommy or me down in anger. After all, I am the one who asks for the special Kosher for Passover chocolates that Daddy sneaks at night when he thinks no one is looking. But of one thing I'm sure, bread is forbidden.

Daddy must be distracted when I ask if I can have lunch with the Janowskis because he agrees. He must realize this within the hour because he's back with a list of precautions.

"You can go, but whatever you do, don't eat any bread. Make sure they know it's Passover and you can't eat bread."

Mrs. Janowski serves sandwiches. She reminds me of the Beaver's mom, always in a dress, manicured and made up, she puts on an apron and wears high-heeled shoes in the house. The only phrases I can manage to get out in her presence are, "yes, please; no, thank you, thank you very much, I'm fine—and how are you?" As hard as I try, I can't tell this perfect-looking woman with such a scary family that I'm Jewish and can't eat the nice sandwiches she's made because it's Passover. And perhaps if dietary law, as I understand it, were less inconsistent, convoluted, and subject to impulsive and erratic contradiction, I might not find myself in such conflict. I'm confused when Mommy orders ham (we don't actually call it that; Mommy points to it on the menu just so the waitress can see), and yet Daddy won't allow her to bring pork into the house. Being a Jew is confusing. Or perhaps I merely lack the necessary mettle.

I eat a sandwich, one only, even though I'm still hungry. I taste guilt in every bite. I'm betraying God, Daddy, and all the children of Israel. Never before have I longed for the confessional as I do now. If I repeat "shema yisrael" as if it were "Hail Mary," will it work?

I long for punishment and ultimate absolution to come in the form of Daddy asking me the fatal question: Did you eat bread? Apparently, he trusts that I have not because the question never comes. And so my punishment is left to me and the imagined fury of a God towards his faithless and fickle servant.

\* \* \*

I am sixteen before I become acquainted with Aunt Kathie. From my perch at the top of the back stairway, I learn that she is coming for a visit. Since extended visits from family members, or from anyone else for that matter, are almost nonexistent, this is a major event.

Aunt Kathie looks like my mother, and then again, she doesn't. She has red hair and freckles, is taller and fatter, and enters our home with an energetic bounce in her walk that hollers freedom. Where my mother seems to be missing in action, Aunt Kathie is so present that her emotions enter the room before she does. Her laughter bellows up the stairway, entering the hallowed sanctum of my father's hour of television news. When my mother tries to shush her, Aunt Kathie only laughs louder. "What, a little laughter's going to hurt him? It ought to do him some good. Anyway, how is it he can hear me laughing all the way down here, and he can't hear the television? The whole neighborhood can hear it!"

I love her on first sight, my Auntie Mame. Not only does she not seem crazy, but she seems the only rational voice in the house. I refuse to leave her side until she is forced to throw me out in the middle of the night in order to get some sleep.

We sit together in what was my room before my sister left, side by side on the small twin bed with the fuzzy little pink lamb on its headboard. Smoking cigarette for cigarette, two criminals in collusion (smoking in the house is strictly forbidden), I ask questions and Aunt Kathie answers them. She never says, "Oh, you'll find that out one day," or "You'd better ask your mother." Sometimes her head rolls back with laughter at what I think I know, and sometimes little lines of past worries appear around her eyes. But on and on she goes like a fabulous smorgasbord until her eyes begin to close, her cigarette waivers and she warns me, "You'd better let me get some rest before I fall asleep with this cigarette and burn down the whole house. Then your father will never let me visit you again." Reluctantly, I leave her, eager to hear the rustling sounds of her movements the next morning so that our adventure can begin again.

Somewhere in that visit, I recognize that Aunt Kathie's freedom gives her power. When Daddy tries to correct her, she waves her hand somewhere off to stage right and laughs with her whole body. "I'm sure you're right about that, Nathan," she replies, as if to say, yes, you're right, but who cares anyway? Although I am sure Daddy never mistakes this for acquiescence, he's left without a response, something I've never witnessed.

And the thing that amazes me so much about her is that his arrows never seem to nick even the surface of her skin. She slides out of reach, while all the rest of us are open to attack. A sense of disloyalty prevents me from inquiring further, but I guess that her presence itself might be instructive. It's of no use. As diligently as I observe, as closely as I imitate, I cannot create this essence within myself. I remain as enraged as ever.

Since I think this might be my only chance to discover the truth, I do decide to sound her out about her stay in the mental hospital. For just a moment, she loses speech and stares at me blankly. "No," she answers thoughtfully, as if she might have possibly misplaced this information, "I was never hospitalized. I wonder what he could have meant." Aunt Kathie is too genuinely puzzled to be hiding something from me. I shrug and privately determine to grill Mommy before Kathie is no longer available for confirmation.

I wait until Daddy is busy in the office and Kathie is resting before dinner to approach Mommy. I shoot straight to the heart of the matter.

"Kathie says she was never in a mental hospital."

Mommy drops her dishtowel and stares at me. "You asked her that?" She seems more shocked by the question than the answer.

"Yes, I asked her."

"Why on earth did you ever ask her something like that? Where did you ever get that idea?"

"I was snooping," I half smile sheepishly. "I overheard you and Daddy talking about her, and he said she was in the 'nut house.'"

It takes Mommy several minutes to decipher this. A smile starts to break which she quickly suppresses. "Ohhhh, that wasn't a mental hospital. That was just your father's way of talking about her going into the convent. He thought she was crazy. Well, we all wondered. Maybe we all thought she was a bit crazy for doing that, but not really crazy. Oh, I'm so sorry you asked her that."

I persist. I'm curious after my own dalliance with Catholicism. "Why did she go to a convent?"

"To become a nun."

"But she's Jewish. She's my aunt. How could she become a nun?"

"Sshh," Mommy cautions in a half whisper, motioning towards the single door separating our kitchen from the inner sanctum of the office, "your father will hear us. She's not Jewish."

"How come my aunt isn't Jewish?" I demand to know.

"She converted. She became a Catholic."

"Because she wanted to become a nun?" Jews do not convert. This is anti everything Daddy has ever taught me. Jews not only do not convert, they do not drink, take drugs, do not turn out to be homosexual, do not divorce, do not steal or murder.....the list is inexhaustible. And if, in fact, Daddy does come across any blatant contradictions, he simply restates that "Jews don't do 'this,'" whatever "this" happens to be.

"I don't know," Mommy whispers. "You'll have to ask her that. Just don't do it in front of your father. You know how upset he gets."

"You don't know?"

"I would never ask. It's none of my business." I decide to make it mine.

That night, after Mommy and Daddy have gone to sleep, Aunt Kathie and I slip out onto the front porch for a cigarette. It's quiet except for a soft breeze playing lightly on the leaves of the oaks and maples lining our cul de sac.

"So," I ask Kathie, "why did you become Catholic?"

"I don't know. It's not that I'm not Jewish. I just like being Catholic."

"I don't understand."

"That's okay. I'm not sure I do either."

"I'd like to have confession," I volunteer. "Once a year doesn't seem like enough."

Aunt Kathie takes a long drag on her cigarette. She blows the smoke out slowly before she speaks.

"You're 16. How much can you have to confess?"

"I don't like my father."

"I don't like him either." Kathie doesn't smile. We sit and smoke. I break the silence.

"So what made you want to be a nun?"

"It's complicated."

"Please tell me. I want to know."

Aunt Kathie crushes one cigarette butt and lights a new one. She sighs.

"Okay. I'll do my best. I don't understand it all myself, but I'll try. It was after Michael, my skating friend."

"Skating friend?"

"Yes, I used to ice skate."

"Oh yes, I remember a picture of you. You were skinny in a short skirt with long hair, like mine only red."

"But I was a few years older than you. I was 19."

"When you met Michael?"

"Yes."

"How did you meet him?"

"We met at the skating rink. He watched me skating and asked me if I'd like to have a partner. We started meeting there and we became friends."

"Did you date? Was he your boy friend?"

"I wanted him to be."

"He didn't want to be?"

"No. He couldn't."

"Why not?"

"I'm still not sure. He said he was going to become a priest. I don't think he was interested in me in that way—or maybe he wasn't interested in anyone in that way."

"Did you love him?"

"Yes, I thought I did."

"Do you still love him?"

"I still think about him, but no, I don't love him in the same way. I realized it could never be."

"Is that why you decided to become a nun?"

"Well, it probably did have some influence on me. I mean, Michael influenced my interest in the Catholic Church. But at the time, I was looking for something, I don't know what, but I felt lost. So I decided to enter a convent."

"What was it like?"

"It wasn't for me. I was always getting into trouble, breaking rules, making people laugh when they weren't supposed to, bringing bagels into the convent."

How cheeky, amusing and irreverent, I'm captivated by her. "You brought bagels into the convent?"

"Yes," she laughs. "I snuck out and bought a huge bag of bagels back with me. It was the last straw. They kicked me out. Anyway, it was about that time that Dolores started coming out."

"Who's Dolores?"

"She was one of my other personalities."

"Like Sybil?"

"Just like Sybil."

"So Daddy was right?"

"No, I was never hospitalized. A priest helped me. He ran a group. There were a few of us. When they kicked me out of the convent, they sent me to him."

"Do they still come out?"

"My other personalities?"

"Yes." I feel a sudden need to look over my shoulder.

"No. I've been integrated."

"What does that mean?"

"That means the priest helped me to get all the personalities to become one."

"How many were there?"

"I was never sure of all of them."

"Wow. Were you scared?"

"Not really. Most of the time I didn't even know I was changing."

I pull another cigarette from the pack we've been sharing. I offer one to Aunt Kathie and then light hers and then mine. We smoke quietly for a time.

"So is it a real tragic love story? Did you have a nervous breakdown?"

"I don't think it was just because of Michael."

"Why then?"

"I think I didn't feel loved by your grandfather. You know, he gave me away when I was a baby. When my mother died in childbirth, my cousins offered to take care of me. He was so sick with grief that he let them take me. When he married Aunt Rose, he could've taken me back."

"Mommy says he tried."

"Well, he did ask, but they begged and begged to keep me. He should've insisted. He was my father."

"Were your cousins mean to you?"

"Oh, no. They loved me. They spoiled me rotten."

I don't know what to say. So we finish our cigarettes and go to bed. I don't fall asleep for a long time. It occurs to me that Aunt Kathie and I have a great deal in common. I wonder what it would've been like if Mommy had died when I was born. Would Daddy have given me away to Aunt Rosie or Aunt Ruthie? I don't think I would've liked it much. I'm so glad Mommy didn't die. Mommy forgets things at times, but she listens to me and always tries to help me. I don't think Aunt Rosie listens to anyone, and I don't think Aunt Ruthie could ever be as helpful to me or as kind.

# [13]

# READING AND WRITING

Even more than I love eating lobster on Sundays ("traif" and only permitted outside of the house), I love Saturdays at the New Bedford Public Library. Every weekend for two years now—since I was four and stopped writing my "s's" backwards and could sign my name well enough to get a library card—my mother, my sister and I have been making this pilgrimage together.

The library is a ten-minute walk into town. It's an ancient stone fortress that is cool in summer and cold in winter. In front there is a statue of an Ancient Mariner. He beckons to all who wish to read and many who do not. Frozen with his harpoon at the ready, he's long past the days when there were whales to sight.

We always walk the same way, the same streets, Clinton to County, County to Union, Union to Purchase. Sometimes I look curiously down other paths that might lead us there, but my mother never alters the route. I wonder if there's someone or something that she fears, but it's probably so that she won't get lost.

At this curious age, there's nothing quite as compelling as the library, except perhaps our attic. There's a special children's room. This room is unlike the rest of the library where volumes line the walls from floor to ceiling. Here the bookshelves stop halfway to leave room for colorful cardboard cutouts of Mother Goose, Dorothy and Toto, Heidi and her goats, Cinderella and her pumpkin coach, with an array of crayoned cardboard letters below them spelling out book titles. I prefer the other rooms and rarely find anything here anymore. I'm already reading adult books that have to be checked out on my mother's or sister's cards.

My mother takes a long time browsing, often not remembering what she's read. When Gay recognizes a title wedged behind my mother's arm, she rolls her eyes back and shakes her head in disgust. "You've read that one three times!" There's no excuse in her adolescent heart for short-term memory loss.

Before I burst into her life, my mother used to read poetry and literature. Now she prefers science fiction and romance. Since she goes through four of these a week, it's more than likely she's exhausted the library's collection. She doesn't seem to mind. When I come home from school, I sometimes find her resting on the living room couch, three-fourths of the way through a novel. "I might have read this before; I'm not sure."

"Do you like it, Mommy?" I ask her. "I read things lots of times when I like them."

"Well, it's keeping me busy," she says. "I finished getting things ready for supper. Do you want to tell me about your book?" And I go on and on as six year-olds do until I run out of words and my sister rescues her by taking me off to my next set of lessons.

My sister shares everything she learns with me. Much of it is over my head, but not all. I never get tired of listening to her, and I'm the only one who doesn't. I'm intrigued by all that she knows, and when she doesn't come to look for me, I seek her out.

"Say egg in French—"oeuf," she instructs me. "That's good, but more like this, curl your tongue." And when I finally get it right, she's pleased and praises me. I lie on her bed next to her while she plays her recorder and teaches me to sing songs in French. She shows me how she makes the notes and lets me try. I'm not very good at it. But when my mother calls us down to eat, I wish I didn't have to go. I know that after supper, Gay will close her door to me to do her homework. I miss her then.

My sister makes reading lists for me. When I've exhausted them, she creates more. On rainy or snowy weekends, I emerge from my room only for meals. I wish I could bring my book to the table, but this is not allowed. If one of my friends comes to the door to see if I'll come out to play, I have to be coaxed. I don't simply wonder what will become of d'Artagnan; I am d'Artagnan, and I'm not to be disturbed.

\* \* \*

I'm bored and irritated with first grade. It isn't at all what I'd expected. I'm overqualified. My teacher makes good use of me. While she teaches the illiterate, I help the more advanced readers stumble through short, shaky and irrelevant sentences. The other children don't seem to resent this, but my questionable status confuses me. In this role, I know I am under-qualified.

My best friend's name is Grace. Purely from lack of exposure, she's in the other reading group. I'm appalled that she's never been to the library, and she is seduced by my endless repertoire of stories. Grace and I have been best friends since the end of kindergarten. I remember that it was winter, thick frost still coating the trees and grass, fogging the car windows. It was hard for my father to see when he drove me to school on mornings when my mother thought it was too cold for me to walk. Patches of dirty snow and frozen dirt predicted a late spring. I was removing my red rubber boots when Grace handed me an envelope addressed to "Philiss's Mother."

"That's not how I spell my name," I said indignantly, immediately taking a pencil from my desk and correcting it.

"I'm sorry," Grace said. "My mom can't write very well."

"It's okay," I said. I felt sorry to have said anything, remembering that English was Daddy's third language and he often couldn't spell the simplest of words. "What is it?"

"I want you to come to my birthday party."

"Just me?" She had only one envelope, not the large pack that was sometimes handed to the teacher to distribute to the whole class, nor the small pack that was selectively distributed on the playground.

"Just you."

I felt special.

My mother showed the invitation to my father that night at dinner. It was written on lined notebook paper.

"Dear Philiss's Mom,

Grace is six years old next week. She asked can Philiss come to her party. Please bring her at 3:00."

This was followed by an address and phone number and signed by Grace's mother. In both instances I had put a pencil line through "Philiss" and written "Phyllis" next to it.

"Who is Grace?" My father wanted to know.

"She's in my class."

"Is she your friend?"

"I guess so." Up until that moment I hadn't known it, but since I was the only one she'd asked, I really wanted to go.

"Grace's mother can't spell."

"You can't spell either, Daddy."

"She's right," my father laughed to my mother. "Okay. I'll take you." My mother looked relieved that this was not going to be a battle.

My father and I set out the following Saturday afternoon for a neighborhood I'd never seen. In my child's sense of time, in my excitement to give Grace the game her mother had told my mother she wanted, the drive seemed endless. It was more likely only fifteen minutes away. Grace lived in a narrow tenement in the North End. My father dropped me off without even coming in and told me he'd be back to get me at 6:00.

Grace's father and mother, her two sisters and three brothers, occupied the lower level of the house. Her father's sister, her husband and their three children took up the second floor, and her father's mother and father lived on the top floor where meals were constantly being cooked and delivered to all other parts of the house.

I could hear the music before I got to the porch, a loud and lively variety totally new to my ear. A tall man with a large belly and a wide smile answered the door.

"You must be Phyllis, Grace's best friend. She talks about you all the time. It's good to meet you. You come on in." He swept the door open and with an exaggerated gesture pointed to an open room packed with bodies gyrating to this foreign music. I must not have moved at all, mesmerized as I was by this unusual scene, because he put a fat hand on my shoulder and gently pushed me forward, calling out in a voice that carried over all the noise, "Grace, your friend's here!"

Black bodies of all shapes and sizes filled the overheated room with aunts, uncles, cousins and family friends. Balloons popped at random, exclamation points to the happy event. The food was as foreign to me as the music, but I ate everything in blissful ignorance of lurking pork or ham. I danced with Grace and all of her relatives long past being sweaty and tired. I don't even remember the gifts being opened, although they must have been. It was not the most important thing.

I was not aware of the time when my father arrived to take me home, but I was pleasantly exhausted and didn't complain. When we got to the car he asked, "Did you have a good time?"

"The best time ever, Daddy," I told him.

"I didn't know that Grace was colored. Did it bother you that you were the only white person there?"

"What?" I looked at my father in complete puzzlement, not understanding the question.

"You didn't know?" My father asked, and I felt ignorant of something I should've known and had missed.

"Of course I know Grace's colored," I lied. "Grace's my best friend." I said this for the first time, realizing that in one evening and one birthday party, it had become true.

\* \* \*

So Grace is my best friend, even if she can't read. She thinks I'm a genius, and I think she has the best family I've ever known. She shares their warmth and love with me, and I share the tales I've read and some I've created. Grace is equally enthusiastic and rarely knows the difference. She's an attentive and admiring audience and accepts all that I tell her as truth. I could not ask for more. She's a wonderful friend, the dearest I've known. It still has no meaning to me that she's colored, but my father makes much of this to his friends. He loves to tell the story of taking me to her birthday party and discovering that they were colored and I was the only white person there. He reports this with a certain pride that feels false, unkind. I grimace when I hear it. But I have no idea why and it's somewhat of a mystery to me that I find myself repeating in each instance that Grace is my best friend.

My efforts to get Grace to come to the library with me fail. The fact is that she would much rather have me tell her stories than read them herself. Her laborious reading takes all the pleasure out of the tale. She gets no meaning from it. She stumbles over the simplest words, and although she doesn't get frustrated, she doesn't understand why she must suffer when it comes so naturally to me.

"You read for a bit," I try to encourage her.

"Why? You do it so much better."

"But you have to try if you want to get better," I insist.

"I don't care if I get better. I like it when you read to me."

"Why don't you care if you don't get better?"

"I don't know. I just don't."

It makes no sense to me why she wouldn't want to improve her reading or how it can matter so little to her, but gradually I stop insisting that she read at all. There's no competitive spirit in her, just acceptance. This is not so hard to take.

\* \* \*

Third Grade. I'm the Jew who narrates the Nativity. I don't object to this on two accounts. My lines are written and all I have to do is read them, and I'm off to the side of the stage in the shadows. My father calls me Sarah Bernhardt, but I have no aspirations for the stage. I want to be Eugene O'Neill. I've already written a play about my family, but instinct warns me that it's better off where it is, hidden under my bed. Since Grace has moved on to another school, the only one I can read it to is myself.

Mrs. Biedermann is my teacher. She chooses me for everything and even though there are times I'd prefer to say no, I'm too afraid to lose my place and so I always say yes.

My sister is busy applying to colleges. My father boasts that she'll be accepted to all of them. He recites the impressive list like a mantra to anyone who'll listen. "Bryn Mawr, Smith, Pembroke and Wellesley. Bryn Mawr, Smith, Pembroke and Wellesley."

I hear my father refracting through the pantry door. I turn the knob quietly and open the door a crack, just enough for me to peek through.

"So Al, how're the kids? Hmmm, we may have to change the right lens."

"Am I losing vision, Doc?"

"No, it's normal aging. You'll probably need bifocals soon. How's the reading with these?"

"Okay. I don't have the time to read too much. The newspaper's about it."

"I know what you mean. We work so our kids can read. How's Lenny doing? Does he know where he's going to college?"

"He's not sure he's going. Maybe U of Mass."

"It's a decent school, Al. Now it's not Ivy League, but not everyone's made for Ivy League. Gay's applying to Bryn Mawr, Smith, Pembroke and Wellesley. She wants to go to Bryn Mawr, but we'd like her closer to home. I told her if she gets into all four schools, she can go wherever she wants. I just may have to live up to that. She's so darned smart."

"Yeah, Doc," Al concedes while my father pulls several lenses from their beds. "I wish Lenny had a bit more of that."

"There's nothing wrong with Lenny. He's a nice boy. Hmmm, let's see how this one is—tell me which is better, number one or number two. One or two." He alternates the lenses over Al's right eye.

"One, I think."

"You have to be certain, Al. You have to know. One or two?"

"Okay, it's one."

"You're sure?"

"It's definitely one."

"Good. Don't worry about Lenny, Al. Look at me. I'm no genius and I got through medical school."

If Al wants to ask him to do the "one or two" again, he'll think better of it now.

\* \* \*

Gay is angry. She doesn't know that she'll be accepted at all four schools. How could she? She wants to be near Grandpop and Aunt Rose. Since she doesn't believe in God, and I have no idea what it will mean for me when she does go, I pray fervently for her.

"Please, God, please let Gay get into all four schools. She has to go to Bryn Mawr and Daddy won't let her if she doesn't. Please, please, God, please help her get in. P-L-E-A-S-E." These prayers are chanted silently throughout the day and every night before sleep. My sister would never approve.

On the same day that Mrs. Biedermann announces the "What the American Flag Means to Me" writing contest, Gay receives letters of acceptance from Smith, Pembroke and Wellesley. Bryn Mawr hangs in the balance. My news is lost in "please pass the salt and pepper" at supper that evening. Anything else is interrupting my father.

"They're all good schools, Gay," my father repeats after the soup and again after the salad. I'd be proud to say you're at any one of them. Dr. Glassman's daughter went to Smith, didn't she? She's the one who married that successful surgeon from Chicago."

Gay stares at her plate, trying hard not to listen. I wait for a long enough pause to ensure that he's finished. It's good that I do because he's not.

"Lenny Davis' father was in the office the other day. He said Lenny's probably going to go to U of Mass. That Lenny must be a slacker just like his father. Al's been working at the same company for years and I've never heard him mention a promotion. Looks like Lenny's going to follow in his father's footsteps. U of Mass." He makes a grunt of disgust, which sends a slight spray of tea in my direction. "I wish you'd think about medical school, Gay. You'd make a wonderful doctor and you wouldn't have to work for anyone else." Gay swishes her fork around a mound of spinach. My father takes another sip of tea. While he's occupied with swallowing, I blurt out, "I have to write an essay about the American Flag for a writing contest."

"That's nice, Honey." My mother shoots a warning look in my direction.

"Medicine is the best career," my father continues. "Look at me, and I'm not as smart as you. I don't have a photographic memory. But still I made it through medical school. I didn't know if I could. Especially when I took anatomy. I threw that skeleton's foot across the room and told your mother I was quitting. Remember, Jeannette?" My mother nods her head up and down but he gives her no opportunity to answer. It's unnecessary, as we all know the story by heart.

"Your mother told me, 'Fine, quit, but you'll go to work for my father.' It was the best thing she could've said. I knew I didn't want to work for her father, (another sound of disgust) so I picked the foot back up and went on to become a doctor. I hated anatomy. If you work for someone else, you could end up like my friend, Max. Twenty-five years smoking cigar after cigar, all for the lousy pension he'll get if he doesn't have a heart attack first. He does the work; his boss takes the credit. Do you want to end up like Max?"

Gay looks confused. It's hard to grab hold of any feature of the short, tubby, balding man with the raspy voice perpetually enveloped in a fog of cigar smoke and known as Max bearing any resemblance to her either now or in the future.

"Well," my father insists, interpreting silence as dissent, "do you?"
"No, Daddy, I don't."
"Then you'd better think about it now."
"I have to write an essay about the American Flag," I shout.
"Phyllis, please don't interrupt your father."
"But Mommy, he NEVER finishes."
"Honey, don't be rude."
"But it's true. How am I supposed to know when it's my turn?"
"When your father is finished," my mother offers in a low voice, knowing full well that this is no answer.

"I'm finished," my father says. He sets down his cup in its saucer and pushes his chair from the table. "Jeannette, I'm going in the other room to read the paper. And you—he points a finger at me—you have to learn not to talk back."

\* \* \*

There must be a way to get my father to listen to me, to see me as significant, to recognize me as someone other than an hysterical child. I will write about him. In truth, I don't have feelings one way or the other about the American flag, even though I have to pledge allegiance to it every morning, five days a week, my hand held over my heart. I don't know what my mother feels for the flag, but I do know it makes my father proud to be American. My sister puts flags in the same category as God.

I sit on my bedroom floor with my composition book in my lap. Now and again I jot down a line; then I read it critically and scratch most or all of it out. A few more lines meet the same fate. I'm not good enough to capture my father's attention, let alone his admiration. I am not Eugene O'Neill. I rip out the page and crumple it, even though most of it is blank.

I begin again. Before two hours have passed, my wastebasket is filled and my composition book is empty. I have based my future on excruciating torture. I thought it would be easy. All those wonderful books, poems, plays. A library filled with them, and yet… I can't write an acceptable sentence.

This is terrifying. The thought that I will not be a writer, that I cannot be a writer, sweeps through my heart like a dry desert wind. I throw the composition book across the room and run to Gay. I remember that she's doing her homework. Her door is shut to everything else. I run two steps at a time down the back stairway. I hear myself shouting, "I can't! I can't do it! I can't!"

My mother has finished washing the dishes and is sitting alone at the kitchen table playing solitaire. "I can't do it, Mommy. I tried."

"What can't you do, honey?"

"I can't write the American Flag composition. I tried. I did. I just can't do it! It's too hard. I wish I were Eugene O'Neill."

"I don't think you'd really want to be Eugene O'Neill. He suffered a lot."

"Did he suffer all the time? Did he suffer when he wrote?"

My mother sets the remaining cards on the table.

"I think he suffered most of the time. He had an unhappy life."

"Me, too. I have an unhappy life."

"Phyllis, why do you say that? You don't have an unhappy life, do you?"

"Yes, I do." My eyes dart towards the wall that separates us from where my father has been reading the newspaper.

My mother sighs. "I'm sorry."

"It's not your fault, Mommy." I give her a quick hug and climb the stairs as quickly as I'd come down. I grab another composition book and get back to work. If suffering is a natural part of writing, if suffering is a normal part of a writer's life, there is hope.

\* \* \*

My essay wins first prize. Mrs. Biedermann announces it to the class and insists on informing the school during our weekly auditorium. She looks genuinely proud of me; I'm embarrassed. I'm not even sure if the essay is true because my father has refused to read it. "Wait until you're older and you know how to write. What can you possibly have to say about anything now?" I'm sure he's right. It doesn't sound all that wonderful to me.

"Nathan," my mother protests, "she won first prize."

"It's not exactly the Nobel Prize for Literature, Jeannette." He laughs and looks at me. "If you're lucky, one day you'll write as well as your sister."

An impossible task. I can't do anything as well as my sister. I wish I'd never written the stupid thing in the first place. Now I have to stand up before a full audience of teachers, parents, other children, principals from other schools for crying out loud, and read the thing. All for a lousy certificate and fifty dollars. Once everyone realizes how childish my essay is, they'll take it back and Mrs. Biedermann will be humiliated. I know I am. I tell Mrs. Biedermann I can't go.

"Why not?" she asks.

"It's not the Nobel Prize for Literature," I say. She calls my mother.

"I didn't know I'd have to read it in front of everybody," I tell her. "It's stupid. No one cares. I don't want to."

"If it was stupid," my mother pleads, "they wouldn't have given you the first prize."

"I'm not going. You can't make me."

Ultimately, I'm no match for Mrs. Biedermann. It seems to be her day more than it's mine. I go and I read the essay.

My father does not attend. My mother does, even though we have to take a taxi because she still can't drive. She is off the horrid pills that make her sleep all the time, but she still sometimes has seizures.

Once we are home, my mother cries and tells my father how moving it was, how well I described his experience as a refugee, pledging allegiance to our flag for the first time. I hear this through the radiator vent. I wait hopefully, but the fictional father I have created, untrue in all respects other than his patriotism, is a far more sympathetic character to my audience than he is to his family.

He asks my mother, "Jeannette, you read Harlequin romances. What do you know about writing anyway?"

I rip up the certificate and give the fifty dollars to my mother.

# [14]

# BRICK WALLS

*"Something there is that doesn't love a wall"*
Robert Frost

In our house on Clinton Place, there is a thick translucent, glass brick wall that feels more opaque to me, as there is little to no opportunity for light to pass through. The wall separates our living room from my father's medical office. I can't remember a time when it wasn't there, but my sister can.

Sometimes when I am at home alone, I wander into this office, a most forbidden place. I like the darkened examining room with its tall windows that line this rounded portion of our house. They frame the oak tree in the courtyard just outside, but I can never see it through the heavy shades. I try to picture the room before it was without light, sun streaming over a piano into what was once a music room. Perhaps it might have been my mother's music room, if it had not become my father's office.

Next to the examining room is a spacious area with a fireplace. In the fireplace is the wood that my father received as payment from his first patient. He never burns this wood or uses the fireplace. On the mantle is a replica of the Santa Maria given to my father by his old friend and walking buddy, Jim. Across from the fireplace and facing a large set of picture windows is my father's desk. Below the picture windows and built into the wall is an old-fashioned window seat. When I climb onto it, my father asks me not to sit there.

A small porch leading onto the main street from this second room has been converted into a comfortable waiting area. My father is proud of his home and his office. He is five minutes from the hospital and ten minutes from the nearest beach. He has many patients. His hard work and sacrifice has paid off, he tells me. It's what I must do, too, he emphasizes, to make a good life for myself. And it is true; he has created the life that he wants.

My mother finally seems to be finished with her surgeries. She's been sentenced to pills three times a day in order to prevent seizures, but they don't always work. Since we've moved into the new house, she has not been in the hospital. My mother is back to being a mother again. She cooks and bakes; she reads to me and tells me stories. But my mother no longer plays the piano. My father says there's no room in the house. Where would she put a piano? In her present condition, my mother has no answer for him.

Our house is dark and still, much too silent for children's play. The large stained glass window above the front staircase is shielded by heavy drapes. My father does not like the idea that outsiders could glimpse within, so they remain perpetually drawn. None of us uses the living room during the day. My mother opens the drapes there first thing in the morning, and my father closes them before he sits down to read his newspaper in the evening. The drapes in the sewing room, later to become the television room, are never opened.

My sister has a radio in her room. At some point in her teens, she also acquires a record player. We sing her favorites from *Oklahoma, The King and I* and *My Fair Lady* while we wash and dry the dishes. The singing is only allowed after office hours. We also have recordings of *The King Who Couldn't Dance, Little Black Sambo, Carmen* and *The Nutcracker Suite*. In the privacy of my sister's bedroom, we listen to *You Ain't Nothing but a Hound Dog*, but my father will never allow my sister to spend money on this kind of foolishness. In fact, we must keep the door closed and the volume down when we play the radio. If we turn it up too high, my father complains that the patients can hear it through the heating vents. My parents don't own a record player. They have a small radio in their bedroom where my father catches the news.

My mother tells me that when she was growing up, her house was filled with music. Now when she talks about it, she mentions it lightly, as if she is surprised by it herself.

"You play the piano?" I ask her.

"Oh yes, we all play, your Aunt Bea and Aunt Kathie and myself. But there isn't any room here for a piano." She seems to accept that as a credible answer, and therefore, so do I.

The glass brick wall separates work from play and day from night. I am curious about my father in there. Does he yell at his patients? I listen at the wall. The sounds are muffled. I can see distorted shadows of figures against the glass. Sometimes my father seems excited, his voice is raised, but I can never make out the words. I like to think that he yells at them, too. He should not be nicer to them than he is to us.

The only time I can clearly hear the patients and my father is when he examines people for glasses, and then I have to put my ear against the door. He uses what continues to be my mother's dish pantry. We leave everyday dishes and glasses on the kitchen counter so that there is no confusion in setting the table for supper. Every once in a while, my mother forgets a crucial dish she needs for baking, and then of course, the timing of our supper is completely thrown off. My father can be sympathetic about this or extremely annoyed. No one can predict.

He might smile easily at my mother and say, "That's okay, Jeannette. I'll just go read the paper," or he might wag his finger at her and demand that she learn to plan ahead. Not so easy when you have short-term memory loss.

I know my father's eye chart by heart, and I listen at the door to catch the patients' mistakes. Not F, that's an E, I correct to myself. My father threatens to change the chart or send me to someone else because he knows that I cheat. I don't want to wear thick glasses like my sister. When I try to see through hers, everything is blurred and nothing is real. It's like looking through the glass brick wall.

When my father is in a good mood, he lets me try on frames. We laugh at rhinestones stuck onto pink diamond-shaped rims. We play a game at guessing which of the women we know would choose which frames.

"Mrs. Katz would wear these." I giggle and model a slinky curved black pair covered with red and purple gems, sticking out my small belly to mimic Mrs. Katz.

My father laughs and says, "I bet she would."

I pull out a small, brown square pair and set them on the edge of my nose. "Here comes Mrs. Goldstein." I strut across the small room. "Dr. Mitnick, I don't think my prescription is quite right."

My father lets me look through the thicker lenses before we clean them. We do this together until I am old enough to be trusted to do it on my own. I like to help my father in his office because he often seems happier there, but you would never know it if you only saw him on the other side of the wall.

The glass brick wall does not always succeed in its design. Since there is only one bathroom in the house, it is inevitable for our paths to cross my father's patients. Once in a while, my father tells my mother to take someone down to the basement toilet closet. He only does this when a workman or a fisherman has not been home to shower and change before their appointment. Large rubber work boots are not allowed on the carpet, but even these trespassers may be taken upstairs if the rest of their attire is clean enough to pass muster and they are willing to remove their boots.

When our bathroom boundaries are about to be violated, my father enters the kitchen first, leaving the patient behind to await the "all clear" signal. If for any reason Gay and I are home from school and one of us might be in the bath or on the toilet, we are lucky if my mother is the messenger. There is a soft knock on the door and "One of your father's patients needs to use the bathroom. Can you hurry?" If we are less fortunate, on one of the rare occasions my mother is out of the house, my father brings the news himself. There is a loud banging on the door and "Hurry up. Come on out of there now. My patient needs the bathroom." If no one is occupying "the room," we are told to stay in our bedrooms until my mother or father gives us the word that we can come back out again. My father is somewhat erratic in all of these rules, and my mother is not always alert, so there are times I am confronted by a stranger negotiating the hallway on their own. And I always peek out of my bedroom door to sneak a look.

Gay and I don't like to share the bathroom with these interlopers. Things are difficult enough already. Since my father bought the house with a bath and no shower, he sees no reason to install one. He is first in the bathroom every morning. This law is never violated. My mother avoids all conflict by bathing at night. I concede to my sister because she is eight years older and she's nice to me. By the time I reach adolescence and bathroom wars could begin between us, she's off to college and my father is my only competitor. But there is puberty at eleven and the problem of sanitary napkin disposal. I am obsessed with how to hide this paraphernalia from potential patient visits.

Besides the bathroom, there is the telephone. We have three of these but only one line, and that is restricted to the office. Two of the phones are on my father's side of the glass brick wall. We are all trained in how to answer it. "Hello, (can be substituted with good morning, good afternoon, good evening) Dr. Mitnick's office. How can I help you?" Outgoing calls of a personal nature must be made after office hours and only with my father's permission. Friends and family are trained and retrained not to call until after 6:00pm unless it is a genuine emergency.

One of the three phones sits on my father's desk and another is just on the other side of the door leading into the pantry/refraction room. The third phone is outside my sister's bedroom door, small consolation for her since she is hardly ever able to use it. And since she is the one closest to it at night, she is rudely awakened for all emergencies and wrong numbers. My father refuses to have it in his room.

When my sister asks to use the phone, my father reminds her, "Five minutes. Remember, this is a business phone. There could be an important call coming in." My sister is creative and I am a quick study. We sneak into the office at night to make calls. But this one-way situation makes it impossible for my sister to date. If my father answers the phone and it's a boy, he demands to know everything about him and why he is calling. In most instances, the boy will turn out not to be Jewish and therefore, unsuitable. If my sister is fortunate enough to answer the phone herself, she will simply be cross-examined until the end result is the same. "Nice" girls calling boys is unheard of in the '50's.

The brick wall fails to keep my father's frustrations sorted into their respective compartments. There is no benefit of travel time from one side of the wall to the other. His dissatisfaction with one works its way to the other through the grouting and between the bricks.

When the dinner hour arrives, the dividing door bursts open and slams shut behind him. "Why don't they learn to speak English? Why do I have to speak Portuguese? I had to learn English when I came here. They're here 20 years and they still can't speak English. What's wrong with them?"

My mother tries to console him. "Sit down, Nathan. Your salad is on the table. I'm boiling the water for your tea."

"I don't understand why they bother to come to a doctor." He continues after washing his hands and seating himself at the table. "I take the time to give them instructions, tell them how to take their medication. They don't listen. I tell this guy specifically, put the drops in your mother's eye three times a day. He comes back and tells me her vision is still blurry. This is my fault? I did a perfect surgery. What does he do after my perfect surgery? He puts the drops in twice a day. What does he tell me? 'But Doc, I have to work. I can't do it three times a day.' I ask him, what about your wife? Can't she put in the other drop? He says, 'But Doc, she doesn't get along so well with my mother.' This is what I have to put up with. You think my life is so easy in there?" He waves his fork to indicate the office and almost hits my mother with it as she sets down his tea. He ignores her and removes the tea bag as if it has materialized on its own. He directs himself to my sister and me.

"You kids don't know what I have to go through to put food on the table. You can't appreciate it now, but you will one day. You think the money for this food grows on trees. I never had the luxury of thinking that and sometimes there was no food to put on the table. You don't know how lucky you are."

My father pushes his empty salad bowl to the side where my mother retrieves it and carries it to the sink. She returns to the table with a bowl of green beans and a larger bowl of mashed potatoes. My father suddenly seems to realize that he is eating supper.

"Where's the meat, Jeannette?"

"I'm getting it, Nathan." My mother arms herself to the elbows with padded gloves and heads for the broiler. When she opens it, clouds of black smoke conceal her from us.

My sister wrinkles her nose in disgust. "Burnt again," she mouths to me.

"Not burnt, well done," I mouth back.

My mother reappears with a platter of blackened things. My father sinks his fork into one and nods. He cuts off a small portion and chews silently. My mother waits, holding the plate.

"Is it okay, Nathan?" She finally asks him.

"I'm eating it, aren't I?" And this is sufficient praise for her to serve the rest of us because it is true that if it did not meet with his approval, he would send it back.

My father chews on, "We didn't have meat when I was a kid. Not in Russia. And sometimes we didn't see any meat in Philadelphia. My patients can't afford to eat like this. I bet your friends don't eat like this." He interrupts himself, "Phyllis, that's enough salt. You're going to get hardening of the arteries."

"But it doesn't taste good without salt, Daddy."

"So go ahead. Keep it up. Don't listen. When you have a stroke and can't move or talk because your brain is half dead, then you'll be sorry."

I look down at the hard, black thing that might possibly be a lamb chop. I have covered it with this latest threat to my well being. I push some of it off with my finger but leave some of it there to make it edible. "Sorry, Daddy." But he has already moved on.

"Do you remember that son of a gun who took his girl friend's eye out? Can you believe that so and so had the nerve to make an appointment with me? I should send him over to Diaz." My father does not have a high opinion of Dr. Diaz. He turns to me, "That's what will happen to you if you take up with some stupid halfwit Welfare bum. He'll get drunk one night and take your eye out, or worse." I am left to consider what could possibly be worse.

"Gay," my father turns to her, "you'll want to become a doctor. You're a smart girl, and anything else you might think you want to do would be a waste. You have all the advantages I never had. You'd be a good doctor. Ophthalmology is the best because you don't get as many emergencies. Remember when I used to do tonsillectomies?"

"How could she forget? You took hers out on the kitchen table." My father's look wipes the smile from my face.

"That was only after the first doctor botched it and they grew back," my father fiercely defends this do-it-yourself tonsillectomy from his eye, ear, nose and throat past. "But that's not my point. Why do you always interrupt me and talk back? Gay never talks back."

My sister grimaces. She sees it as pointless. She's lost her appetite. I can tell by the way she's pushing her food around on her plate that she is still picturing the patient having her eye poked out. Gay hates it when my father talks about these things at the dinner table. She doesn't want to become a doctor and she hates burnt meat.

"Anyway," my father goes on, "if you want a job done right, sometimes you have to do it yourself." No one contradicts him. "You'd make an excellent doctor, Gay."

Gay taps her meat listlessly with her fork.

"What about me?" I demand.

"I don't know if you're as smart as your sister."

"Of course, she is." My sister finally speaks, in my defense.

The phone rings. My father drops his fork onto his plate in irritation. "Answer that, Jeannette. Whoever it is, I'll call them back."

My father shakes his head as my mother stumbles out of her chair and the strap of her apron catches on its back. Gay reaches up just in time to free her. My father picks up his fork again but holds it in mid air, as if he is about to conduct.

"Good evening, Dr. Mitnick's office. Can I help you?" There is a long pause.

"Well, he's having his dinner right now. Can I have him call you back?" My father lowers his fork and lifts both arms in supplication. There is a pause. "Well, hold on please while I get a piece of paper and a pen." There is another longer pause. "Okay, yes, yes, I have it. Okay. Thank you." My mother comes back into the kitchen and pulls out her chair to sit down.

"Who was it, Jeannette?"

"Oh—wait a minute. I left it by the telephone." My mother pushes her chair in again and disappears into the office. She returns with a torn piece of paper. She hands it to my father.

"Jeannette, Jeannette, how many times do I have to tell you not to tell a patient I'm eating my dinner. I'm the doctor. You should never tell them what I'm doing. It's none of their business. Why can't you just tell them that you will have to have me call them back?"

My mother looks down at her plate of food. Maybe Mommy and I are both not so smart. Maybe I don't even want to be smart. I blurt out, "Mommy's a mommy, she's not a secretary. She makes great pies." My mother looks instantly grateful.

"Thank you, dear."

"Yes, and who do you think pays for all those pies? If we don't answer the phone the right way, people will get the wrong impression. They'll think I'm a quack or lazy like Diaz. It's a question of respect. Phyllis, I don't want you to answer that phone unless you can do it properly."

"I'm sorry, Nathan. I was thinking about the dinner." My mother only wants to keep the peace.

My father's brick wall is impenetrable but not impermeable. As hard as we all try to keep our lives and my father's business separate, it is impossible. Gay and I tiptoe around, voices hushed. When I come home from school, I whisper the events of my day to my mother. The only voice that is always loud enough for all of us to hear is my father's.

# [15]

## MUSIC LESSONS

I'm ten years old, and my father has decided to buy me a violin. I've been laboring along in the school orchestra for two years now, and the teacher thinks I show promise. Since I can read the notes and have managed to demonstrate this somewhat precariously on the school's violin, the teacher has recommended that I have my own instrument. My father is flattered. I've finally distinguished myself in something he values. What I am interested in is my voice. Perhaps because I feel I have so little of my own.

It's mid-August, hot and humid without a breeze. I'm busy eating peaches and reading Jane Eyre on the front porch.

"But I'm reading, Daddy. I don't want to go in the car. It's too hot."

"Don't tell me what you want or don't want. I told you to get in the car NOW."

"I have to go to the bathroom first."

"Get up there now. I'll wait for you in the car."

Reluctantly, I bring my book into the house and carry it slowly up the stairway to the bathroom. There I finish the chapter, flush, and saunter down to the car before I realize that I really do have to go to the bathroom. I find my father fuming and smoking a cigar. The car is filled with hot air and soot. My nostrils tense and my throat gags like it does when we drive by fresh tar being laid on the road. My father starts backing out of the driveway. I roll down my window.

"Roll that window back up."

"I can't breathe."

"Why are you always so difficult? My window is down. You'll forget to roll yours back up."

"I CAN'T BREATHE!" I can't see or think either. I am consumed with rage.

The car screeches to an abrupt halt just out of the driveway. I am thrown forward and feel a mixture of peaches and bile surging up the back of my throat. I swallow hard, forcing it back down.

"Why do you always have to talk back to me?" The cigar is waving in front of me, smoke billowing up my nostrils, the bile and peach mixture rising uncontrollably into my mouth. I open the car door quickly and lean out just enough to retch the awful mess into the street.

My father looks around for witnesses, and seeing none, shakes his head at me. "You really bring these things on yourself. You're much too old to have tantrums." He does not relinquish his position on the window but puts out his cigar in the ashtray. "I shouldn't be smoking these things anyway." It is all I will ever get in the way of an apology.

I don't dare to ask to go back into the house, so I wipe my face with Kleenex from a box on the floor of the car. The bitter taste left in my mouth only aggravates the bitterness in my heart. We ride in silence, the odor of the cigar lingering between us. My father's eyes rarely leave the road ahead of him but every now and then, I catch him glancing at the ashtray. I hate him.

"You told Mommy you were going to quit."

He doesn't respond.

"You lied to Mommy. You promised her you'd quit." I attack with all the vengeance of my ten-year old heart.

He sighs. He is not happy with losing, nor is he used to it.

"Okay." He grabs the three cigars resting on the seat and yanks the half-smoked one from the ash tray. He rolls his window all the way down and slams his foot on the brake, sending my miniature breasts straight into the glove box. With a flourish that can only mean finality, my father flings out the cigars.

"I just quit." He smiles at me. He is in control again. His losses turned to winnings, he will tell his version of the story for years. There is no rolled up window, no vomit and no disagreement. He presents me as a coy mirror of my mother, chiding him on possible health hazards. And I never contradict him because it is one of the few instances in which I am presented in a more positive light. I bask in that moment of light and make believe it happened that way.

Now we are locked together in silence. I will not make a move to acknowledge him. I am filled with feelings of hatred and despair. He has outsmarted me. The fact that he lit the cigar at all appears inconsequential to tossing them all out the window. In his own narrative, he is the hero.

I am trapped. It is like the nightmares I used to have when I was five and six. I would open the large linen closet door in our mirrored hallway, and the monster would be waiting for me. I would turn to run, to move in any direction at all, but it was as if my whole body had been dipped into a vat of glue. Only with the greatest of effort could I even begin to lift one foot. I held myself prisoner of my fear. Now I hold myself prisoner of my anger.

My father parks the car on a side street where I don't recognize the shops. It is a section of the city where I have never been. I follow my father down a winding cobblestone lane. We pass an antique store, a mask and costume shop, and a souvenir shop filled with whalebone carved to every imaginable shape and design. Scattered in the dusty window are whale paperweights, whale T-shirts, paintings of whales, posters of whales, whaling ships and whaling implements. I forget that I'm angry.

"Are we near The Whaling Museum, Daddy? Can we go look at the whaling boat?"

My father wags his finger at me in exasperation. "How will you ever get anywhere in this world? You have to learn to pay attention. Do you want me to get your violin or not?"

While I remember very little of the musical instrument shop, I see it as old and dusty, like the man who sold us my violin. There is a memory of trying out several while my father tells the shopkeeper how he has always wanted to learn to play. I will never know how much the "poor boy in Russia" story influences the ultimate price, but it is my first exposure to haggling.

My father opens the trunk of the car and gently wraps the violin case in a blanket. "You have to be very careful with it," he says, whether to me or to himself, I'm not quite sure. He is quiet now and almost tender. He waits before he starts the car.

"I wish I could have had the opportunities that you have when I was a child," he says.

"You can share my violin, Daddy," I offer.

"No," he smiles, "I never had any talent for it anyway. This is your violin, and I want you to practice every day........" The lecture continues, I suppose, until I realize that he is parking the car in front of The Whaling Museum. I am too overwhelmed with joy to do anything but clap my hands with excitement.

"Well," my father says, as if an explanation is more necessary here than at any other point in our outing, "I have the rest of the day off anyway and we are in the neighborhood."

\* \* \*

I still try to untangle meaning from my years with the violin. My lessons became a metaphor for all of my father's past struggles. I was his mirror, the worst of his fears staring back at him, and soon this was all he could see. The more I searched for the pleasure in my music, the harder my father fought to instill discipline. The study of anything meant serious work, and there could never be enough. There was no such thing as too much. And if pleasure was to be gained, it could only be from achieving discipline. Pleasure in the process meant an inappropriate attitude towards learning.

My father discussed my musical progress every evening at dinner. His comments were never directed to me. Nor were they related to the quality of the drifting notes he could barely hear through the thick glass brick walls of his soundproofed office, or that were conducted by the occasional movement of air through the heating vents. My father was concerned with time. And with time, I became defiant.

After my eleventh birthday, my father hires one of his patients to be my private teacher. His name is Mr. Horowitz, and he has been first violinist under Toscanini. He refused to teach me at first because my father is his ophthalmologist, but my father begged and pleaded until he eventually got his way and probably, a reduced fee.

Mr. Horowitz is a kind and patient man. I enjoy my lessons and look forward to his visits. He knows that I ask him to play each lesson again and again because I am in love with the sounds he creates so effortlessly. When he glides his bow across the strings, he no longer seems a middle-aged man, short and paunchy, graying around the temples. There is a magic that takes place, a metamorphosis. In his presence, I pray that I too will be transformed. Each time I raise my violin, I imagine that my notes will be as glorious as his; that this gawky awkward child will be replaced by an accomplished young woman. There are even those rare moments when I believe that I have created this alteration through my music. Sometimes I catch Mr. Horowitz smiling. On these evenings, he rations out subtle nods of confidence and leaves fewer cigarette butts in the ashtray.

My father has far less compunction when it comes to expressing his doubts. At the end of the day, he blasts through the office door like an angry wind blowing up a thunderstorm. He shoves my mother aside from the kitchen sink to wash his hands. Bacteria be damned, she no longer complains about this, even though I know by the look on her face that she doesn't like it one bit. Sometimes she raises her eyebrows at me, and I roll my eyes in support.

I try to make myself invisible at supper. Silently I count the rhythm of chewing, one—two—three—four, and a one—two—three—four. I punctuate these measures with occasional swallows. It's such a clever way of playing with my food that even I am unaware of my own intentions.

My father, skilled in his surgery is helpless in his kitchen. He bangs his fist like a little Nikita.

"Jeanette, where's the ketchup," "Jeannette, where's the salt," "Jeannette, where is my tea?"

My mother jumps up from the table at each command, dropping her napkin on her chair. She runs to retrieve whatever is missing. At this very moment, it is her napkin. She has forgotten that she is sitting on it and begins to grope for it on the floor. She gets up to get another, unaware that one untied apron string is trailing the napkin behind her. My father doesn't see it, and I don't tell her.

The crash of my father's teacup onto his saucer throws off my chewing count and I am forced to swallow. It feels like a golf ball going down, and I choke it back up into my napkin. Nobody notices. I roll it up in my lap. Without looking up, my father admonishes, "Jeannette, will you sit down and eat your dinner already?" She catches sight of the lost napkin from the corner of her eye and calls out to it, "Oh, there you are. Now I have two." I want to tell her that I could use one, but a demon inside me just giggles.

My father glares at me but addresses my mother. "Did Phyllis practice her violin today?"

"Yes, she did."

"How long did you practice? Did she practice a full hour, Jeannette?"

"She must have. She was up there for a long time."

"How do you know if she's practiced an hour is she's in her room with the door closed?"

"She goes up to practice on her own, and then she comes down when she's finished. I ask her if she's done, and she says yes, so it must be an hour."

"Jeannette, Jeannette. How many times do I have to tell you that you're too easy with her. You have to set the timer. It's not good enough that SHE says she's finished. She'll never learn discipline that way."

"I was up there practicing for two and a half hours." My indignation is obvious. "It's more fun when I don't have to think about the time."

"Don't talk back to me. It's not supposed to be fun. We're paying good money for these lessons. Do you know how lucky you are to be getting private lessons? I would have given anything to have violin lessons when I was your age. If you don't learn about discipline now, you never will. Learning the violin is learning discipline."

"But Nathan, she was up there for a very long time, and I was using the timer for dinner. I never used a timer when I played the piano."

"YOU were not Phyllis."

I ingest his rage along with mine until I am full without eating. The only sound I can hear is my father chewing and the click of his fork against his plate. To drown him out I picture myself smashing my violin. The noise I make in my head is numbing. When I wish that he would die or simply disappear, I feel guilty and afraid. My violin is a less complicated target. But not completely because I love my violin. And so it becomes even more complicated as I destroy what I love because I cannot destroy what I am not wholly able to love.

\* \* \*

The violin is suffering a slow and painful death. The same child who can imagine herself a Hagannah fighter named Ari is engaged in full battle with the enemy. I begin to practice my hour in the living room, directly on the opposite side of my father's glass dividing wall. I am hoping to "entertain" his patients. Religiously, I set the timer for 60 minutes. For fifteen of these minutes, I tune the violin and rosin the bow. There are forty-five minutes left in my hour of vengeance. With the same degree of enthusiasm that I have so recently devoted to creating music, I produce jarring and scraping noise. It's not long before I discover that this technique often results in broken E strings, requiring a delay of practice until more can be obtained. My mother innocently does me the favor of presenting me with a large supply. Nonplused, I begin to scrape away harder at the G strings, more difficult to break and therefore, a bit harder to procure. This often requires a special trip to Boston.

Even at eleven, perhaps especially at eleven, I am a formidable opponent. My father cannot bring himself to complain about the dreadful racket breaking his rule of silence during office hours. After all, he is the one insisting that my practice hour be "visible." Although the continuous breaking of the strings has to be suspicious, I am far too devious in my performance to be accused of malice.

And so I break strings, break the silence, break my heart, and then finally, break my father. The violin lessons come to an end. Mr.

Horowitz quits. He apologizes to me, but it is years later before I understand that it has broken his heart as well. A cigarette dangling from his lower lip, he confides to me, "Phyllis, I have tried to reason with your father. But this fighting is too much for me. The fact is, he wanted the violin for himself. You know, you have a good ear for music and a lovely voice. Maybe you could study singing." He hugs me farewell and wishes me luck. I think I have won. I have no idea how much I have lost.

# [16]

# THE ARTS OF CIVIL AND CULINARY DEFENSE

*Or*

*Coming of Age in a Bomb Shelter*

My father is vigilant when it comes to the Cossacks. My mother is vigilant when it comes to the bomb. Even though I'm only in the fourth grade, it's pretty apparent to me that diving under my desk will do me no good at all. Yet I dive. It's a break from routine, a place for passing notes, pinching skin and pulling hair. I don't think past the drill.

My mother posts the Civil Defense Code above the kitchen table. She collects clippings from periodicals, bomb shelter designs, "ten basic steps to living through disaster," anything she can lay her hands on, and she places them strategically where she thinks my father will find them.

Squatting at the top of the back stairway in my snooping stance, I listen to my parents and their friends. How much does it cost to build a shelter? How large does it have to be? What do you do if your neighbors try to get in? Can you turn them away? Do you think it's a good idea to buy a gun? Well, what if it turns out to be old Mrs. Genensky banging on the shelter door? What would you do? Slam the door in her face? Shoot her? Late into the evening, they struggle with these questions. The women debate what to take, what to leave. The men grapple with politics, jockey statistics, study engineering plans. I know from his tone that my father will take this no further.

But my mother is the happiest I've seen her. Since her surgeries, she has not returned to painting or writing, other than the mishmash she attempted to write about the experience of her illness. Bereft of the skills she once had and has lost, Civil Defense has given her purpose. Under my mother's watchful eye, we haul jugs of water into a forbidding and long forsaken room in the basement. This is our "temporary" shelter until my mother can convince my father to have one built underground. The unsteady shelves are lined with canned goods, candles, matches, flashlights and batteries, blankets, a first-aid kit, emergency clothing, an old radio, paperback novels of mystery, romance and science fiction (my mother's recent favorites), some religious paraphernalia and family photos my mother fears might be stolen by the invaders.

My mother has never had to wait in line for bread, but she knows how to hunt and gather. And as if to prove how idiosyncratic and unpredictable this quest can be, she has accumulated a supply of saccharin that my father claims could kill the rat population of North America. The pantry shelves are lined with My-T-Fine Pudding. I like the chocolate when I'm sick. Somehow under cover of night or while my sister and I are in school, my mother manages to fill an attic room from wall to wall, floor to ceiling, with cartons of Kotex sanitary napkins. Swinging high on the pendulum of menopause, she's vowed that no daughter of hers will ever be caught without, and so she constructs a tower of maxi-pads to protect our femininity should the bomb drop and prevent them from being manufactured. This tower will collapse with the invention of tampons, but my mother cannot know this now.

The bomb is bringing my mother back to life, and it's hard for my father to disapprove. Her picture appears in the New Bedford Times, a Civil Defense Certificate suspended mid-air between her hand and the Mayor's. There she stands, digging in her heels, her mouth set in a thin line of determination. She will not give an inch. She has stumbled onto altruistic hoarding. She will save us. And she can justify buying out every grocery store in town in order to do it. I watch her calling taxis to take her to the grocery. Hours later, she's back, lugging bags and boxes and a grocery receipt several yards in length.

My sister, not yet off to college at this point in time, joins up with my father, and I simply don't know how to stay neutral. I admire this new mother of mine. I don't care if she's fighting windmills. I like that she's picked up a sword, but I worry that she'll be the first to lay it down. This thought nags away at me. It's too hard to always be on the losing side. So I collaborate. I refuse to descend to the basement for civil defense drills. The harder my mother tries, the harder I resist.

My father pokes and jabs and calls my mother foolish, but I know he's nervous. It's sort of like religion. What if it turns out that he's wrong? He's more afraid of Russians than Germans, perhaps even God. Sometimes I think he makes fun of my mother to cover this up. He attacks during meals, since little else brings Gay, his vocal ally, out of her room and into the general population.

"Jeannette, Jeannette, if the Russians drop the bomb on us, we won't have time to get to the basement. We'll be vaporized."

I look at my sister. "Is that true?"

"Mhmm." Gay is a sixteen year-old of few words.

"Is it?" I demand of my mother.

"It has to be dropped on top of you for that to happen." My mother gives my father a look. "And I don't think they're going to choose New Bedford as a target."

"How far away does it have to be dropped so we're not vaporized?"

"I don't know, honey, but I'm sure we don't have anything to worry about."

"Yeah, nothing to worry about," my sister dismisses her. "If we're not vaporized, we can die slow and painful deaths from radiation. That's if we don't die first from eating the crud in the basement."

"What's it like to die from radiation?"

"You get burns and sores and throw up all the time, and then you go blind and can't breathe."

"Is there a cure?" I'm weighing my options.

"No, you get sick and die."

"I think I'd rather be vaporized. Does it hurt? Would it feel like Daddy's uncle did when he was burned in the synagogue?"

My mother gets up from the table and busies herself at the sink.

"Well, it must've hurt a lot to burn to death," I persist.

"He probably was trampled or suffocated before he caught on fire. I bet he didn't feel a thing." Gay is not without remorse. She knows I have nightmares.

"Do you think?"

"Yup, I bet he never even knew the synagogue was on fire."

My father gulps down the last of his tea, sets the cup down in the saucer, and pushes his chair back from the table. "I sure hope he didn't."

My father leaves the room and a shred of doubt in my mind.

I'm disappointed in my mother. She's never mentioned radiation sickness. And what's this about being vaporized? I've never thought hiding under a desk would help, but I have held some belief in the basement. I feel stupid and angry. Gay and Daddy are dismissive and sarcastic at my mother's attempts. The concept of World War III has created an unholy alliance. As we chip away at my mother's resolve, she shifts the battle ground to the kitchen.

I don't know if I believe the story that my mother seduced my father with a seven-layer chocolate cake, but I do believe that there is no one who can equal her baking. She erects gingerbread houses with rose gardens and trestle doorways and children peering out from pansy-box windows. With her icing tool in hand, she is Rembrandt, Vermeer, Picasso, and Pollack. The paintings she's struggled to create since her "accident" are stacked in the basement. But the works of art she pulls off with flour and sugar and butter are immediately devoured and never duplicated.

I'm not above the theft of these treasures when her back is turned. I pull off a flower from the edge and fill in the hole with icing to cover my crime. She pretends not to notice. Once she's finished and surveys the cake, she's always surprised at "missing" a spot.

As talented as my mother is at baking, she's a frightening cook. Conflicted by her desire for creative license and my father's demand for artistic control, our home cuisine offers little to recommend it. Vegetables are boiled to a soggy mess. Potatoes are safe, unless my mother decides to "vary" them with marshmallows and maraschino cherries. Rice is unreliable. Since the cooking of rice involves the same pot as the sterilization of my father's medical instruments, my mother makes her protest felt by "forgetting" it. Someone always has to shout, "The rice is boiling over!"

Since I don't like meat, except for lamb chops, I don't have complaints about how it's prepared. Of course, how it's prepared may be the reason I don't like it. Gay insists that when the meat is not transformed into a casserole, we have half a chance of identifying the animal of origin by its bones. For the most part, it's a generic blackened slab of dried gristle, challenging first our knives and then our teeth. My mother suffers in silence. Occasionally, she reminds us that this is how my father likes it. She prefers hers rare.

For a time, my mother resorts to fail-safe measures. These are boxes or jars that say they contain either all the necessary ingredients for a complete meal or lack only the meat or chicken, milk or egg "to be added." During this period, meals are dull but edible. But since our abandonment of the bomb shelter, my mother is fed up with all of us. She adopts new measures.

Chung King Chicken Chow Mein—straight from the can except for the chicken—is replaced by a sticky concoction my mother sometimes refers to as "Hawaiian Delight" and other times as "Hawaiian Surprise." The chicken is dried up and left over from Friday's Shabbat dinner and is the one constant note in a medley of fatal sauces. These include Dole canned pineapple, Dole fruit cup, Dole inspired recipes from Dole cans which always call for Maraschino cherries. My mother stirs these mixtures with a vigor that would chill the heart of Titus.

"Do you think she's trying to poison us?" my sister asks.

"I don't know," I tell her. "Maybe it's what we deserve for being so mean. Anyway, it beats being vaporized or getting radiation sickness."

My sister raises her eyebrows. "I don't know about that. Slow death by Maraschino Cherries. Just think about that." And I do, every time I swallow another one.

Over time and troop desertion, my mother begins to waver. She no longer insists that we change the jugs of water or the canned goods that begin to bulge at the sides, threatening botulism. I come home from school one day to find an empty outline on the wall where the Civil Defense chart used to be. It's as if the threat of the bomb, along with my mother's rebirth, never took place. The poster-bearing activist mother in the newspaper photo fades into the crossword puzzle doing, soap opera watching mother who's caught in a time warp. "Civil Defense Mom" was at least there with us, alive and on the front lines. I miss her.

I climb slowly down the dilapidated stairs, past the metal arms of the octopus heating system, deep into the bowels of the basement. I creep into the shelter cautiously, afraid of spiders and other creatures that might be living there. The dust is thick, coating cans of peas and beans and soup with a greasy film. I study my mother's work, beans with beans, soups with soups, peas with peas. I run my fingers over her mother's picture, wiping away specks of dust. My grandfather's picture is stacked underneath hers, clean and protected.

Why does she always give up? Why does he always win? Why does Gay take his side? And why don't I stick up for her? No, I'm a coward and a collaborator. For several years now, I've hidden down here, and in my imagination, I've pretended to be a boy, Ari the Hagannah fighter, protector of the children of Israel. It doesn't seem that if I am me, I can ever possibly win.

Ari, the long-suffering phantom of my fantasies, must die. From now on, I will be Sara, heroine of World War III, savior of her family and country, America, not Israel. I become heiress to the bomb shelter. Sara is blond, beautiful, slender, brave, intelligent, and beloved by her family and country. She is all that I am not. Whenever I waver, I try to restrict Sara to the basement and keep Ari alive upstairs, but Sara is insistent and pops up in the midst of the Ari fantasy I use to lull myself to sleep. Ari might be in the midst of pulling survivors from a bombed building, when he discovers Sara, unconscious but unwounded. They fall hopelessly in love, and it no longer matters whether I am Ari or Sara or how impossible the time periods or geography, I cannot keep them apart.

Inevitably, nature takes its course. I can no longer deny the daily evidence. I'm forced to replace my undershirt with a bra and I no longer go down to the basement. John Lennon and Bob Dylan replace Ari. Somehow I can be more of myself with them, and so Sara, too, disappears. I've always known Ari would have to go, but since I don't have the heart to ever officially kill him off, he stays with me, my Hagannah warrior at the ready.

We never talk about the bomb shelter anymore. The Cold War continues, but the heated debates between my parents and their friends turn to other things, more immediate and within the realm of resolution. My mother returns to reading science fiction, romance and murder mysteries, her form of shelter from both worldly and internal wars.

# [17]

# THE TELEVISION WARS

My mother's father believes in progress. He's the first in his neighborhood to own a car and the first to purchase a television set. Grandpop initially becomes addicted to soap opera through radio. If there is any advancement in technology that leads to the enhancement of "his programs," Grandpop can see no earthly justification for depriving himself of this pleasure. No one interrupts him during these hour-long sacred departures from reality any more than they would think to disturb him during a televised boxing match.

My father, on the other hand, believes in education. Television is the evil eye that might penetrate society on the whole but will have little hope of crossing his threshold. My father is convinced that television will bring about the downfall of education and will corrupt us, his children, as well as all of America, leaving in its wake a country of "illiterate morons." In retrospect, he was not so far off the mark.

My father also believes in reading the newspaper. He did not survive the pogroms, several wars and The Great Depression by "hiding his head in the sand." He waits impatiently for the local paper to arrive every day, running from the office to the front door in between patients to see if "that lazy good-for-nothing boy has gotten here yet." Sometimes he cracks open the office door to the kitchen and whispers to my mother, "Tell Phyllis to see if the paper's here."

If 6:00 p.m. dares to arrive before the paper, my father's last patient long gone and the dinner dishes cleared, he paces the front hallway, glancing anxiously out the window for "the boy." Soon he's on the phone calling the newspaper office to ask if the newspaper is being delivered that day, and if so, where is his? And heaven forbid if the paper is damp or torn or chewed by a neighborhood dog; these and any other newspaper misdemeanors are reported directly.

I worry about the paperboys. I wonder how many of them will lose their routes over my father's phone calls. I think he's just being mean. But for my father, serious events might be taking place in the world, events that could mean that everything he's worked so hard for could be snatched in a moment. He's vigilant in his efforts to protect the fragile life he's been able to create. What do I know about how precarious our existence is? I read the funnies and depend on my father to keep us all safe. And I look forward to my next rendezvous with any television.

My mother never plots to be near a television. My sister ignores the tiny box in favor of a movie screen. But I make sure that I come down with all my childhood illnesses in my grandparents' house in Philly. I try never to be sick in New Bedford and succeed, other than the chronic bronchitis that plagues me equally at both addresses. The more grandiose disorders, designed to elicit more sympathy and time free from responsibility, all take place on the couch on Fleming Street, directly in front of the square black and white.

I am the happiest of chicken pox victims. A whole week of Howdy Doody and The Mickey Mouse Club, not to mention aunts and uncles bearing gifts for the poor, sickly child. I scratch and scratch until my mother makes me wear gloves, and then I take them off and scratch some more.

I know all about Gunsmoke from the radio broadcasts we're sometimes lucky enough to catch on a Sunday evening on our way home from visiting Aunt Dora in Boston. They also have a television, but I would have to put up with weird Uncle Morris in order to watch it. Not so bad, but I do have to keep an eye on him to make sure he doesn't do anything bizarre. But here I am, covered from head to toe with red, itchy bumps, and I can actually see Miss Kitty. There she is, that seasoned dance hall diva, delivering her saucy western wisdom right before my eyes. I practice all the secrets I've learned for sending the thermometer above normal just to spend another day in the wonderful world of television.

As I grow a bit older, my obsession becomes film noir. I can't get enough. My father complains that he's never shown me anything of Philadelphia. I've yet to see the Liberty Bell or Betsy Ross's house. As soon as we hit the Pennsylvania border, my television-tuned body begins to flaunt symptoms. I don't care much about Philadelphia's history. I only want Hitchcock. And for a small price, I can have a week of silent, swarthy men pursuing dark, mysterious women. It's well worth the measles, the mumps and the chicken pox.

I'm almost ten when my father announces, just before another trip to Philly, "I don't care what bloody disease you get this time, I'm taking you to see Philadelphia." The "bloody" and his afternoon tea are the only remaining evidence of my father's actual birthplace in London where he spent all of a month. But I know that when he uses it, he's "bloody well" fed up. This is more a threat than a promise, but once the body is so well trained, even the most extreme torture is not guaranteed to turn it around.

My body clicks into automatic illness the first evening. It's the hottest time of summer. I wake up in the middle of the night in a cold sweat, coughing and wheezing. My sister is sharing the room with me. She slowly gets out of bed to roust our mother, as my illnesses are always real and never a matter of malingering. I hear her muttering as she goes out the door, "Nothing's going to stop him this time. You're going sightseeing no matter what awful disease you've managed to come up with." She's jealous. All she ever gets are migraines. Invisible ailments don't count for much in my family; infectious diseases are the best.

My sister is right. Even though the thermometer (with no monkeying around from me) registers a clear 102 degrees, even though my mother and Aunt Rose protest that I should not be allowed out of the house and in fact should be in quarantine, even though it's hotter than hell in the car (no air conditioning), my father shows no mercy. He's taking me to see Philadelphia. If I die in the process, so be it. At least I will die less ignorant.

I can't swallow or breathe. We inch along in gridlock. The heat of suffocating exhaust fumes combine with sweet, heavy air. None of it fazes my father. Fully decked in a suit and tie, he doesn't sweat, he doesn't even crease all day. He looks as fresh as he did when he first came down the stairs in the morning. By the time he gets me to the Ben Franklin Institute and all of its scientific games for children, he's won me over. I'm still sick, in fact, even sicker, but I'm having a wonderful time. My father is handsome and charming. I'm proud to be with him. And on this one day in our history, I think he's proud to be with me, too.

The grand finale is a lobster dinner at Bookbinders. Head pounding and fever raging, I can't taste a thing. But my father is so satisfied with himself, a boyish grin giving his pleasure away, that I eat everything on my plate and order desert. His parents could never afford to treat him to a dinner like this, and how he has dreamed of being able to bring his own child here one day.

My stomach turns over just as I've downed about three-fourths of the Philadelphia cheesecake. I feel it move with my spoon poised in mid-air, and I know if I act quickly, my father won't have to know. Gently setting the heap of cheesecake already nestled in my desert spoon ever so lightly back onto the plate, I excuse myself. As soon as I'm out of his sight, I run the rest of the way to the toilet with my hand over my mouth. Sometimes fate is in my favor. The ladies' restroom is vacant. I'm mercifully able to keep my ablutions not only a secret but a private matter. And so it's with a light heart and empty tummy that I return to finish up desert and what has been as close as it gets for me and my father to an almost perfect day.

\* \* \*

Soon the ease of prepubescent days comes to an end and adolescence rears its ugly head. Junior High School. No one should ever be sent there. As if there aren't enough awful things about me that are different, we're the only people in town who don't have a T.V. This status, and therefore the rest of my life, is inalterably changed by such tragic events that I can still feel the blood cut off in my chest when I'm forced to put them together. If not for the shooting of John Fitzgerald Kennedy, the most beloved man in Massachusetts, I don't think my father could have come up with sufficient rationalization to break down and buy a color Zenith.

Wrapped in a metaphorical American flag, he gets that set home so quickly that we have to wonder if he's had it stashed away on hold somewhere. One day we have no set and a room designated as "the sewing room." Suddenly our President is assassinated, and there we are watching it all in living color in the room now known as "the television room." All in the name of patriotism. My father is off the hook. It is almost admirable how he manages to do it.

And for a brief time, at least until JFK is securely in the ground and we see the film of Caroline and John John waving until we can replay it in our minds by heart, this is the only television we watch. In between his patients, my father sprints up the stairs with renewed energy into the television room to catch any slight news item he might have missed. My mother and I are not allowed yet to turn it on ourselves.

Soon we return to our lives. Eyeglasses have to be fitted, meals have to be prepared, and homework has to be done. Even Walter Cronkite turns to different matters. Along with John Fitzgerald Kennedy, there is Martin Luther King, Robert Kennedy and Vietnam. The innocence of the 50's is swept away into the 60's. We watch it all in dismay from our designated positions on the old pull-out sofa bed. My father sits closest to the door. My mother sits next to him. When she reads instead, her afghan reserves her place. I sit on the very end or on the floor.

As soon as Walter announces, "and now a word from our sponsor," my father wields his new secret weapon, the remote control. Initially, he's content to cut the commercials with a click of the mute. He laughs and points at the actors' antics, smug that he's defeating them by eliminating the sound. Soon he grows impatient with this diversion and begins to surf the channels. We have five, three of which come in clearly. "Ah," he sighs, "sports and public television."

My father is infected. The very thing he's despised and barred from his home now dictates our supper schedule. Meals are served between the departure of the last patient from his office and the 6:00 news. Should this trailing patient somehow manage to insert himself between my father's glances at his watch and the door with foolish questions concerning cataract surgery aftercare, my father easily makes up the time by eating his soup or salad along with his entrée and desert. His furtive peeks at the clock on the wall are unnecessary, except as incentive to my mother, who hurries about making sure that nothing is wanted. We know exactly what he's up to and before too long, there's no pretense.

My father's addiction, like all addictions, is not without its broader implications. Like any alcoholic or drug user, he's only willing to share when it's his choice and under his conditions. My sister has escaped prior to television and cares little for it when she's home. And so we are three. Since we all agree on *American Playhouse, Hallmark Hall of Fame* and *The Alfred Hitchcock Hour*, these are standard family fare. The battles begin around *The Ed Sullivan Show*.

My father loves the animal acts, the puppetry and circus acrobatics, even though he insists he only watches them "to make your mother happy." But Ed Sullivan makes some fatal decisions. One is to hire Sammy Davis, Jr. whom my father can't forgive for converting to Judaism. He cringes at this more than his music, which my father also despises. He makes so many comments throughout that we can't hear anything anyway.

"I refuse to accept that he's Jewish," my father shudders as soon as Ed finishes flourishing his arm and introducing Sammy to his audience. "Why did he have to convert? To make himself more popular?"

"Since when did being Jewish make anyone more popular?" My mother always defends Sammy.

"Exactly, and on top of being colored."

"Black, Daddy. No one says colored anymore. It's not nice."

"Black, colored, whatever, he was already a Negro. Whatever could've made him want to be Jewish? He has to be nuts. Just look at him."

My mother and I strain our eyes for signs of insanity in Sammy. Neither of us can spot anything unusual.

"He wasn't persecuted enough? He missed being a slave? He should've been in the shtetl, freezing cold with nothing but potatoes to eat. Maybe that would've helped him find his way back to Jesus. And pretty darn quickly, I bet."

"Maybe he just wanted to be Jewish, Daddy. And what about the Ethiopian Jews? They're black."

"Nobody in their right mind just wants to be Jewish. You have to be born to it. You know how I always say I'm proud to be a Jew, but I was born Jewish. I wasn't given a choice. Neither were the Ethiopians."

"So if you were born something else, you wouldn't think Judaism was a good religion? If you had a choice, you might choose something else?" I've become prone to these kinds of arguments.

"Don't be disrespectful. I was born Jewish and so I don't imagine anything else."

"Shhhhh," my mother scolds us, "I can't hear with all of this talking."

"You're not missing anything. He can't sing. You call that crooning singing?"

At this point, my mother gets up in despair and retreats to the bedroom to read. Sometimes I follow her out and sulk back to my own room and other times I hang on, either for the sole purpose of irritating my father or because Ed Sullivan is breaking ground with a new rock and roll band. This is another fatal booking error on his part because it is there that I first see the Beatles. It's one of the few times that my father is the one to retreat.

My father wrestles with his acquisition of the television set. It's ill-gotten gains. No one ever comes out and says this to him, but his constant protestations that he never would have had a television in his home were it not for the untimely death of the President soon becomes interpreted as he "—doth protest too much" by many of his friends and most of his family. My father is not one to be stopped even by his own mind. Given long enough, he comes up with enough justification to put even his own restless doubts to sleep.

During the Ed Sullivan skirmishes, we are also engaged in the Channel 13 public television battles. When it comes to marshaling us in the name of education, my father is Napoleon. His orders are issued from the second floor landing at the top of his lungs. Thus he could be assured that we would hear him and obey.

"Jeannette! Phyllis! Leonard Bernstein's on! Get in here now! Hurry up!"

We scurry away from whatever we're doing to convene in the television room. It's not that my father is any great lover of music. He knows that it's something he ought to love, that is, music of a certain nature. He's never owned a record player and later, he will never own a stereo. This is not important. What is important is that Leonard Bernstein is a highly respected musician of the right sort of music who is Jewish and is not black.

As soon as we enter the room, my father begins a discourse on the difference between Leonard Bernstein and Sammy Davis, Jr. and his "sort." To his credit, he doesn't descend to race or religion. In this instance, he sticks strictly to the music. Of course, and as a direct result, we are never able to hear Leonard Bernstein either.

My father doesn't only stick Leonard Bernstein in as the only fly in our ointment of public television. There are endless documentaries. My father never considers whether or not they might be of any interest to either my mother or to me. It's educational. And on this note alone, it absolves him of the sin of bringing the "darned box" into the house in the first place.

There's only one way for me to enjoy the television, and that is to watch it when I have it all to myself. This can only happen on Sunday afternoons. My father has designated Sundays as my mother's day of rest and our day out as a family. The first break in this irreversible tradition is my sister's departure for college. The second break in this now "sisterless" tradition is me. I can't bear it without her. And there is the additional pull of "Sunday Afternoon at the Movies." Some kids would go just for the lobster, but since I've been raised on the stuff, movies are much more important to me. Soon my parents only ask me if I want to join them in the polite way one inquires, "And how are you?" without expecting an answer other than "fine." My mother piles the freezer shelves with all my favorite and appropriately named "T.V. dinners." I'm on my own.

It is true that once you begin to break with tradition, what has once been sacred can quickly become profane. There are strict rules of etiquette in our home and they don't have to make sense. One of these rules is that we always have to wear shoes in the house so that the sweat from our feet won't discolor the carpeting. My father has not yet been exposed to Japanese culture or I'm convinced he would have instituted some sort of slipper regulations. Another hard and fast rule is that no food, under any circumstances including a lengthy list of possible exceptions, is to ever enter the television room. As soon as I am on my own, I break both of these rules.

Every week I look forward to Sunday. By noon, 12:30 at the latest, I'm free to kick off my shoes, heat up my dinner, and be back upstairs with an aluminum foil container of Swanson's turkey with stuffing, mashed potatoes and gravy, side of peas and cranberry sauce, a bag of potato chips, soda and Twinkies just in time for the 1:00 pm show. I don't have to be sick to watch television. I don't have to compete with anyone for the remote or the atmosphere. And the movies I watch. Who wouldn't want to spend a lazy Sunday afternoon with Bogie and Bacall? *Casablanca*? *The African Queen*? I'm in love with Susan Hayward, Gregory Peck and *The Snows of Kilimanjaro*. And Ava Gardner is the woman I want to become as a woman and the woman I would want to love as a man. My television Sundays become my night dreams and daydreams for the week. Sunday is all the stimulation I can stand.

My mother recognizes that she, too, can only be happy watching television alone, but this is much more difficult for her. My father's used a national misfortune to claim his set. My mother uses the benefits from a personal injury claim.

My mother is frustrated by countless attempts to qualify for a driver's license. Certainly, part of this is due to medical restrictions. The law requires a certain amount of time for anyone with a history of seizures to be free from them before they're allowed to drive. But I suspect that the overriding factor in my mother's repeated failures is my father's driving lessons. When she finally accepts that she will never drive herself to the grocery store, she insists that neither will my father. She'll take a taxi.

Jammed into the back seat with somewhere between twenty and thirty bags of groceries, my mother's return from the grocery store is a neighborhood event. Whoever happens to be about runs to her assistance. "Mrs. Mitnick, can I help you?" By the time I get there, most of the bags are already lined up on the kitchen floor and table. My father's manner evokes sympathy for her. "That poor woman, I don't know how she puts up with him."

I've just finished my freshman year of high school and it's summer vacation. I'm off to the beach with my friends whenever possible, so I'm rarely there when my mother comes back from shopping. When I get home late one afternoon, she's lying on the couch in the living room with a hot water bottle on her leg and a heating pad on her back.

"Mommy, what happened to you?" I throw my beach bag onto the floor in the hallway and rush over to her.

"I was in an accident. The taxi ran into another car when it stopped short at a red light. The taxi driver tried to stop in time, but he hit him anyway." Mommy has a curious expression on her face when she says, "I have whiplash. I went to the hospital. Your father came and brought me home."

"Are you okay?"

"Just the whiplash to my back and my neck. I'm going to sue."

"You're going to sue?" I'm incredulous. "Does Daddy know you're going to sue?"

"No, not yet, but it's not his accident."

My mother finally has something all her own. Courageously cashing in on her own misfortune, braving the wrath of my father, using his own profession against him, my mother is able to bargain her whiplash for a small black and white television set for the kitchen, the mink coat she's always wanted and a telephone and telephone number of her very own. It's a one-shot deal, so who can blame her?

The new television and telephone shift the balance of power in our house. It's too late for my sister, but my mother never says no to my requests to use her phone. Calls can be made and received at all times of the day, and since I can run much faster than my mother, I easily intercept calls from the boys at school. My father doesn't answer my mother's phone, although she is still responsible for answering his.

As for the television, it is a constant in my mother's kitchen. The only time it's outlawed is during meals. My mother is no longer lonely or alone. She returns to the world of her father's soaps. *One Life to Live, Days of Our Lives, The Young and the Restless, General Hospital*, and her favorite, *Another World*, these and others keep her company throughout my school day and my father's workday. Now when I get home from school, she isn't sitting in the living room with a book she can easily shift to her lap in order to hear about my day. Now I must wait for a commercial.

"Shhhhh, I want to know what's going to happen to Rachael. She's pregnant but she hasn't told anyone yet." I don't begrudge her. I join her. It seems fair.

My mother loves science fiction. Once a week, the two of us go down to the kitchen to watch *Star Trek*. I never become much of a fan, but my father makes so much fun of my mother that I join her for moral support.

"Where are you going, Jeannette?" Daddy asks as Mommy pushes aside her afghan and begins to get up from the couch in the television room.

"Downstairs. It's almost time for *Star Trek*."

"Do you want to watch it up here?"

"No, that's okay. I'll go watch it on *my* television." My mother knows that if she stays upstairs, my father will make so many derogatory comments that she will feel too demeaned to enjoy the show. There's also the "food is forbidden" rule upstairs, and we can eat ice cream to our hearts content in the kitchen. I follow my mother.

"You, too?" my father barks after me. I feel like both a hero and a traitor.

Once we're inside the kitchen, the door shut behind us, ice cream bowls at the ready, we're allies in pleasure without purpose, something my father regards with disdain. I want so much to just feel good, but there is always this nagging shame. A little voice tells me that there is something dishonorable in this kind of happiness, and I no longer can distinguish if it is my voice or my father's.

Sometimes when the episode has just begun, my father will holler down the back stairway, "There's something really good on Channel 13. It's a documentary on Greek art. You like Greek art, Phyllis."

"I'm watching *Star Trek* now, Daddy," I holler back. I'm twisting inside. I do like Greek art. I want to go upstairs. I want to be downstairs. It's all been spoiled.

# [18]

# MOVING VIOLATIONS

"I couldn't see obstacles in my way
I missed the roadblock I'm happy to say
But sideswiped a Porsche with my Chevrolet
The cop who stopped me said I'd have to pay
Love can lead to reckless driving

There is no neutral here
The shift's in forward gear
And if I drive too fast
I may run out of gas

I've always been a klutz
And love can drive you nuts
So if we run away
Let's fly TWA"
(Lyric, Phyllis M Skoy)

We live in fear of my father's driving. He never likes to give up the driver's seat. When he is forced to do so by unusual circumstances, his foot tenses on an imaginary brake, his hands press against the dash, and I can hear his rapid breathing when anyone dares to take the ignition key and assign him to the "death" seat. He never sits in back.

My father ignores all pleas to slow down and ridicules my mother's sidelong glances at the speedometer. He never admits he is wrong, even when caught red-handed. Tickets are frequent. When the lights begin flashing and the sirens screaming, my father first searches and determines that there is no other target in sight. But when the police car is biting the rear end of ours, he has little choice but to pull over to the side of the road. Mumbling something under his breath, he rolls his window down to the inevitable.

"Officer, is there something wrong?

"Your license and registration, sir."

"They're fine."

"I'd like to see them."

"Jeannette, get the registration." While my mother digs in the glove compartment, my father retrieves his license from his wallet. Gay and I sit quietly in the back seat, hot from the beach and sticky from ice cream.

My father hands over the license while my mother shuffles through the confusion of dated street maps of Philadelphia and Boston, nail clippers, can openers, coupons, old gas receipts, and papers that make no sense to her at all. Still unable to spot the registration, she removes everything from the glove compartment, scooping it into the skirt of her sundress. She sifts through it, a bag lady unsure of her treasures.

"Which is the registration, Nathan?" He leans over and begins to sort through her skirt, muttering something after "honestly, Jeannette" which I am unable to hear. I look at my sister, but she shakes her head, warning me. I watch the officer watching, and even though I cannot say why, I am convinced that my father will get the ticket.

"It's right here, Jeannette." He holds it up to show her before passing it through the window. I see the expression on the officer's face and I feel ashamed. He takes the paper from my father's hand and says, "I'll be right back." My father breathes heavily over the steering wheel and rolls up his window.

"Now I'm going to get a ticket just so this guy can meet his quota."

My mother pauses from returning the papers to the glove compartment and gives my father a long look.

"Jeannette, Jeannette. You know if you didn't nag me to slow down, I wouldn't have—he never would have stopped me. You need to leave the driving to me."

My mother shuts the glove compartment and stares out her window.

"I put my foot on the brake. That's when he pulled me over. It's a mistake to slow down once they've spotted you."

As silent as a snowy midnight, we sit in the car until the officer breaks the spell with a tap on the window. My father rolls it back down.

"Do you know you were going 70 in a 50 zone?" He looks my father directly in the eye.

"No, Officer, I didn't. I'm on call at the hospital. Did you see the M.D. on my license?"

"Hmm. Are you heading to an emergency, Dr. Mitnick?" The officer's eyes wander to the wet bathing suits, beach towels and toys scattered around us in the back seat.

"Well, no, not exactly," my father grins sheepishly, "but I am on call." My mother ignores him and continues to stare out the window.

"So you're on call, but there's no emergency that you have to speed to right now?"

"No, sir."

"What kind of doctor are you, Dr. Mitnick?

"I'm an ophthalmologist."

"Oh, now I do see! Ha, ha, just a little joke, Doc."

No one laughs besides the officer, and no one dares to speak while he writes the ticket. Even my father is quiet the rest of the way home.

\* \* \*

I am eleven when my mother announces that she would like to learn how to drive. She's traveled by trolley in Philly, even though my grandfather was the first on his block to own a car. No one drove it other than Grandpop and Uncle Ben. New Bedford doesn't have trolley cars or much else in the way of public transportation. Because my mother hasn't had a seizure in months, my father agrees to teach her. When my father insists, I go with them. Gay is tucked away at Bryn Mawr, so I am on my own.

My father drives out to the beach parking lot in Westport early on a Sunday morning. It's October and too cold for crowds. A few cars belonging to hard-core walkers dot the paved area behind the dunes. The only other potential victims are two lone seagulls grazing the area for crumbs. My father warns my mother that she must watch out for these cars, as they are not conveniently parked next to each other. He tells her that he would have preferred this, but after all, there they are, and there is nothing to be done about it. He doesn't express concern for the seagulls. They are clearly more on my mind than his.

Our car is a 1957 Plymouth, automatic, modern but not fancy for its time. My father parks the car, changes seats with my mother, and begins to explain the levers and buttons, on and offs, ups and downs, ins and outs. I worry that she will remember none of this once she turns the key in the ignition. I think my father is only resisting what is certain or perhaps taking a crack at discouraging it. He will teach her out of this.

Finally, my father laughs nervously and asks, "Okay Jeannette, are you ready?"

My mother places her hands on the steering wheel exactly as my father has instructed, right hand at two o'clock and left hand on ten o'clock, and lightly presses the gas pedal. My father shakes his head. "You have to start the car, Jeannette."

"Oh," she says. She turns the key, presses the gas too lightly, stalling the car.

"Again, Jeannette."

"What did I do wrong?"

"Just do what I said. Turn the key and press your foot on the gas pedal."

"I did that."

"You didn't press it hard or long enough," I chirp from the back.

"What, you're teaching her now? What the heck do you know? You're eleven. Just be quiet back there."

"Is she right?" My mother wants to know.

"Let me show you" is my father's answer. They trade seats. He carefully demonstrates how to start the car several times before they trade seats again. I'm surprised by the ease with which my father seems to be giving up what has been his and his alone.

My mother starts the car and eagerly presses the gas a second time, not understanding why the car still doesn't move forward. My father shakes his head again. "You have to put the car in 'drive,' Jeannette. It's still in 'park.'"

"Oh. There's so much to think about." She shifts to "drive" and stamps on the gas, lurches forward, slams on the brakes and looks at my father.

"Gently, Jeannette, gently. Take your foot off the brake and gently press the gas pedal." I see that my father is holding on tightly to his seat and so I do the same. My mother "gently" removes her foot from the brake and slowly places it on the gas. We move forward at about ten miles an hour.

"Nathan, I'm doing it." She smiles at him.

"Look where you're going, Jeannette, not at me. Look out the front and out of your mirrors."

"Mirrors?"

"Yes, your mirrors. Is there traffic behind you? Next to you?"

"But Nathan, there isn't any traffic here at all."

And on it goes until my mother is so fixated on the rearview mirror that she drives into a curb.

"Eeeeeeh, Jeannette. You have to look where you're going."

"I don't see how I can look out the front and the back at the same time," my mother complains. "Where is reverse, now? Oh, the 'R.'" I'm awfully glad that the car's an automatic and she doesn't have to consider a clutch and three speeds like my father's last car. She backs up successfully and brakes, but forgets to put the car back into "D" before she puts her foot on the gas. "Oh no, what did I do?" She brakes again and looks at my father.

"You're still in reverse, Jeannette."

I want to ask if I can get out and go for a walk, but I don't want my mother to think I'm afraid to stay in the car. I am more aware of my father's tone every minute.

"You have to think about what you're doing, Jeannette. Until you can do it automatically, you have to think first. Eventually, you can do these things without thinking, but until then, think, Jeannette, think!"

My mother can no longer think. Her mouth drooping, tears in her eyes, she moves the gear shift to "D," places her foot lightly on the gas and turns the wheel to the left, away from cars and curbing.

"That's good, Mummy," I encourage.

"Thanks honey."

"Look where you're going, Jeannette. Are you looking where you're going?"

\* \* \*

The driving lessons continue this way for some weeks or months, until my father is forced to acknowledge that my mother must drive on actual streets in order to qualify for her license. This is not easy for him. He didn't expect it to go this far. But since my mother is willing to up the ante, he braces himself and goes along. And my father is not one to go along.

We are back in the car on a Wednesday afternoon. My mother needs to pick up her prescription from the pharmacy, and my father suggests that she drive. "You have to start sometime," he says, handing my mother the keys. "You can drive to the drugstore and then to the beach. How's that?" There is chivalry in his gesture.

My mother looks pleased. My father has parked in front of his office on the street, so she will not have to negotiate backing out of the courtyard where both the car and the antique street lights might be in jeopardy. My mother starts the car rather nicely, looks out of the rearview mirror to make sure no one is coming and pulls confidently into the street. She doesn't forget the stop sign on the corner and in fact, slows down and comes to a stop as if this is something she's been doing all her life. She looks both ways before she proceeds across the street. I want to shout, "Great going, Mummy," but I don't want to jinx anything.

The next block is a two-way street and narrow. Cars are parked on both sides.

"You're getting too far to the left, Jeannette. Watch it; watch it; now you're too close on the right. Think, Jeannette, think. Oyyyyy, Jeannette, careful, there's a car coming, more to your right. Oh, my God, that was close. You have to think, Jeannette. There's a whole car here. When you pull that sharply to the right, the back will stick out more on the left. Look! Look ahead! Stop! Didn't you see the car pulling out of the driveway? For crying out loud, Jeannette, you're only going 25 miles an hour."

"Here comes a light, Jeannette. It's yellow. Slow down. It'll be red by the time you get there. Okay, pull up a bit. No, no, not too close to the parked car! Oyyyyy, Jeannette. For crying out loud, I just told you not to get too close on the right. When I tell you to pull up, I mean straight ahead. You have to listen."

"I am listening, Nathan. You're telling me too many things at once."

"I have to tell you, Jeannette. This is a moving vehicle. This is not the empty parking lot. I have to tell you and you have to listen." My mother is silent, but I can feel her shifting from whiney to angry to belligerent. These are sensations I recognize. I feel her fantasies of driving herself to mah-jongg, to the new shopping mall in Dartmouth, even as far as Boston for the day, disappearing into a wet fog of tears and disappointment. So close, so within her grasp that for a moment, it felt possible.

I'm not hearing my father anymore, and I imagine that my mother isn't either. We are enveloped in this descending fog of what we all know now is defeat. But my mother strikes out in her last hurrah, my father's instructions still coming at her, "on the left," "on the right, on the right, Jeannette," behind you, look behind you, Jeannette," "in front—IN FRONT!" Too late. The pharmacy is approaching quickly; we are going up its stairs and my mother still has her foot on the gas. She does not apply the brake until we have crashed through the door.

"As long as we're here, we might as well pick up my prescription," my mother says. When I look up from where I've ducked behind the seat and see the astonished faces around me, the most flabbergasted being my father, I think I have never loved my mother more.

My mother's driving lessons do not end here, although it certainly is the end of her driving lessons with my father. She will fail one road test and pass another, but what she cannot do is to keep the breakthrough seizures at bay. Whenever my father tells the story of my mother's drive up the pharmacy steps, it is my mother who adds the footnote that she was able to pass her driving test, although she was never able to get her license.

* * *

I know that my mother once drew maps for Curtis Publishing, but on road trips she has the greatest of difficulty reading them.

"Jeannette, look at the map and tell me where I get off."

My mother searches in the glove compartment until she has her hands on whatever state we happen to be lost in this time.

"Hurry it up, Jeannette. We'll be in California before you find it. Route 90, we need Route 90. Don't you see it?"

"Not yet."

My father grabs the map from my mother, thrusts it over the wheel and into the windshield, obstructing his view and our view from the back seat. I look at my sister. She looks more disgusted than frightened, so I relax. My father holds the map up and waves it around, above his head.

"Can someone, A-N-Yone, PLEASE find this darned Route 90?" He never says "damned."

My sister grabs the map, studies it for a few moments and winces. "Daddy, you passed it."

"Where?" He turns his head to look.

"Nathan, stop the car!"

"And just where should I stop the car, Jeannette? In the middle of the highway?" My mother glares at him and then out the window.

"Where did I miss it?"

"Back where Mommy told you to turn."

"Good Lord, Jeannette. That was thirty miles back."

"She told you to turn," my sister and I sing out.

My father yells to my sister, "Find the next exit. Jeannette, you look for a place to turn around."

"There's one," my mother points as we pass it.

"JEANETTE, you have to tell me so I have time to turn."
"But Nathan, I just saw it. You're over there, and you didn't see it."
"I'm driving. Gay, where's the next exit?"
"I'm looking for it, Daddy. Oh."
"What do you mean, "Oh?"
"It looks like a long way, Daddy."
"How long?"
"I don't know but it's more than the distance from the last exit."
My father sighs.

I know that this is the worst moment I could possibly choose. "Daddy, I have to go to the bathroom."

"Do you see a bathroom here? Have you been paying attention? There's not even an exit here."

"I have to go, too, Nathan."

"Me, too, Daddy," my sister winks at me.

"THERE IS NO BATHROOM!" The three of us squirm in our seats in silence until my mother calls out, "Rest stop, three miles, Nathan."

"If you can see a rest stop with three miles to go, Jeannette, why is it you can't see a turn in the road?" My mother doesn't answer. We are grateful when he pulls onto the exit ramp. My father doesn't like to stop for the bathroom even when he's going in the right direction. He longs for his army days in Texas when my diapers hung from our Studebaker, a toilet and laundry on the go.

My father has a hard and fast rule about rest stops. No purchases of any kind. We are to go straight to the bathroom and back to the car. We will eat when we get there. Sometimes when we are lost for hours, it is just too painful to go to the bathroom. The tantalizing smells of popcorn and hotdogs are hardly worth it. Since my father also has a hard and fast rule about asking anyone for directions, I often wonder if I will ever eat again.

"Nathan, there's a gas station, don't you want to stop and ask for directions?"

"No, Jeannette, I don't. I'm going to ask some idiot? Then we'll end up really lost."

"Aren't we lost now, Daddy?" I'm really hungry.

"No, we are not lost. We took a wrong turn. I know exactly where we are."

"Let's sing a song," my sister tries to distract me. We manage the first stanza and chorus of "Oklahoma" before my father yells, "Can you please be quiet until I find the road!" My sister hugs me and I curl up with my head in her lap and go to sleep. It is my way of staving off starvation and other things.

\* \* \*

My father is afraid to drive in big cities, but he never lets on. Instead, he berates construction as an annoying foil introduced just to confuse him. He is most upset by Philadelphia.

"What did they do to this road? They've changed it. It wasn't like this the last time we were here."

My sister grunts. If only she could have taken the train to Bryn Mawr, but my father has insisted on driving. So here we are in the cool of September and the oppressive heat of the Plymouth. My father does not believe that car windows should ever be lowered.

"She couldn't have gone to Wellesley or Smith, no, she had to pick Bryn Mawr." My father addresses an aggravating tailgater, "Can't you see I'm looking for the road? Why don't you just pass me?"

"You're in the left lane, Nathan."

"Jeannette, don't you think I know I'm in the left lane? I have to turn left, I think—how can I possibly be sure with all of this crap—and I can't turn left from the right lane now, can I. Gay, look at the map."

"This is an old map. Can't you stop and ask, Daddy? My orientation starts at 4:00."

"Don't worry, I'll get you there." We have no doubt that this is true. It's the when and how that is in question.

I sigh and look at my sister. I don't care if we ever get there. Once we do, she'll gather her belongings and leave me for tea parties and new friends to share in her secrets. I dread the drive back without her.

"Maybe we won't be able to find it, and we'll have to take Gay home with us," I offer.

"Don't be silly," my sister snaps, annoyed at my father's refusal to admit he's lost.

"I wish you didn't have to go away."

Gay takes my hand. "You'll come visit me, I promise."

"Really?"

"Yes. You can sleep in the dorm with me."

"Can I go to a tea party?"

My sister groans. She is less enchanted with this aspect of Bryn Mawr than I am. But then she adds, "Sure."

I squeeze her hand, momentarily consoled.

My father breaks into this moment with, "Where's the darned road and why aren't there any signs? These sure are crappy directions." No one volunteers an answer.

At some hour before sunset, Bryn Mawr materializes amidst the brilliant fall foliage, ivy masking a castle of stone. Victorian windows peer into dark and mysterious halls. My sister's room has a musty smell. I worry that I will never be able to find her there. Her roommate is lively, Jewish, from New York. I fear she will replace me. The drive back to New Bedford is quiet. My father lets me listen to my favorite radio shows, but there is no Gay to giggle with me or to ask if I want to lie down and put my head in her lap.

\* \* \*

I am recently eleven, freshly pubescent, and in the car again. It is late March of 1960. My mother, my father and I are taking a road trip through Philadelphia, Washington, D.C., Virginia and other historical points of interest my father wants me to see. The final destination is a meeting of the American Ophthalmologic Society being held at the Fontainebleau Hotel in Miami Beach. This will be the farthest I have been from home since Tijuana.

Our first stop is Philadelphia. We visit Bubbe and my father's brothers and sisters. He is so excited by the idea of this trip that he doesn't even quarrel with Aunt Rosie. Every time my mother thinks he might, she kicks him under the table. Grandpop and Tuffy are no longer with us, but we visit Aunt Rose in her new apartment where she lives with her brother, Alec. Alec has a parakeet who sits on his shoulder. I like to watch them sing to each other. My Aunt Rose no longer seems like my grandmother in this strange place. The house on Fleming Street has been sold to a colored family. My Aunt Rosie and Uncle Sammy call them "schvatza." My father winces and tells me never to use that word. It's not nice. My mother insists that we drive by Fleming Street. When she sees the house, she cries.

My father is fiercely patriotic. He tells me how hard things were in Russia, how his family feared the Cossacks, the anti-Semitic farmers near his shtetl, and the predictable eruptions of violence. America saved his life and he wants me to know its history. On the drive to Washington, D.C., he praises the United States government, Eisenhower, Washington the President, Washington the Capitol, Abraham Lincoln and the freedoms and foods we have that he could never have hoped for in Bershad. He talks about his childhood, stories I have heard and some I have not. For the moment, I am glad that Gay is not with us. She is tired of my father's stories and would be rolling her eyes.

We drive into the busyness of Washington, D.C. after breakfast and before lunch. My father refuses to take public transportation. Buses, trains, trolleys, the subway or the metro, they exist for people who cannot afford cars.

Since my father refuses to leave the car at the hotel, he is perpetually seeking a place to park. Garages are too expensive and city lots are too far, so we drive around never-ending blocks while the three of us intensely search for some slot that is not a fire hydrant or a meter. It is some time before my father is willing to concede that these parking places do not exist. I am hungry, tired and cranky and have to go to the bathroom. My father tells me I will just have to hold it. My mother turns and gives me a warning look that tells me there will be no help coming from her. Once we rid ourselves of the car, and I cannot say how, my father entertains me with monuments, museums, cemeteries and stories. We jump from present to past, to changing worlds. I try to shape these images in my mind. My father tells me about the Civil War, but I am stuck in the schtetl. I am too afraid to ask my father if he thinks such things could happen here.

In too short a time for my liking, and I suspect my mother's as well, we are back in the car. My mother and I occupy ourselves checking out the window for Burma Shave billboards and billboards that boast a festive little fellow with a ten-gallon hat who perpetually points to large colorful letters that read, "Only (X number of) miles to the South of the Border Motel."

"Can we stay there, Daddy? Please?"

"If we get there when it's time to stop and it doesn't cost a fortune." I am pleased that he doesn't say no. I have no idea how two conditions can stack the odds against me.

Breakfasts below my northern borders are beyond my New England experience. Pancakes and sausage and eggs with hot biscuits and gravy. No potatoes. Grits. I order grits for breakfast, lunch and dinner. There are no limits on food. As long as I can eat it, I can order it.

We pass the South of the Border Motel in the middle of the day. Other than the intriguing advertisements, it looks like every other motel. I am not disappointed. My father doesn't know this and says, "I'm sorry, Phyllis. Maybe we can stay there on the way home."

"It's okay, Daddy. The signs look better than the motel."

My father laughs. "Yes, that's often the case." My mother smiles.

We pass uneventfully through South Carolina and find ourselves in Georgia. The road narrows as we pass through towns that hardly seem inhabited. Snow flakes begin to dot the windshield. My father asks, "What is this?"

"Snow," my mother replies immediately.

"Jeannette, I know what it is. It's not supposed to be here. We're in Georgia, for crying out loud."

The flakes become heavier, the kind that stick and build quickly. The windshield wipers are moving slowly, weighted down by the freezing water. Cars are skidding around us and my mother is frightened. There are huge ditches on either side of the road and already several cars have veered into them.

"Okay," my father says, "we'll stop for the night in the next town. Let's hurry up before everyone else gets the same idea."

My father puts his foot on the gas, skids past a few cars still on the road, and takes off down what no longer feels like the highway. The road narrows and my father says cheerfully, "Must be a town." For a moment, none of us think the sirens and lights are aimed at us. My father doesn't stop, and soon we are surrounded.

"Now what." My father stops where he is as there is no possible way to determine where the side of the road ends and the ditch begins. Several men climb out of two police cars. A large man with a sheriff's hat steps up to the car. My father tries to roll the window down, but he can only force it a couple of inches due to the amount of snow. All I can see of the sheriff under the hat is one beefy reddened cheek.

Where y'all headed in sucha hurreh, Mistah?"

"In the first place," my father retorts, "I'm a doctor not a mister. In the second place, I wasn't hurrying anywhere. I want to get my family to a motel for the night and out of the storm."

My mother looks around nervously. "Nathan," she cautions him, touching his arm.

The third man edges up in back of the sheriff. "Yanks," he sniggers.

"Where y'all from?" the sheriff asks.

"New Bedford, Massachusetts," my father says a bit too proudly.

"What y'all doing down here? We don't see too many yanks in Nahunta."

"And we don't care to see 'em, no way," says the man who sniggered.

My father ignores him. "We're on our way to a medical meeting in Miami Beach."

The second man who got out of the same car as the sheriff mutters, "Surprisin' y'all didn't fly, seein' as you're a rich doc n'all."

"I'm not rich," my father informs them.

"Well, doc, it's like this. Y'all have your way a doing things up north, and we all have our way a doin' 'em down heah. Now my friends heah, they come out in the weather to help me, and they gotta feed theah families. Now, we can settle this right heah and now, no judge, no court. You just give us the $300 fine, and we can all walk away easy. Watcha say?"

"You want me to just hand you $300? I haven't done anything wrong."

"Got three of us who'll say you was doin' something wrong, Yankee doc." This comes from deputy number two. "We got you clocked at 50 in a 25."

"Well, then," my father shakes his head. "I guess you'll have to take me in. Take me to the judge. This is America. I'm not paying."

"Nathan, what are we supposed to do?"

"Y'all can come along with him. You ride with us, Doc."

"My wife can't drive."

"Okay. Not likely you'll try to run off in this storm. You just follow me, suh." The sheriff and deputy number one in front, deputy number two bringing up the rear, we form an eerie caravan in the quiet of the steadily falling snow and silent flashing lights.

"I'm not paying these gonifs." My father has to know that by now I know that "gonifs" is the Yiddish word for "thieves." Obviously, as he continues, he doesn't care if I know.

"That was a speed trap. They've been sitting there all day waiting for some out-of-towner to come through so they could go home with an easy hundred bucks a piece. I'll go to jail first."

"Nathan, you can't just go to jail and leave us here."

"It's a matter of principle, Jeannette."

"Nathan, if you go to jail, I'm taking Phyllis and flying home." This sort of pronouncement is rare. I know she means it. How can I go back to school? I'm supposed to be writing about my experiences for the sixth grade class. It's the only way my teacher would let me miss this much school. What if they make me repeat the whole year? Tears in my eyes, my voice cracking like a pubescent boy's, I plead, "Daddy, please, you can't go to jail."

We arrive at the courthouse/jail in silence. It doesn't look official to me, just a large wooden building, old and decaying. A metal sign attached to two poles by chains swings dangerously in the wind. It announces "Nahunta Courthouse" in fading blue metallic letters. I look for bars on the windows. I don't see any, but I can barely make out the windows themselves in the drifting snow. Before we get out of the car, my father warns, "I'll do the talking."

My mother looks him straight in the eye. "I meant what I said, Nathan."

"Daddy, please, please don't go to jail. I'll give up my allowance." My father gives me a surprised look. I have no idea what it means.

My mother and I are seated in a waiting area. It is drafty and furnished only with a few wooden benches. I picture my father in handcuffs and chains, *The Birdman of Alcatraz*. I have to go to the bathroom.

My mother points to green letters painted directly onto a wall, "Toilets," and an arrow pointing down a narrow hallway. It's dark and creepy. "Do you want me to come with you?"

"No, it's okay."

I walk slowly down the hallway and take a left at another arrow that says "Women." I wonder if the toilets are as cold as the hallway. I find myself at a dead end with two doors. In bold jagged white painted letters, one reads "Coloreds" and the other reads "Whites Only." I stand there and stare.

What am I? Are Jews "Whites" or "Coloreds?" I honestly don't know. I know I'm not dark like my Portuguese friend, Cecelia, or my colored friend, Mary, who is chocolate brown. I use their toilets when I go to their homes and they use ours when they come to mine. I'm confused. Is this like the Jewish ghettos and my grandfather not being allowed to travel for work in Kiev? My father says things like that don't happen in America, or at least not since the Civil War. I have to pee badly by now, and something I can't name is boiling inside me. If Mary were here, she'd have to go in the "Coloreds" toilet. I will too.

I open the door cautiously, peek inside, take a deep breath before I step in quickly and shut the door. Something brushes me across the cheek. I stifle a scream and realize it is a string connected to a bare light bulb screwed into an outlet in the ceiling. I yank at it several times, but the light does not go on. I wait for my eyes to adjust enough that I can see the toilet seat and lift the lid to find an indoor outhouse. I hold my breath, pull down my pants, pee, slam the lid back into place and pull my pants up with one hand while opening the door with the other. I jump outside and into the body of a hefty blond woman. I shriek as the door slams behind me. The woman pushes me away from her back against the door, the expression on her bloated face far more violent than her brushing me off her like an annoying gnat. Words fly from her dark cave of a mouth, due to several missing front teeth.

"What were you doing in there, kid? Ain't you big enough to read? Can't you read the sign? It says "Coloreds." You don't look like no colored to me. Where your parents at?"

"My mommy is sitting over there on a bench and my daddy is seeing the judge. They don't care which bathroom I use." My tone becomes slightly indignant because I don't feel afraid. "Go ask them, if you like. I have lots and lots of colored friends and we use the same bathrooms in New Bedford."

"Oh, y'all r Yankees. Where's Bedford? Ain't that Connecticut?"

"No. It's New Bedford and it's in Massachusetts. And my father says they don't know how to clean the roads here when it snows like they do in Massachusetts."

The woman's mouth twists and turns in a sneer. "Well, since ya can't read and don't know which toilet yar supposed to use, I guess ya'd be bettah off up North wheah they know what to do with snow. Now you'd best git back to your mamma."

"My best friend is colored," I yell back at her as I head for the waiting area. I feel triumphant in getting in these last words before I remember my father telling me that it's not necessarily a good thing when people say, "Some of my best friends are Jews."

I find my mother doing crossword puzzles from a book she's carried on the trip. She looks up from her anagram and asks, "Did you find the bathroom okay, honey?"

"Yeah." I cuddle next to her and we work on word puzzles together.

It feels like both a moment and many hours before my father returns. He is alone. "Let's get the heck out of here," he says as he passes by our bench, not even pausing long enough for my mother to collect her bag and coat. We follow quickly after him and find him in the car with the motor running.

"What took them so long? "My mother asks.

"We had to drive to the bank."

"Why?"

"Because, Jeannette," my father sounds like he does when he is explaining something to one of his "stupid" patients, "I guess the judge and his secretary needed their cuts, too. The three hundred became five hundred, and I didn't have that much cash on me. I swear, if Phyllis hadn't been so worried about my going to jail, I wouldn't have given them one penny."

"So it's because of Phyllis that you paid them?" There is a touch of irony, barely discernable, in my mother's tone.

"Yes. I could tell she was really scared."

"You should have paid them in the first place and it wouldn't have cost another two hundred."

"How do I know that, Jeannette? They could've hauled me in there anyway and still asked for five. And after what Phyllis said to the secretary, I'm lucky they didn't decide to lock me up anyway and throw away the key."

"What?" My mother turns around and looks at me."

My father winks at me in the rear view mirror. I'm not in trouble. He's proud of me. "Well, after she came out of the "Coloreds" toilet....."

"You went in the "Coloreds" toilet? She went in the "Coloreds" toilet? I didn't think they did that anymore. I thought it was only in books."

"Well, when I had to hand over the cash to the secretary and she was writing the receipt, she said, "I guess I know wheah she gits it from. Y'all bettah learn that we don't do things down heah the way y'all do 'em up theah. That little girl o' yours, she bettah learn how to read. That could git y'all in a lotta trouble in these parts.""

"I told her, what are you talking about, my daughter is the best reader in her whole school. Then she said, 'If she's such a good reader, how come she couldn't read the toilet sign?' I knew Phyllis did it on purpose."

My mother laughs and turns around. "We've had a lot of protestors in our family. I guess we have another one." My mother tells me about my great grandfather, how he made his house a hideout for slaves on the run. My father tells me about Aunt Dora, how she founded and fought for the ILGWU.

We find a funky motel for the night. We are united in our Yankeeness, in our Jewishness, in our rebelliousness, drawn tightly together in another configuration of us against them. We are safe, warm, dry and cozy against the elements of nature. We trust, at least for this one night, that we can live for some minutes without discord. Perhaps we might have the capacity to stumble across a few hours in our lives when we, too, can feel secure against both the inner and outer elements of human nature.

\* \* \*

I am sixteen and I have learned from experience. I save my allowance for driving lessons and take them after school when I am supposed to be studying at the library. Not a soul knows about this with the exception of my driving instructor. He knows my father, and perhaps that is why he has agreed not to tell. Sometimes when I see him grabbing the sides of his seat with both hands and pressing his foot against the floor, I am convinced he will tell my father, but he never does. I promise him that I will do it myself as soon as I receive my license. I live in fear that I will pass my father on the road and one of us will be shocked into a deadly accident. I have visions of me driving into him or him driving into me, the looks on our faces, our last thoughts as we slip into unconsciousness, sirens fading in the background.

I pass my written test and then my road test. I hold the coveted paper in my hands, but still I cannot speak. Days, weeks go by, but when I try to force the words from the back of my throat, where they seem permanently lodged, no sound comes out.

Summer is coming and I will be visiting my cousin in Michigan. She has promised me a car to use every day. Suppose she mentions this to my father? I must fess up. I dream that my father is old and I have to drive him to the hospital. He yells at me to call a taxi because I don't have my license. I dream that I drive away with my mother in a pink Chevy convertible. My father is yelling after us that we will be arrested because I don't have my license. Every morning I check to make sure that my license is where I put it before I go to sleep.

We are seated at the table after breakfast on a Sunday morning. My father asks me if I want the funnies. I take them from him and begin to read *Dick Tracy*. My father says, "I hear you're a good driver." I freeze.

"Pat O'Conner came in on Friday to get his glasses adjusted. He told me I should be proud of you. And you learned on a stick shift."

My mother is frozen in her chair. Apparently, my father is amused by this deceit and wants to get genuine reactions. I push my eyes to the next frame of *Dick Tracy*.

"I was going to tell you, Daddy. I paid for it with my allowance. I was going to tell you but I was afraid you'd be so mad."

"Well, just don't think you'll be driving my car. I had to buy my own car and you will, too. And I'm not one of these fathers who will allow you to drive mine all over the place. I didn't buy your sister a car and I didn't let her drive mine. Look at what's happening to your cousins."

"What's happening to my cousins?"

"Never mind," my father replies, "but I'm not about to let it happen to you."

\* \* \*

It is many years later, and I am inspecting my father's new Cadillac. Since my mother's death from a metastasized cancer several years ago, he calls to ask my opinion and permission about major purchases and events. I know I have offended him by not accepting his offer to make a gift to me of the last car. Somehow the idea of driving around New York City in a lemon yellow Lincoln Continental is more frightening than my father's response to rejection.

The new car is a respectable deep blue. It is a doctor's car. I "ooh" and "ahh" enthusiastically as my father opens the door for me. Unpredictably, he wants me to drive. I am less enthusiastic about this prospect because he is even a worse passenger than he is a driver, but the shiny new chrome tempts me. He instructs as I insert the key. The speedometer jolts ahead to thirty miles an hour upon contact.

"Dad, something's wrong with this car. It's starting at thirty miles an hour. This is scary."

"You just don't know what you're doing. It's run by computer. It's supposed to do that."

"Dad, computers can be wrong. It can't be possible that it would start at thirty miles an hour. This is dangerous. We have to call the company."

I know what's coming now. Even though I am 37 years of age, my father interprets my response as defiant. He starts to breathe heavily; his face wrinkles in annoyance.

"Okay. Let me drive." The implication of my incompetence is clear.

"Dad, please, this is not a question of driving ability. There is something wrong with this car."

"Nothing is wrong with this car! It's a brand new car. Get out and I'll drive. You just don't know how to operate it. Believe me, there's nothing wrong with it."

I question myself. Could this be some new invention? I shake my head and get out. We switch sides. I am determined to lighten the mood and enjoy this experience. I slide into the passenger seat and begin to play with the seat adjustment.

"Wow, Dad, look at this! This is fantastic. It goes all the way....and now slides down..." as I turn to smile at him, I see that his expression is frozen.

"Put it back the way it was."

"Why? It's adjustable."

"Don't ask me why; just put it back."

"Dad, I'm not five years old. What is wrong with adjusting an adjustable seat? I'll put it back before I get out. I'll leave it exactly the way I found it."

No, it is not possible for him to accept that the car should be altered in any way. It's perfect the way it starts at thirty miles an hour. One should not question these things.

"Put it back now. It came that way for a reason. That's the way it came, and that's the best position."

"Why did they bother to make it adjustable then?" I know this question is futile, but the devil in me insists on poking away.

"Because they'd sell the car in the best position to make people want to buy it, the most comfortable." I adjust the seat back to its original position. I find it too difficult to argue with his logic.

"You know, Dad," I forge ahead, "people come in different sizes."

"Of course I know that." He informs me, "I'm not stupid."

Several weeks later my sister visits. After one driving attempt, she announces she will not step foot in the car again until he has it serviced. Doesn't he realize that cars don't start up at thirty miles an hour? She is the first born. She has the voice of authority. He submits. The company easily admits a computer glitch and fixes the car. He confesses this to me only after he knows that my sister has told me. He is careful to report that my sister did not have a need to adjust the seat.

# [19]

# HAIRY LEGS

*The air is heavy and thick with fog. I am alone in a small boat, a rowboat....yes, it is a rowboat because I do have oars, and I am rowing. My arms are tired. The air is so dense, and now it feels as if I am rowing the air. Somewhere off in the distance I see a figure standing and waving to me. I struggle to steer the boat toward the figure, but my arms are so fatigued that the boat no longer seems to be moving. I cannot even lift them to signal back. Although the figure is too far to see, I recognize my sister. I work so hard to reach her, but then she is gone and I drop both my oars from exhaustion. I yell for help, but I know no one will hear me. When I wake up in a sweat, I remember that my sister is leaving to go away to school.*

\* \* \*

The neighborhood boys are serenading me again, *"Hairy legs, hairy legs. Do you have a hairy twat?"* I am not sure what a "twat' is, but I know by the lewd gestures and sneers that I have to be careful how I find out.

*"Hairy legs, hairy legs, why don't you shave your hairy legs!"* The chant of the Hebrew school boys is more musical, contains no mysterious vocabulary and presents me with a possible solution. But much

like everything else in this period of affliction known as early adolescence, it's not as easy as it sounds. The only shaving I've ever witnessed is my father's morning ritual. If he's in a benevolent mood and allows me to sit quietly on the toilet to watch, he warns me that I must never, ever, under any circumstances, no matter how dire they may seem, even if one of my friends begs and pleads with me, touch his razor or shaving implements.

When I was little, he'd wave the razor at me, shaking drops of water in my face. "It only looks easy because I know how to use it. You could sever an artery and die." By the time I'm old enough to know what an artery is, he elaborates. "This is not a toy. You are never to play with it. I know you wouldn't mean to, but you just don't realize how easy it would be to hurt someone with this. Next thing you know, I'd be driving that crazy friend of yours, the one who's always scratching you—

"Jean, Daddy, she has a name, and she isn't always scratching me."

"She has a bad temper. That's what happens when you adopt a child. Her parents are nothing like that—first thing you know, she's cut you or you cut her, and I have to drive you to the hospital. I end up getting sued for everything I've got; we all end up out on the street, ruined. Is that what you want?"

"No, Daddy, but I don't touch the razor."

"Just see that you don't."

I vow over and over not to watch him anymore, but something draws me back there every chance I get. I'm fascinated, hypnotized.

At eleven, I'm more aware of the subtle gesture. I see how his hands caress the shaving brush. "It's real horsehair," he confides. Lovingly he swirls it around in a wooden dish of British shaving lather. He sweeps the brush across his face in a continuous counterclockwise motion. He never lifts the brush until he is covered with white. Then he places it delicately back in the dish until he's completed the entire shaving procedure. Next he lifts the razor, and while he shifts his head into a variety of poses and postures and presses his skin taut with one hand, he glides the razor across his beard with the other. These acts are accompanied by absolute silence. Unless—

The phone rings. My father lifts the lather brush from his cheek. He waits. Poised. Brush in hand.

"Naaaaathan. It's for you," my mother wails through the kitchen, up the long staircase, across the landing and into the bathroom.

"Who is it, Jeannette?"

There is a long silence. My mother has forgotten to ask, and she is quietly returning to the telephone to do so now. But she has to walk back from the staircase, through the kitchen and into the office and then back again. The whole future of the day rests on the nature of this phone call. If it's an emergency, my father will have to remove all the lather from his face, take the call, and lather all over again. I raise my butt ever so slightly from the toilet seat in case I need to beat a hasty departure.

We hear my mother's footsteps and then a deep intake of breath as she braces herself for the shout upward, "It's Johhhhhhn. Johhhhhhn Diaz."

Through the layers of lather, I see his face relax. John is another ophthalmologist in town. He's always late, he's clumsy, he's too fat, and he doesn't know how to take a vacation. The verdict is clear.

"Tell your mother I'll call him back when I finish shaving."

Happily I race to the top of the banister and deliver this message to my mother. "He'll call him back. He's busy right now." My mother is literal. I want to save her from a lecture from my father on how she should handle the office phone. I'm feeling that all is right with the world. When he's in a good mood, my father lets me touch his cheek just after it's freshly shaven. I run back to claim this privilege.

But now that I'm eleven and in puberty, this shaving business takes on new meaning. Is it possible for my legs to achieve such smoothness? My father is downstairs in his office. My mother is in the kitchen. My sister is locked away in her bedroom. I reach for the razor. Lightning does not strike. I screw open the handle and see that there is a blade inside. Would he ever know? Do they even know that my legs are hairy?

I hear a door and quickly drop the razor into its case. I run some water as a decoy, but it's only my sister. "What are you doing?"

"Nothing."

"Well, if you're doing nothing, I need the bathroom."

There is only one bathroom in our house. There's a toilet in the basement, but since it seems to be a transient home for spiders, we never use it.

"Okay," I sigh deeply. One bathroom. Always occupied. How can I ever shave my legs? Do I even know how to do it? Suppose my father's right and I fatally wound myself? I'll be mortified. "New Bedford Junior High School Student Found Fatally Slain Shaving Legs." I could see myself sprawled for all to see in the accompanying photo. I sulk out of the bathroom and plunk myself down on the chest in the hall.

My sister's already closed the bathroom door. I can't go on being called "hairy legs," and I know I will never use that razor. I am done for. Not even twelve. I won't go outside again. I'll become a hermit. I'll stop going to Hebrew School. Good.

My sister walks by me on her way back from the bathroom.

"What's wrong with you? Do you need the bathroom again?"

"Nothing."

"Come on. Why do you have that look on your face? Something's wrong."

I don't want to tell her. I'm too embarrassed.

"Come on, you can trust me." She coaxes, seeing signs of my weakening. She's only home for a week from college. It's now or never. I burst into tears.

"Did I do something?" she asks.

"No."

"Daddy?"

"No."

"Mother?"

"No."

"Well, what's happened?"

"Some kids are making fun of me."

"Which kids? What are they saying?"

"Boys."

"Ohhhhhhh. Yeah," she sighs, "I know all about that. What are they saying?"

"I don't want to tell you." I start to sob again.

She comes and sits down next to me on the chest. "I love you, Sweetie. You can tell me."

I tell her. She promises she'll be right back. I hear voices in the kitchen. Heavy debates ensue. Mumbling drifts up the back stairway. Whatever the outcome, I'm relieved. I'm not alone with this anymore.

My sister helps me shave my legs and teaches me how to do it myself. Then she goes back to college. I cry. My father stresses to me that education is the most important thing in life; there's no need to cry; one day, if I don't screw up too much, I'll go off to college, too. Since I'm eleven, I don't care about college. It seems to me that while my sister has finally found her freedom, I've been left behind in the prison yard of my puberty.

# [20]

# HIDING PLACES

I have several hiding places. The first is where I hide to listen to what my parents are saying. Mostly I do this at the top of the back stairs, as many of their arguments about me take place directly below in the kitchen. Occasionally, I use the radiator in my room to overhear what my parents are saying in their bedroom. This conversation is muffled and hard to follow. But sometimes I get a hint of what's to come, and that is worth the slight red burns I get on my ear from pressing it so close to the heat in winter. When their voices are too low for me to make out, I can shift from the radiator to the inside of the tiny closet that borders their bedroom wall. This is uncomfortable and feels risky, so it has to be important.

I also have hiding places where I run away from my father. When I'm older, this becomes the duck pond in the park, but for now I'm only seven and too little to travel that far. Before I'm allowed to cross the street, I hide in Mrs. Brody's garden. It is huge and overgrown with magnificent flowering bushes, ancient trees, wandering vines and living creatures. There is an old New England stonewall surrounding this magical place, and I can sit for hours reciting what I can remember of "The Mending Wall" and other poems. Mrs. Brody stops going into the garden. She's too old and too ill. But even when she did, she never chased me out. One summer day, the ambulance comes for Mrs.

Brody. She doesn't come home again. Her children sell the property to the Catholic Church. They turn it into a convent and nursery school. We get on well with the nuns, but I can never forgive the Church for tearing up Mrs. Brody's garden and paving it all for a parking lot. Only my little friend Roger, the brother of the Janowski twins who live down the block, knows I come here. It's our secret place.

Another place where I run to hide from my father is Roger's tree house. Well, it is actually not Roger's alone. He shares it with his twin sisters and his horrid older brother, Dean. We are all afraid of Dean. His parents must be terrified of him as well, as he is never punished for the most evil of deeds. And their mean tempered dog, Lady, is as scary as Dean, so I have to be either desperate or looking for Roger to choose this spot.

If it is too cold outside even for me, as rain or snow is not sufficient to stop me, my last resort is the bomb shelter in the basement. As I often have to share this spot with spiders and even more unpleasant and unwanted companions, it is never my first choice.

I also have at my disposal legitimate hiding places. This is a separate category because it is not so easy for my father to identify that I am hiding specifically from him. I stay overnight at my friend Nancy's house when I am feeling more kindly toward him but want to be away from what I sense is stormy weather over the horizon. When I am not so kindly disposed and in fact want to inflict pain, I spend the night at my friend Karen's house. My father dislikes Karen's father even more than he dislikes Karen. Mr. Cohen doesn't know how to be a quiet and careful Jew. He spends hours expressing his leftist views on talk radio. Even when my father agrees with him, he would never go public with his opinions. Mr. Cohen is fat and slovenly, and since Karen's mother died of cancer, there is no mother to supervise. My father is suspicious of my affection for this man and a bit jealous. I am never sure if my fondness for Mr. Cohen is genuine or merely revenge.

My last sort of hiding place is illegitimate and forbidden. Nancy and I discover it together and no one knows we go there. We make several plans to visit our secret place in the dead of night, but this is bravado. As foolish as we are, even we know this would be dangerous. It is *verboten* even by daylight, but we are reckless and in need of some adventure. So, like children everywhere, we discover the old railroad tracks down by the fishing pier. It is the fishing pier that is off limits to us. Fishermen are notorious for their drinking and other things that our parents whisper about or only allude to in our presence. They never think to include the old railroad yard as a no trespassing zone as it is on the other side of the pier. Nancy and I have a special secret code we use to refer to this place. We draw blood from our respective fingers and mix it to seal this oath. I can remember it to this day but cannot bring myself even now to break our vow of silence. Some things should stay sacred. What I do violate is our vow not to go there separately. There are times when only a sense of imminent danger can mitigate my rage.

No one knows I spy on my parents except for my sister, but everyone knows that I hide from my father. Even he suspects my various means of escape and is resentful. He was forced to hide when he was a child. Perhaps because his life was at stake and he does not feel that mine is, he interprets my hiding as oppositional and unnecessary. This disagreement as to what constitutes survival is an ongoing debate between us.

None of my friends ever chooses to hide at my house. There is only the one time Roger gives it a try. Roger is good-natured and can take an awful lot from his brother before he finally draws the line, but this is no guarantee that Dean won't immediately choose to cross it. One summer evening, when I come home from playing at Nancy's house, there is Roger waiting on the front doorstep. My friends don't just come up and ring the bell because they are all too terrified of my father. So I am a little surprised to see Roger standing up over his bike, rocking from side to side with a duffle bag slung around his neck, and even more surprised to see my father chatting easily with him and looking amused.

"Hi, Roger. I can't come out now. We're going to eat dinner."

"That's okay. I'm eating dinner with you. I asked your Dad if I could come live with you, and he says it's okay."

"What? Is that really okay, Daddy?" I'm happy because I feel so sad for Roger, but I am more than a little suspicious of my father's sudden generosity.

"Well," my father grins, totally pleased with himself, "Yes, I did say that, Roger, but what else did I say?"

Roger looks unhappy now, like he would if he had suddenly found a dead fly in his ice cream soda.

"Did I give you a condition to living here?"

"Yes, sir," Roger mumbles.

"And what is that condition?"

"That I leave my bike at home, sir."

"Okay," my father is smug and confident. "I'll be inside and you can think about it. You see, Roger, Phyllis doesn't have a bicycle. I don't allow it. So if you live with us, you'll have to live by our rules. That's fair, isn't it?"

Roger nods his head in defeat. My father retreats indoors, confident in his victory, secure in his child psychology. He knows that Roger will never sacrifice his bicycle. Poor Roger is left to ponder which is worse; his home with a bike or mine without. My father is right. It's no contest. Roger doesn't even stay to eat. He will have to find a way to hide at home.

My parents have their own hiding places. My father hides at the beach or takes a walk in the country. Since he's not happy unless he has an audience, he usually requests that one or all of us accompany him. He is hiding from his patients. If he happens to see a car he recognizes parked by the shore, he will keep driving until he feels safe. When he wants to hide from us, he barricades himself behind the glass brick wall of his office after hours. But mostly, he is hiding from himself, from the fears that haunt him when he is confronted with the responsibilities he is faced with as a husband and father.

My mother hides from all of us. She escapes into science fiction and mystery novels. Later she will add romance and religion. She reads so many of these books, four to five a week from the local library, that she often brings the same book home two or three times without realizing it. When I am thirteen years old and television finally enters our house, both of my parents discover new variations on the theme of hiding.

My mother and father also have hiding places for things. They're not terribly successful at this. There is the tin painted box that always sits on the top shelf of my parents' bedroom closet. Important items are "concealed" here, birth certificates, bond certificates, a marriage license, old passports, new passports, the extra set of keys to the car, the key to the safety deposit box (where some of this stuff ought to be), the mortgage book for the house, my father's dog tags and so on. Whenever anything momentous occurs, my father will ask one of us to bring him "the tin box." We all know where it is and what it contains. We later learn that so do most of our neighbors and relatives.

My parents have a hiding place for money. This is simply a wallet stashed under lace and linen hankies in a drawer in my mother's dresser. No thief with any self-respect could possibly burgle the house without discovering it. We all know where this is too, as we are often sent there to pay the paperboy or to get grocery money. There is not a doubt in my mind that certain neighbors and relatives are also privy to the "cash drawer" banking system. There is also no question that my father is declaring every penny of this cash to Uncle Sam. He is far too grateful to his adopted country to even consider cheating the government out of a single penny and has no patience for anyone who does anything fancy with their income taxes.

I would love to discover my sister's hiding places, but I never betray her by looking. I know that she hides within herself and that's why she has those awful headaches. She disappears for hours at a time in her room, the shades drawn and the covers pulled up over her head. Sometimes she lets me in to rub her back, but there are other times she just mumbles, "Go away." My father tells everyone that my sister is a model child. She never talks back. When I catch her eye in the middle of one of my father's lectures, she rolls both eyes and then winks at me, but then she quickly slips into herself again. She never slams doors or runs out of the house screaming. I do all of these things, but I never have headaches. Though according to my father, I give my parents plenty.

I often go through my parents' hiding places, sometimes alone, sometimes with my sister, searching for some added clues as to their true identities. We're never quite sure about these people who live with us, who they really are. There must be some hidden explanation.

So Gay and I search but our efforts are poorly rewarded. Our boredom eventually leads us to the Chinese chest, but there's little hope of anything hidden in there. Musty sweaters, my mother's old bags, my grandfather's treasure box of buttons, crocheted wraps, linens, odds and ends, loose old family photos. In desperation one day, because we know there are bats up there, we decide to make a go of the attic. There must be an answer to the riddle of our parents somewhere.

We tackle the attic in stages. First we try to open the door. This takes some tugging and maneuvering as it sticks in the heat. When it finally creaks and groans its way open, we scream and run in the opposite direction. This is to give ample warning to any attacking bats. Slowly, I climb the stairs. Gay is deathly afraid of the bats and I must go first to assure her that it's safe. Once I've gotten all the way to the top and nothing has flown past, Gay cautiously climbs up the dusty stairs to join me.

The attic is an interesting place. There is an actual hidden space almost the size of a small room. Inside are an old spinning wheel and an antique washing jar and basin. We have no idea how they came to be there and we're always thrilled to find them undisturbed, as if some ghost might have come to reclaim them in our absence. We create mysteries and dramas around their owners' lives that explain why they were separated from these things when they left.

Next to the hidden room is a large room with books and boxes. My father's old skeleton from medical school permanently resides in this room, but his head lies in a drawer in the part-time pantry and part-time examining room for my father's patients. I love to open this drawer suddenly to shock my friends, pretending I don't know it's there. And if that doesn't get them, I bring them up here to meet the rest of him. Many things come to die in this attic room, old textbooks, my father's golf clubs, toys no longer played with but too loved to be given away or discarded.

My mother keeps old clothing up here. There are pointy shoes covered in peacock feathers, jackets and coats with the furry heads and tails of various creatures attached to them and an assortment of hats we never tire of trying on each other in bursts of giggles.

There is another large room up here where my mother stores surplus supplies. Boxes in varying sizes all bearing the Corning Ware label are stacked against one wall. These are assorted wedding gift sets, engagement presents, anniversary and holiday notions, and they are awarded with care according to the receiver's status in my parents' lives. It must have been one hell of a sale.

This room also houses all the broken items my father has attempted to fix. Clocks from the antique to the simple bedside table alarm are scattered where they lie permanently frozen in increments of time. Three or four radios and an assortment of lamps are among this collection, along with pieces and parts of minor appliances. If my father tries to fix something and fails, he cannot tolerate allowing someone else to do it. We all know that once he raises a tool to one of our beloved possessions, it is doomed forever to this dusty and disorderly useless condition.

We head for the "library" room first. We always visit our old books. Sometimes we discover something we haven't yet read or an old friend we want to revisit. There's hardly ever a time we don't leaf through *Mother Goose*, Hans Christian Anderson and Grimm's. The shelves are lined with animal stories, childhood fables and tales. Here and there are old 78 recordings. Some of these periodically make their way back downstairs, like *The King Who Couldn't Dance* and *Little Black Sambo*.

"Want to go through some boxes?" Gay winks at me, knowing I will agree to just about anything she suggests.

"Sure, let's go." I lead the way into the other room.

If not for the extreme heat in summer and cold in winter, the attic would be heavenly. It is everything an attic should be, complete with bats, unsolved mysteries, treasures, the outside possibility of a haunting, and seemingly endless discovery.

I am up to my knees in odd assortments of material and yarn, when Gay hits pay dirt. "Over here, you won't believe this." She's holding a stack of letters tied together with a velvet ribbon. She's slipped one out and finished reading it. She hands it to me.

"My dearest Jeannette," it begins. That's all I can remember. As carefully as we place the letters back where they've been hidden, they are as absent as my father after his death. It's the only proof we have of romantic love between them, other than a single sentimental valentine from my mother. If we were not both there to read them, it might have been the most deeply hidden place of all, a place where only they had gone and one we would never witness.

The letters we read do not seem to be from the man we know as our father. This language is beautiful and reads like poetry. There's no doubt that the handwriting is his, but how can these declarations of love possibly be from the same fuming and raging being who is in a continuous state of displeasure with the once adored object of his affections, my mother? Instead of settling any of our questions, the letters only raise more. Who are these people who call themselves our parents? We shake our heads in despair of ever learning the truth.

My mother and father never seem to search out my hiding places. The diary I keep in junior high school is always intact, no matter how many devious means I employ to catch them at prying. If they do, they are extraordinarily careful. Somehow I cannot imagine either of my parents going to such lengths and precautions as to make sure that a single strand of my hair is placed diagonally across a page (never the last written page, as that would be entirely too easy, but the next to the last written page where it could easily fall out if one didn't know it was there) or that a tiny dead insect is inserted at either the top or the bottom of the inside binding. Perhaps they are such creatures of habit that they simply lack the curiosity. And perhaps they do have a respect for my privacy, more than I clearly have for theirs.

Our house is old and rambling, and so there are hiding places where even an adult can disappear. In my horror movie phase, I live in fear of ghouls jumping out at me from closets and from behind stairways. Even some of our cupboards go way back into the unknown, where I'm afraid to crawl or stretch for dread of what might be lurking there. While I'm still small enough, my friends pick up on my fears, and so they refuse to be bribed to wriggle into these spaces in my place and report back to me their findings.

When I'm in high school, I forget these childish games and focus on boys and Beatles. It isn't as if I lose my awareness of these creepy places, but my thoughts are busy elsewhere. If I should happen to have a date who takes me to a scary movie, or if there is a slumber party where we watch a horror film, I might be more careful opening the attic door or slipping down into the basement, and I might check out the occupancy of my closet or the space under my bed before going to sleep at night, but other than these exceptional moments, ghosts and ghouls are not so much on my mind anymore.

It's late spring and I'm nearing my last days of high school. My parents decide to go away for a couple of days to attend a wedding in Western Massachusetts and completely out of character, my father suggests that I might like to have a few friends over the Saturday night they plan to be away. I call Karen and Sophia. Since Sophia is quiet and shy and absolutely blameless, I have to suspect that what happens next is Karen's doing. By 6:00pm on Saturday night, the neighborhood is a giant parking lot. Cars are double parked around several blocks. There are 800 kids in my graduating class and at least 300 of them know that my parents are out of town.

People stream in through doors and windows. I have to threaten to call the police if anyone dares to make out on my father's examining table or for that matter, even open the door to his office. This rule does not come into being until it's already been violated by several of the more brazen couples. I'm in anguish, running from room to room praying that my parent's beloved home will not be destroyed. I'm the only one who is not having any fun.

Soon all of this changes. I have been singing "I want to be Bobby's girl" for two years, and suddenly there is the Bobby of my dreams standing directly in front of me in my own house. He is happily alone. I forget what can happen if I'm not vigilant. I allow myself to lose sight of the other 298 potential disasters running around in my parent's house. I only see Bobby and to my surprise and joy, he only seems to see me. We kiss at long last, and he asks if there isn't some place we can be alone. I look around and shrug hopelessly until I remember the one spot no one else will dare to go. We disappear into my father's office.

There's hardly enough time for a second kiss before I hear screaming and shouting and the sound of running footsteps all over the house. Bobby and I rush out to find people pushing each other out through windows and doors. Someone I don't recognize yells to me, "The parents are home. We have to get out." When I turn to warn Bobby, he's no longer there.

The house is emptied in seconds. I'm standing in a vacated room with my parents who I see for the first time. Only a moment ago they were a rumor. My father explains in an uncannily calm voice, "Your mother wasn't feeling well, so we decided not to stay. I'm going to take her upstairs. Why don't you clean up the house and then come up."

I sit down in the mess and cry. My mother is surely dying. If not for that, my father would have killed me by now. But I hear their voices, and she still appears to be very much alive. The television goes on, and even my father would not watch television if my mother were about to take her last breaths.

Slowly I move around and straighten the house. I wash all the glasses, bag up all the bottles and empty all the bowls of pretzels and potato chips. When the inside is finished and I have vacuumed all the floors, I go outside and clean off the lawn. For such a brief party, there are bottles and cans everywhere. It's another hour or so before I go back inside. I find two stray jackets discarded by owners who must have been in too much of a hurry to care and head for the coat closet. No longer suspecting arms to reach out and grab me from its depths, I'm too shocked to let out the blood-curling scream that chokes me when an arm appears from behind the coats and grabs hold of one of the jackets. A whisper follows the retreat of the arm.

"Are the parents still here?"

A face begins to take shape in the darkness. It's a boy I've only seen once or twice in the hallways at school.

"Is it safe?" He asks again.

"Yes. They're upstairs. Everyone else left hours ago. You've been hiding in here all this time?"

"Yeah. You've got an awful lot of umbrellas back here." I almost think he'll demand one, but he's silent until he finally asks, "This is your house? Those are your parents?"

I sigh deeply. "Yes. They weren't supposed to be here until tomorrow."

"Wow, you're in big trouble. I guess I'd better get out of here."

I let him out the front door and turn around to see my father on the stairway behind me.

"Who was that?"

"Just a boy, Daddy. He's been hiding in the closet all this time." I stifle a giggle.

"Since we got home? He was so scared he was hiding in the closet?"

"Yes—." I burst into laughter. When I look up, my father is laughing with me.

"I've never seen kids run so fast," he cackles loudly, "they were pouring out of the windows. All I said was, we're Phyllis's parents and you have to leave now. I didn't even yell at them."

"Oh God, I wish I could have seen you come in the door." Now we're both bent over with laughter. "He was so scared that he scared me. He stuck out his arm and grabbed for his jacket from the back of the closet. I didn't even know he was there. Is Mom okay?"

"She'll be fine. It's just an upset stomach, but we couldn't have much fun with her feeling sick, so we thought we'd might as well come home."

"I didn't invite all those kids, Daddy, honest. I guess one kid told another kid and soon the whole graduating class was here. I'm sorry."

"It's okay. I'm surprised none of the neighbors called the police." He starts to grin again. "You should've seen their faces when we walked in the door." We laugh again. Who has stolen my real father and replaced him with this forgiving and understanding substitute with a sense of humor? And where is my real father? In hiding?

My father keeps all of the correspondence he supposedly never wants us to see hidden in the bottom drawer of an old-fashioned wall unit in his office. There is reasonable argument, of course, that had he really wished to keep these revelatory gems from us, they would have disappeared as completely as the love letters. They don't. We find the lot after his funeral, stuffed not so neatly in the drawer we are checking for additional piles of prescription pads. We've been ripping them madly for hours now, intently, silently.

I open the drawer with difficulty. The wood has swollen and contracted with heat and cold, and the house is one hundred years old. There is a large wrapped wad of papers on the top, and I pull it out to get at the rest. I unwrap it to see what it is and immediately wave it at my sister.

"What is it?" she asks.

"Unbelievable. I didn't know he had this. It's the transcript of the deposition he took for his malpractice suit. But he never went to court. They settled. Remember?"

"Barely," my sister says, taking the manuscript out of my hand. "I wasn't supposed to know anything about it."

"I know, and I still feel bad that I didn't tell you then. But he was insistent and so embarrassed. He refused to tell anyone. I'm still not sure why he decided to tell me. Maybe he thought I'd screwed up enough times in my life that I wouldn't judge him, or maybe he only wanted more legal advice. As snooty as he could be about credentials, it's amazing to me that he would come to an ex-court reporter for legal advice, but he did."

"But it was free advice," my sister laughs, "don't forget that."

"I guess," I smile, "but as much of my education as he paid for, I guess he had a right to a bit of "free" advice. For whatever it was worth."

"True," my sister agrees. She opens the packet and immediately becomes absorbed in the papers.

"Wow," she calls out moments later. "I'm definitely retiring before I lose it. His filing system and records were a mess."

"That had nothing to do with old age," I grimace, "remember, I worked for him."

"He was that bad back then?"

"C'mon, Gay, he had the "C's" filed under "G" and the "B's" filed under "D." There was no logic to it, unless he was following the Russian alphabet."

"No, that wasn't it." My sister has studied Russian.

"I didn't think it was. I was being sarcastic."

"I knew that," my sister laughs. "But seriously, the way he went on about details, I never would've expected it. This is sad."

"What do you mean?"

"Well, you can read it for yourself. He's just so confused. He can't answer the questions and the dates are all out of sync. I feel sorry for him. It must have been awful."

"He was always a good doctor and a lousy record keeper." I hesitate, picking up a letter from my Aunt Bea. I read it slowly, then read it again, and laugh out loud.

"What's up?" Gay looks up from the deposition.

"Maybe he wasn't such a great doctor after all, at least not according to Aunt Bea."

"What did you find?"

"Listen to this." I read out loud.

*Dear Nathan,*

*I want to let you know that you are not the great doctor you are always telling everyone you are. The glasses you gave me were the wrong prescription. I had to go to another doctor to have it redone. He could not believe the prescription you gave me.*

*And by the way, I've written a letter to the military on behalf of my sister, Jeannette. She is in no condition for you to be running off and abandoning her with two children to go to Korea. Your sister-in-law, Beatrice*

"Why do you think he kept this and not the love letters?"

My sister shakes her head. "Who knows? Maybe he wanted us to find these things. Maybe he wanted us to know the truth."

"But he only wanted us to know the truth after his death, obviously."

"Maybe he wanted us to understand why he hated Bea so much."

"Poor Aunt Bea," I laugh. "He was probably still holding a grudge against her for the one time she asked him to carry her luggage, so he gave her the wrong prescription. Fortunately, it was only for glasses. A wrong prescription is what ended him up in this malpractice suit. You're right. He should have quit practicing sooner."

"You know, he might've kept them to reread them, so he could keep his anger alive."

"Now that sounds like our father."

# [21]

# I SCREAM

> I Scream
> You Scream
> We All Scream
> For Ice Cream
> (The Beach)

Nathan can't forget. The bite of ice cream my mother never offered him becomes the story he tells even after her death. When Nathan meets my husband for the first time he says, "Let me tell you about Jeannette, the kind of person she was. She was the most unselfish person I ever met. She never demanded anything, you know, like some women, not Jeannette. That woman was a saint. When we went on vacations and I laid out all the brochures, she'd always say, 'You pick, Nathan, wherever you want to go.' She was a wonderful wife. That's why I won't marry again. She asked me if I would when she knew she was dying, and I was honest, I told her I didn't know. But I could never find a wife like her again." He pauses and a smile creeps over his face. "Of course, there was one time I can remember when she was selfish. We were courting and taking a walk through the park…"

There was this ice cream cone. She never offered him a bite. He never asked for one. Ah, those little pricks and jabs to the heart. So many years later. So much water under the bridge. So much giving and taking. But of one thing I can be sure, it's always the story he chooses to tell about the woman who was to become my mother, in spite of and not because of a bite of ice cream.

\*   \*   \*

My mother is different from other mothers. I think I first become aware of this at the beach. No matter how hot it is, she leaves the house in a long-sleeved dress with a high-buttoned neck, topped with a cotton sweater buttoned or zipped closed. On her feet are her sturdy walking shoes, brown, black or white in color, lacing up the front, they all look the same, but they are never sneakers or sandals. On one arm she carries a large, floppy bag filled with articles of clothing, gloves and scarves and a variety of crossword puzzle books and pencils. She carries three different-sized hats for differing degrees and angles of sunlight. These vary from your basic baseball to a floppy canvas mid-size to the all-out straw wide brim. Underneath whatever hat she chooses, her tight chignon is guarded by a scarf wrapped several times around her head and tied securely under the chin.

My father, on the other hand, looks like other fathers, only more so. He's fit, more handsome and always more tanned. He swims farther and faster than other fathers, and he's always more serious about it. He takes his clothes off at the beach, while my mother layers them on. The contrast is unsettling.

My father scorns the sandy portions of the beach. This is where he could run into people he knows. He worries that he'll be confronted by a patient who might wonder why he's laying about on the beach instead of tending to bleeding and swollen eyes and measuring for glasses. My father says they'll think he's not so busy and therefore, not so good a doctor. Seeing him outside of his suit and tie with his family might diminish their image of him. This is not good for business. So my father leads us from the hot and sticky car to a small and rocky portion of seashore where there is barely enough sand for us to spread our blanket. We've learned not to protest. It will do no good. He makes a strong case. And don't we all prefer the rocky side anyway? Sometimes I still believe that I do.

My father and sister and I spread out a blanket which we stay from the winds with rocks. My mother retrieves a lone beach chair from the trunk of the car. We three lie on the blanket while my mother sits off to the side. She covers her lap with a woolen army blanket and selects a crossword puzzle book from her bag. My father continues to talk, but no one is listening. Something about doctor so and so and a patient who would not have gone blind if only they'd followed his instructions. My sister appears to be sleeping. My mother is busy counting the number of letters in a word. I pretend to sleep, allowing my thoughts to drift with the sounds of the tide and the rhythm of my father's voice.

"Okay. Time to swim. Let's see if you girls can beat me." My father is standing up, grinning. My sister reluctantly pushes herself off the blanket. She knows not to fight the inevitable. I never learn this lesson.

"We don't want to go now, Daddy." I dig my fingers into the sand as if to anchor my body.

"Look at your sister. She's not complaining. Look—she's already in the water."

What he says is true. Gay is now sticking one foot gingerly into the cold. She knows that my father's favorite stunt is to dive in rapidly and splash us until we join him. This is unlike the happy splashing we see around us. No, swimming is serious business.

I hesitate. I am seven, and there's nothing I want more than to be exactly like my fifteen year-old sister. But surely she hates this as much as I do. Why does she march down to the water at his beck and call? I stand up but stay by the blanket, digging my toes into the comforting warmth of the sand. Anyway, I always lose. My sister comes in second. My father always wins. Big deal. He can beat a seven year-old and a fifteen year-old. Not unpredictable. But that never enters my mind. I think I have a chance. I'm defeated every time.

I labor down to the water's edge. My delay has put me at a disadvantage. They're both emerged in the water. I'm the only one left to splash. If I close my eyes now, I can still feel my seven year-old arms and legs struggling against the current and the waves. I can taste the salty water and feel my breath resisting the effort. I'm afraid that I'll swim out too far and end up in water over my head. My ears are plugged. My heart is beating so loudly that my eardrums feel like they'll burst. I panic and turn my head to breathe straight into a large oncoming wave. To my relief, I'm swept back to shore. By the time I stand up again, after coughing and choking the water from my lungs, the race is over.

My father is doing a butterfly stroke on the edge of the horizon. He stops only once to call, "Watch me, Jeannette."

"Don't swim out too far, Nathan," she replies without looking up from her book.

I sit at the water's edge, letting the cool waves rush under me and feeling the wet sand pull me along with the tide. I'm sad without a reason I can understand. I love this place, the rocks and the roughness of the surf, the cries of the gulls as they circle and dive for fish. But there's something about this beauty that is as melancholy as I am. I feel my sister's hand on my shoulder. "Let's go hunt for shells." I jump up eagerly at this simple but honest extension of hope.

\* \* \*

The sun is going down and we're all wrapped in damp clothing with the exception of my mother. It's been several hours since we've eaten sandy tuna fish sandwiches and juicy peaches from a nearby farm. I'm shivering and hungry. My mother closes her crossword puzzle book, the signal that it's time to pack up and leave. Drugged by hours of sun, we load the car slowly and sloppily, dragging sand onto the floor in spite of my father's strict instructions. "Shake out that blanket." "No, no, wipe off your feet first." Somehow we're all finally inside.

Now I close my eyes and pray. Please, God, if you're out there, please make him stop at Gulf Hill. I've been good all day. Please, please. I pray to the rhythm of the wheels. I try to keep my eyes on the road to see which direction he's taking, but the motion of the car rocks me to sleep.

"Jeannette, should we stop for ice cream?" She's still thinking about the answer as my father swerves the car into the Gulf Hill Farms parking lot. I can see the cows lined up for milking, their tails busily swishing away the flies.

"Look, Phyllis, they're milking. Daddy, can I take Phyllis to watch?"

My father looks back and forth from my sister to his watch. "Okay, but make it quick. What kind of ice cream do you want?" He takes our orders and walks off in the direction of the windmill structure where the ice cream is sold.

It's too late in the day. The cows were milked hours ago. But I'm content just to be with my sister and these large, warm animals with their soulful brown eyes. I pet one affectionately while my sister stands back and watches. We see my father approaching, grasping onto our cones.

"Eat it out here until it stops melting," He cautions us. "I don't want it all over the car. Your mother ordered peach," he says this as if it is something new, but my mother always orders peach. Once in a while she stretches herself and orders pistachio, but it's always one of the two. My sister and father have chocolate chip, and I've ordered something chocolate with fudge syrup and nuts. It is sticky and melting faster than I can wend my tongue around its dripping surface. I spot a tear drop of chocolate on my T-shirt and use the napkin my cone has been wrapped in to quickly erase the evidence, but another drop hits my shorts in the meantime. This battle is beyond me.

My father rushes us into the car. "Come on, it's getting late. I don't want to hit the traffic. Eat the rest of it in the car. Phyllis, be careful. I don't want ice cream all over the car. Hurry up, get in!"

We scramble into the car where my mother is quietly eating her cone. My father has finished his, and my sister is inhaling the last of hers from the bottom of her sugar cone, a trick I've not yet learned to master. My father starts the car and pulls onto the road. I lean forward, bite off the end of my cone, sucking strenuously. "Look, Daddy." I draw in as hard as I can but forget to keep the cone upright.

"I can't look at you now, I'm driving. Jesus Christ! Look what you've done now! Jeannette, you'd better stop me. If I get my hands on her, I'll kill her!"

I still have no idea what I've done. My father pulls over to the side of the road, jumps out the door, cursing and jumping around like a man possessed. Only now, as I look down at my empty cone and wonder what has become of my ice cream does the unthinkable enter my seven-year old mind.

My father manages to wipe most of the chocolate mess from his shorts, but he's left the door open and the window down. The lump of cold wetness landing so suddenly in his lap has left him without reason. Furious and exhausted, the rest of us tense and tired, we once again head off toward home. My sister is the first to see the bee, and I'm the first to hear it.

We both scream, "Stop the car! Kill it! It's a bee. Get it out of here!"

"Sit down both of you, right this minute. How do you expect me to see? I'm trying to drive. The bee won't hurt you as much as I will if you don't sit down and stay still this minute."

"I can't," my sister pleads, "stop the car."

Resigned to his family, the bane of his existence, the vicissitudes of life, my father once again pulls over to the side of the road. We all jump out while he remains fixed behind the wheel. There is a point to be made here, but by now even he's unsure what it is. The bee is as relieved as we are at its release. We quickly get back in and shut all the windows. The drive home is long, stuffy and silent. As we enter the road back into town, my sister catches my eye and winks. I snuggle up next to her and she whispers in my ear, "Just another family day at the beach." I'm not sure why this is funny, but I take her cue and we both laugh.

\*   \*   \*

I'm thirty-five, and my mother is slowly and painfully dying from metastasis of the pleura. She chokes when she swallows and no longer has any will to eat. Since she broke her femur several months ago, she's been unable to walk and confined to bed in the Jewish Convalescent Center. She wants to die at home, and she's angry with my father for denying her this last request. Just as she once ate huge pots of macaroni and cheese, she now protests with starvation. It's the only thing left within her control.

Watching my mother and father communicate is excruciating. He's now profoundly deaf. Mother can only whisper with enormous effort. He spends his days by her side. He talks and she listens. Little has changed.

It's just a week before Mother's Day, but I'm afraid to wait that long to visit. My mother's face lights up when I enter the room. For just an instant it's the face I remember from our shopping and theater days. She tries to say something, but my father doesn't notice. He tells me, "She won't eat anything. Tell her she has to eat. The only thing she wants to eat is ice cream. Tell her she can't live on ice cream."

I reassure my mother that we're going to get her ice cream. Then I take my father for a walk. I hold his hand as I remind him that she won't live no matter what she eats. He must let go of his need to feed her. He doesn't want me to see his tears. He turns back toward her room and asks me to please go and get the ice cream.

I now have to feed the mother who once fed me. She struggles to suck in the moisture of the ice cream from the edge of the spoon. I see that this is to please me. She's lost the desire for it now. The sweetness of memory and the steady drip of morphine lull her to sleep. The ice cream turns to soup as we sit and watch her.

"We ought to go and let her rest," Dad says.

I know that our conversation won't disturb her. We couldn't wake her if we tried. But Dad has been sitting here idly for days and welcomes my company and some relief from this routine. He assures me she'll be awake later on, and we'll come back and visit with her until she goes to sleep for the night. He asks me if I'd like to drive out to the beach and stop for ice cream. We silently consent to pretend that this is for me.

This drive is so familiar that I can close my eyes and predict exactly what I'll see when I open them. Frost's *mending walls* stretch before us, creating a giant patchwork quilt inlaid with shades of green and brown. Just beyond is the slight hint of blue and green and white, where the sky meets the ocean. I open my eyes expecting to see the little mill house by the pond that's my mother's favorite, but it's too soon. Or we've passed it. My father tells me it's just up ahead.

He asks me if I remember my mother's favorite flavor of ice cream.

"Peach," I smile.

"Yes, that's it, or what was that other green ice cream she used to order sometimes? What do you call it?"

"Pistachio." I don't tell him that I was the one who used to order pistachio.

"Pistachio. That's it. Your mother always loved ice cream. When I met her, I couldn't see how I could ever afford to marry her. I remember the butter she'd buy just for baking, and I'd think to myself, all that butter! It was beyond anything I could imagine. That much butter for one family."

"But it was her seven-layer chocolate cake that won you," I remind him teasingly.

"Oh, yes. That was really something special." He rolls his eyes at the memory and is lost somewhere within himself for a moment. "Over there, to your left," he points.

"Ah, yes. It's still lovely." I lean out the window, as if I can pull it in close to me and hold it there. My father slows the car to give me an extra minute.

"That isn't really how she won me," He says. "She was always so kind and generous. She thought about everyone before she thought about herself. I had to take her shopping for clothes because she'd always tell me she didn't need any. Whenever I showed her travel brochures, she'd tell me, 'Wherever you want to go, Nathan.' Israel was the only place she insisted on."

"And Russia," I remind him.

"Well, yes. That's true. I didn't ever want to go back there." We're both quiet.

"She was a very generous woman, your mother."

"Yes, she could be generous," I respond carefully, thinking of my sister. "She certainly was generous with me."

My father doesn't really hear me. He's floating off into the past.

"Except for that one time."

"Which time was that, Dad?" I know exactly which time it was but I want to hear him tell it again. These familiar stories are suddenly precious.

"When I was courting your mother, I didn't have a nickel. My sister, your aunt Rosie, really liked Jeannette. She'd give me the money to take the trolley from South Philly to Roxborough and enough money sometimes to buy flowers or candy. But I never had the money to take her anywhere, so we'd go for long walks in the park—Wissahickon Park in Philly was beautiful back then. In the fall, the leaves on the trees—," he sighs, sad for a moment, but then he perks up, remembering where he's going with this.

"Your mother always loved sweets, especially ice cream. Anyway, we were walking along on this particular day—it must have been summer because it was hot—and your mother bought an ice cream cone from a - a—what do you call it?" He's beginning to struggle with words that once flowed easily.

"A vendor?" I offer.

"Yes, 'vendor,' that's it, a vendor in the park. Do you know she finished that entire cone without ever offering me a single bite? I couldn't believe it."

It's clear that he still can't come to terms with this momentary lapse of my mother's, if in fact it even was a lapse. It's as if it's just happened. All the deprivation. I picture him as a boy, arriving by boat in America, seeing strange looking round orange fruit and biting into one for the first time. He can still recall that first delirious moment of contact, that instant of profound joy, spoiled almost immediately by the knowledge that there might never be another orange, or certainly not one as sweet.

"Maybe she wasn't being selfish," I offer.

My father is very quiet. He almost appears thoughtful. I risk more.

"Maybe it never occurred to her that you couldn't get one yourself."

"You know," he pauses, "you may be right. That was the only selfish thing I ever saw her do."

I note that he continues to use the word "selfish," and even though he may have arrived at some greater degree of understanding, his pain is still fresh and raw. He doesn't see how she couldn't have known and for this there is disappointment and some resentment.

We arrive at the dairy farm in silence. Although it's still early in the season, the cows are out and being milked by small groups of children. Some of them are squealing with glee while squeezing the udders with a frightening confidence. Others are hanging back, less sure of the cows' temperaments and their own capacities at this mysterious task.

Dad smiles. "Do you remember doing that?"

I laugh. "How could I forget? That was me over there." I point to a serious child who is cautiously petting the cow's head before approaching the udders.

"You were always good with animals."

"Except for the time the Schwartz's dog bit me in the mouth!"

"He was a very old dog, and it was hot."

"Remember Mom's face? It was redder than mine, and I was covered with blood."

"She was pretty scared. The only other time she ever called me out of the office like that was when Kennedy was shot."

I think to myself that she wouldn't have dared. My father wanted his patients to believe that there wasn't anything on the other side of the wall. He was careful to caution us that from 9:00am, and sometimes earlier, until 5:00pm the Mitnicks simply didn't exist. My father was allowed to break this law by barging in on us unannounced with some desperate patient in tow who needed to use the bathroom. But we were refugees of another dimension until the opening of the office door at exactly 5:00pm announced that dinner could be served. Now and then dinner would be late because my mother had forgotten to get the dishes from behind the sliding doors in my father's examining room. I would find her with one ear pasted to the door, trying to determine whether or not my father actually had a person in the room or was talking on the telephone. Since he often refused to allow his patients any response time at all, it was difficult to distinguish.

We would hear, "Mr. Pimento, why didn't you put in the drops the way I showed you? What's the point in coming to a doctor if you aren't going to do what I say? Now I'll explain one more time, and I want you to do exactly what I tell you. If you don't, there's no point in coming back here at all. Okay, here we go. Did you get that? Now take these back and I'll see you in a week. Good-bye Mr. Pimento."

We eat our ice cream in the car. My father doesn't hesitate to tell me to be careful, even though I'm now thirty-five. He reprimands me for the time I dropped my ice cream into his lap. I was seven. Thirty-five, going on seven, Russian Standard Time. I'm too tense now to enjoy it, but I eat it anyway.

We're strangers again. Old battles are silently being reenacted within each of us. My father's lost because he knows he's injured me but has no idea how or why. And I've lost my self in his presence. It's a war neither of us ever wins.

Mother pretends to be sleeping when we return. I can tell by how quickly she begins to stir at the sound of our voices. I bend down to her ear to hear what she's whispering.

"Did you have a nice drive?" She knows exactly where we've been.

"Yes," I smile. "You made us hungry for ice cream."

"Don't tire her out with too much conversation," my father warns. I want to ask him what difference it will make, but instead I hold her hand and stroke her head. Against her will, she's soon asleep.

I leave for New York the next morning. My father brings me by the convalescent home to say good-bye and I promise I will be back the following week for Mother's Day.

"I want you to promise me something else," she motions me closer so that she can speak into my ear. "I worry about you and your father. I want you to promise me that you'll look out for him, that you'll take care of him. Promise me you'll get along with him. Don't leave him alone."

I want to tell her what a ridiculous request she's making of the one person least likely to be able to accomplish it, but I can deny her nothing now. Knowing that I'll be bound by her deathbed wish, I look her straight in the eye and I promise. She sighs with relief. Her mission is achieved. Mine looms before me. It will be many months before I learn that she's asked and received the same promise from my father. She's determined to attain through her death what she was never able to in her life.

"Please come back," she whispers, her voice barely audible. "I feel so much better when you're here." I kiss her forehead and reassure her that the week will pass quickly. We both know that for her this is a lie. I hate myself for leaving her, but I go anyway.

\* \* \*

Late that following Thursday evening the phone rings. I know who it is before I hear the voice. It's cracked, broken. I have difficulty recognizing this man who cries.

"I'd just gone home for an hour when they called me," he explains, as if his presence could've prevented anything. He wasn't there at the end to hold her hand and to comfort her. I don't remind him that I wasn't there either. I'm still angry and unforgiving that he didn't allow her to die at home. Holding onto this anger distances me from both his grief and mine. And so to his reference to the hours he's spent by her bed, I make no reply.

\* \* \*

My father has congestive heart failure and has just been released from the ICU in Naples, Florida. It's the first time I've been to see where my father has been spending his winters since the early seventies. When my mother was living, she reluctantly went with him. She never succeeded in escaping from the beach. Her only victory, small as it seems, was that they did not buy. It's now 1995; she's been gone since 1986, and he's still renting. We've never been invited.

The dream vacation home is a small apartment, cluttered with the belongings of its real owners. They are two elderly women whose bathrobes and nightgowns are hanging on hooks in the bathrooms along with my father's. They no longer bother to clean before his arrival, if they ever did. It's unclear whether this is due to their age or his, or the fact that he doesn't like to "make a fuss" or "complain." He pushes their things to the side and "makes do."

It's a five-minute drive to the beach and my father has not been able to make it there the entire season. Now he's content to sit by the pool.

The doctor has cautioned him that walking on the sand might be dangerous. His gait is wobbly and his sense of balance is not good. My husband and I consult in whispers behind closed doors.

"Let's take him to the beach," Arthur doesn't have to convince me.

"Yes, tomorrow."

When we tell my father, he's pleased. He's timid about the sand, but we reassure him. We've been out scouting, and we already know where there is a bench close to the parking area where he can sit and watch the waves. I clinch the deal with the promise of a picnic lunch. My father busies himself with preparations that I know bring both of us to our past and him to an even earlier past I can only share through black and white photographs.

We're all up early the next morning. My father is excited by the prospects of a day at the beach. My husband and I have barely slept. The apartment is unbearably close and the mattress is soft and lumpy. When I go to the bathroom, I see him sitting on the edge of his bed. He's tiny and fragile. He struggles to remove his pajama bottoms, fails and rocks forward, breathing heavily with the effort. I ask Arthur to help him to dress. Now he's the one who has to bundle up for the beach. He's always cold.

When I enter the kitchen, I see that my father has been there first. The coffee is made and so is the picnic lunch. The cooler is packed with tuna fish sandwiches, pickles, peaches, cookies, potato chips and coke. Next to it is a bag filled with paper plates, plastic forks, spoons and paper cups. Out of curiosity I inspect the sandwiches. He's even remembered that I like my tuna with mayonnaise. These are neatly piled off to one side. I feel Arthur wrap his arms around me from behind.

"Can you believe this? He must have been up all night."

"He's quite a tough old bird, your da." Arthur adopts a cockney twang to lighten the mood, but I can see that he's as touched by all of this as I am. "No wonder he didn't have the energy to dress himself."

"Shhh, he's coming." I hear the tap of his cane on the tile.

My father's eyes are alive, young and twinkling. He knows he's done great work. We hug him and compliment him. "You even remembered the mayonnaise," I tell him. It's a side of him I rarely see.

"But there's no ice cream."

"Do you want some? We can stop somewhere."

"No," he says, "I don't think so."

It's a glorious day. Florida has been rainy and cold but seems to recognize that we have special needs. The sun is strong for January, and I'm comfortable in a T-shirt and chinos. Thank you, God, I say silently, thank you for giving us this day.

We help my father to the bench. He's shaky on the sand, his own misgivings and the doctor's warnings momentarily robbing him of pleasure. But once he's seated with the sun on his face and the ocean stretched out before him, he becomes so much a part of the landscape that we leave him alone there, just for a time. I flash a picture of him in my mind. I can see him sitting there now, so at peace, all of his demons at bay, for these few moments.

I go and sit by him and finally, he breaks the spell. "Thank you," he says simply. I squeeze his hand, unable to respond to such unusual appreciation. Arthur waits in the background. I stretch out my free arm, and he joins us on the bench. Me and my men, I smile to myself. Who would have ever thought that he could share me? It's not my husband I'm thinking of.

My father is tired in an hour. He wants to go home. We pack him and our uneaten picnic lunch into the car. We laugh and assure him that some of the best picnic lunches are eaten at home, and of course, the tuna sandwiches will not be sandy. My voice breaks. I've been looking forward to crunching sand. It's a memory, good or bad. I had fantasized reliving it with him, and like many fantasies, it's not to be. But it's the best that all of us could do. It's another day at the beach.

# [22]

## "MIRROR, MIRROR ON THE WALL, WHO'S THE FAIREST OF THEM ALL?"

> *Strange that there are dreams, that there are mirrors*
> *Strange that the ordinary worn-out ways*
> *of every day encompass the imagined*
> *and endless universe woven by reflections.*
> (Borges)

I think Mommy likes me, most of the time. When she's feeling good, she likes to listen to me. I can make her laugh. When she's sick, she disappears inside herself. The bedroom door stays shut. I know without asking that I'm not allowed to knock.

I am eleven, and I love to go shopping. Mommy lets me pick out whatever I want. She says I have a special eye.

"Show me what you like."

Mommy settles into one of two flower-covered wingback chairs sitting on either side of a large three-way mirror outside the entrance to the dressing rooms. I'm happier when the other chair is free and not filled with some impatient husband. Usually husbands ignore me and that's okay, but every once in a while an eye will wander and look at me in a way that makes me uncomfortable. The wives leave behind the smell of dead lilies.

I saunter through racks, pressing fabric between my fingers, savoring textures with my eyes closed, opening them only to examine the colors more closely. Mommy's favorite is blue, but she tells me she likes me in every color in the rainbow—except for green. She never insists on blue; I try not to want anything green.

"Mommy, look at this!" I pull a lemon yellow blouse from the rack. Mommy watches the salesgirl, waiting for the lines in her face to stretch and spread, her eyebrows to reach for her scalp.

"The child has taste, doesn't she?"

"Yes, she does."

"It will cost you a bit, but it's made from the finest silk."

"Of course it is," Mommy nods, "Phyllis has a gift."

I am gifted. Mommy and the saleslady agree. It's surprising when anyone suspects I might be talented at anything, and so I spend the next few hours entertaining Mommy, the saleslady and myself by striking seductive poses in the three-way mirror. Mommy tells me how pretty I am.

"You look so good in everything, Honey, so pretty. You have such a tiny waist. You're so lucky. I hope you won't ever lose that small waist. I wish I could've had a waist like yours. 'Fatty, fatty, bumbalatti,' that's what the other children used to sing to me."

"What's a 'bumbalatti,'" I ask, knowing her answer. I've asked this question so many times before but I keep hoping new information will emerge.

Mommy looks puzzled. "I'm not really sure," she says. "I think they just made it up to rhyme with 'fatty.'"

"Did you cry?"

"I did. I cried a lot."

"I'll try hard, Mommy, to keep a tiny waist."

"Honey, I'll love you no matter what. It's just so much fun shopping with you. You can wear all the pretty things I never could. Don't ever say this to your sister, please," she lowers her voice, as if Gay might be somewhere near, "but your figure is much nicer than hers."

I like it when Mommy tells me that anything about me is nicer than my sister, but I don't think it's true. I know Daddy doesn't think so. He tells me even he's not as smart as Gay. So I can't be smart, but I can be thin. It doesn't seem to require much. I think about the three or four candy bars I buy several times a week from the vending machine at

Hebrew School. Mommy has no idea because I use my allowance. She brings me double packages of Hostess chocolate cupcakes with chocolate icing and Twinkies coconut covered cupcakes every time she goes shopping. I peel off and eat the icing and coconut and hide the cake in the garbage. When I get caught, Gay rolls her eyes and Daddy complains about waste. It's only the icing I want.

Daddy yells at Mommy for buying me junk. I worry that one day I'll wake up fat and disappoint her. She seems to depend on me not to. Then Daddy will have been right all along and Mommy might not like me best anymore. These thoughts make me feel crummy.

But I love to eat. Daddy brags to his friends that they haven't ordered for me from the child's menu me since I was five and able to finish off a two-pound lobster. I eat and I eat and I don't get fat. I'm the only one to achieve this on both sides of the family. Sometimes I have bad dreams. I blow up like a fat lady balloon. When I try to fly, I come crashing down and pop wide open, spraying the contents of my stomach everywhere. I'm as fat as Mommy's second cousin, Beatrice, whose bottom slides over the sides of just about any chair. When I wake up from a nightmare like this, I have to rush out to the hall to look in the mirror. I have to make sure I'm still me.

I can talk Mommy into buying me anything, but there is always one condition. I have to promise never to tell Daddy how much it cost. Mommy swears me to this. "He doesn't have to know," she tells me. "It'll only make him angry. He doesn't understand how prices have changed." When Daddy does ask, my mother shrugs and whispers, "I can't remember." It's hard to ever be sure what she remembers. As if my father can't pick up the checkbook and see for himself.

I push my skills to persuade Mommy. I want to know how far she will go. And she'll go pretty far. The rabbit coat I wore in kindergarten. It was mostly white with little black and brown spots here and there; just like the coats on the bunnies I'd seen on the farm in Padanarum. I'd wanted to take one home, but Daddy said no. I loved the way those bunnies felt, so soft and warm and squirmy.

"She's five years old. You buy her a fur coat? Jeannette. What is wrong with you? *You* don't have a fur coat."

"I must be the only woman at Tifereth Israel (our synagogue) who doesn't."

"Phyllis will be the only child who does."

"Good. I'm glad." There are these unpredictable places where my mother stands her ground firmly.

"I love my new coat, Daddy."

"She'll outgrow it in a year, Jeannette."

"It wasn't expensive."

"How much did it cost?"

"I don't remember."

"Phyllis, how much did the coat cost?"

"I don't know, Daddy."

And I don't. I'm five. But I'm learning to make a point of not knowing.

I don't remember how it is that I'm allowed to keep the coat, but I wear it until the sleeves stop somewhere between my wrists and my elbows and Mommy refuses to let me leave the house in it anymore. It doesn't seem fair that I have to grow up and out of it, that I have become too long and too tall.

This summer I've talked Mommy into "an itsy bitsy teeny weenie yellow polka dot bikini" that I wear for the first time before breakfast on a Sunday morning with a matching pair of yellow flip flops. Daddy is spreading a thick layer of Philadelphia cream cheese on one half of his poppy seed bagel. He drops his knife onto his plate and stares down at a serving platter of lox.

"Jeannette, what's this?"

Mommy turns to look at the plate where my father's knife has landed. She rubs her wet hands on her apron.

"It's the same lox I always get, Nathan. It's from the delicatessen at the Stop and Shop."

"I'm not talking about the lox, Jeannette. I'm talking about Phyllis."

Mommy seems to notice me for the first time; Daddy stares into the plate of lox.

"What's wrong with Phyllis?"

"Did you buy her that?"

"The bathing suit?"

"Jeannette, Jeannette, what the heck else would I be talking about?"

"I thought you were talking about the lox."

"She might as well be wearing the lox."

"It's the style, Nathan. She's just a little girl. All her friends are wearing them."

"And how do you know that all her friends are wearing them? Did you go to each of their homes and look in their closets to see? Or did you call their mothers one by one and ask them? You believe everything Phyllis tells you. That's your problem. I don't care if every single girl in her class is wearing that so-called bathing suit. No daughter of mine is going to the beach dressed like that. Phyllis, go straight up those stairs now and change."

"But Daddy, I don't have another bathing suit that fits."

"This one doesn't fit either. Jeannette, how much money did you waste for this crap?"

"I don't remember."

Daddy isn't buying it.

"Jeannette, I want to see that receipt right now. Go get it."

I remember what it cost. It took me half an hour to talk Mommy into it. We're at the start of the summer of '61. It's possible to buy a bathing suit for $25.00, even $15.00, maybe a cheap one for ten. Mine was $48.00; many thanks to the popular song. I don't know another teenage girl with a radio and any sense of the changing of tides who doesn't picture herself in that same suit, prancing and dancing across the sand in a sea of Frankie Avalons. I wish I'd thought to cover myself with shorts and a shirt until we got to the beach.

Mommy comes back with a long receipt. "Here it is, Nathan."

"*Forty-eight dollars*? Are you crazy, Jeannette? She's twelve years old. I don't see why you can't find a perfectly good bathing suit for ten. Phyllis, you go upstairs right now and take that suit off. It's going back first thing on Monday." I stay where I am.

"You can't buy a bathing suit for ten dollars, Nathan."

"I'm sure you're right about that, Jeannette, if you shop in the most expensive stores you can find. I bet some of her classmates wear suits that cost ten dollars. My Portuguese patients aren't buying *forty-eight dollar* bathing suits for their twelve-year olds unless they're buying them instead of paying for their glasses." My father adjusts the glasses on his nose. He seems to consider whether this might be true.

"My father always said that it's better to buy something well made than to have to keep replacing things because they're cheaply made and fall apart."

"You call that well made? Come on, Jeannette. Your father bought real butter during the depression. He had his own clothing factory, for crying out loud. He didn't have to worry where his next nickel was coming from. Phyllis will outgrow that suit before the leaves start turning. And how the heck is she going to swim in that thing? One big wave—there's hardly any material. Jeannette, you just don't think."

"It's the style, Nathan."

"I don't give one darn about the style. I am not about to let her walk around the beach half naked for everyone in the world to see. Suppose we run into one of my patients?"

"Oh, Daddy, P-L-E-A-S-E. You care more about your patients than you do about me. My old bathing suit is way too small. If I can't wear this one, I can't go to the beach. I don't want to go to the beach with you anyway." I run up the back stairs into my room and slam the door.

Mommy hates the beach. She's afraid of skin cancer and dresses like a nun in a habit. She'd be just as happy to stay home. Daddy doesn't mind going by himself during the week, but on the weekends the beach is packed with families and Daddy will stand out. Daddy doesn't like to stand out. Someone might ask, "Why is Dr. Mitnick at the beach without his family?" By the time the question is tossed back and forth over the sand dunes, there could be speculation of divorce. I win. Daddy insists that I model last year's suit so he can see for himself how it rides up in the buttocks and pulls tight across the chest. He surrenders.

"Today you wear the suit. But next week you and your mother will buy a suit that covers your stomach. When you go to the beach with me, that's what you'll wear. What you wear when you go with your friends is your business. Just don't let me see you wearing that thing again."

I think that's more than reasonable, so I don't ask him what his patients might think if they should see Dr. Mitnick's daughter roaming the beach in a yellow polka-dot bikini without him.

\* \* \*

But the aftermath of these shopping trips is troubling. Daddy yells that my wardrobe is "putting us in the poorhouse." His accusation reaches me through cracks and crannies, heating ducts and the back stairway. I have Dickensian dreams of us standing by as my father's body is lowered into the ground in a Potter's Field because the cost of my clothing has "worked him to death." Sometimes I ask Mommy if we shouldn't return everything, something, anything, so that we won't end up hungry and poor. Mommy shakes her head and says, "That's your father, and you'd better get used to it because I can't keep fighting your battles for you. You'll have to learn how to do this on your own." Cowed by the thought of it, I feel my stomach turn. I cannot imagine doing this on my own.

We lug bags and boxes up to my room and dump piles of clothing onto the bed. In spite of my father's threats, we are distracted by the feel of fabric, the abundance, the luxury. My mother holds up each item to re-examine. "Ooooh, put this one on. Let's see how pretty you look. Oh, you can wear so many colors." She makes it sound as if I have accomplished something rare, remarkable, as if there are only a few of us in the world who can do this.

Gay is home for spring break. She comes to see what we are up to. She stops short in the doorway.

"Are these all for *her*?"

Mommy looks up but doesn't answer.

Once when I was five, Daddy caught me playing "doctor" with Danny, Peter, Martha and Caroline. Even before he was able to scoop me up and storm away, I could feel this same kind of shame, hot and heavy, flooding my veins.

Mommy tightens her grip on the scissors. She snips off paper price tags until they begin to gather in a pile on my bed. I think Gay might say more, but she tosses her hair and walks away.

I stare at the clothes on the bed. I hate that I want them anyway, spoils of some bloody war I don't begin to understand. An evil demon in me is glad; he grows as malignant and insistent as the weeds in Mommy's tiny flower garden.

\* \* \*

Before I can outgrow my clothes, I outgrow the stores in New Bedford. Mommy and I begin to shop in Boston. We catch the early morning bus in and take the last one back at night. Daddy has his dinner alone, something Mommy's prepared ahead for him. Mommy and I eat in Chinatown, after a matinee. Gay is at Bryn Mawr. She's Bohemian. She wouldn't be caught dead in any of the matching shoes and purses Mommy bought her before she left. When I see her, she is in the same black wool skirt and turtleneck sweater. Her hair is long and bushy. I think she's beautiful. So does her sexy French boy friend. I have a hopeless crush on him.

By now I'm an experienced shopper. I know exactly what I want and don't waste time prancing in front of mirrors. I've discovered that all saleladies will say I'm gifted and pretty whether they think so or not. I want to get on to the theater, the Chinese food, the cake and ice cream we have for lunch. I can put together a wardrobe lickety-split. We send the packages home; then we play.

Daddy doesn't share our love for the theater. Mommy and I like it much better without him. He makes all kinds of comments. Mommy has to shush him because he doesn't seem to know how to whisper.

"This is trash, Jeannette, *pure* trash. I don't see how anyone with half a brain can enjoy it. Why are you clapping? These people are morons." I'm not sure if he means the actors or us, the audience.

Daddy is furious when there's even a hint of sex in the script. I think it must have something to do with me. He's been unhappy since I've grown breasts, and now that I have them, breakfast can be as bad as dinner. Daddy likes to tell me about young girls he's known of who've "gotten into trouble." His eyes inspect me silently over coffee and cereal. If I am "decent," he ignores me. But if any color of fabric or length of garment gets his attention, he begins to talk about nice Jewish girls who don't listen to their parents and who've gotten into trouble. I'm not sure what he means by "trouble." I ask my best friend, Jeanie.

"He's telling you you'd better not get pregnant."

"What? I'm twelve. How could I get pregnant?"

"It happens," she says, "that's what 'getting into trouble' means. You can get pregnant as soon as you get your period. Don't you know that?"

"Of course I know that." I did, but I hadn't given it much thought. "Anyway Jeannie, you have to go all the way to get pregnant. I haven't even kissed a boy."

"God, you're retarded." She laughs. "Too bad your father doesn't know how slow you are."

I remember the bathing suit. "Jeanie, that's disgusting."

"I'm just telling you; that's what 'getting into trouble' means."

"No. He doesn't mean that. Daddy hates anything to do with sex. He won't even go to the movies. He says there's too much sex. No. I can get into trouble if I don't come home when I'm supposed to or if I don't get good grades in school, or if —-."

"He's not talking about that kind of "getting into trouble." He's talking about getting pregnant. Don't believe me. I don't care. You asked." Jeanie sulks; she has to be right. By now, I guess that she might be. She somehow knows more about these things than I do.

"So, you don't believe me?"

"I don't think I will."

I liked Jeanie better before we had breasts, though to tell the truth, Jeannie doesn't have much of anything yet. She had her first bra before I did and stuffed it full of Kleenex. I don't like hooks and straps or girdles with garters that torture my thighs and leave marks on my skin. Stockings are stupid. I wear them once and they rip and run. Mommy has a drawer filled with nothing but nylons. When I watch her dress, my future feels grim.

I'm disgusted by the bulk of menstrual pads; yet they're not so thick that I don't find bloody stains on my underpants. Everyone must surely know I am wearing one, and yet there is nothing to be done. They must be worn, carried about and changed. Even when I keep track, the damn thing catches me unawares, off at the beach or a swimming pool, no bathroom or Kotex in sight. I haven't bargained for this bodily business. I miss tearing the sheets from our beds, tossing them over carefully spaced chairs and tying the ends to their wooden-slatted backs to build tents and tunnels we can crawl underneath. I miss pretending the old carriage house is a jail. Now my jail is this body.

Boys and sex, sex and boys; that's all Jeannie wants to talk about. "Isn't he cute?" "Do you think he likes me?" I would be so glad to turn back time. I would protect our tunnels and tents; I would hold on fast with all my might. I would never let her cancel me to sneak off to meet some boy in the park. Boys don't want to play anymore. When I walk by, they turn their bodies away, but stare like dolls with their heads twisted on backwards. I want to run this all by Gay, but she might as well be living on Pluto. Whenever she calls, Daddy is there, an accountant of seconds, keeper of the watch.

"Your sister wants to speak to you. Say hello. Hurry up. Remember, this is long distance." Daddy waits with outstretched arm, fidgeting, hovering, desperate to pluck my sister away if I don't hand her back quickly enough. What makes him think "hello" will do? Paragraphs are left out.

\* \* \*

I'm going to be thirteen, a full-blown woman in the Jewish faith. This is ridiculous. I won't be a woman for years. To be honest, if it's more of the same, I've had quite enough.

The cantor's wife is my teacher. It's her job to prepare me for the bat-mitzvah service. She believes my voice belongs to her, and she dreams of waving to me from her front row center seat when I make my debut at the Metropolitan opera. I only want to survive this humiliating experience.

Boys have to do their bar mitzvahs alone, but we're just girls and so we get to double and triple up. It's all arranged by dates of birth. Nina is my partner. Daddy hates her mother. She wears gobs of makeup, gigantic jewelry and much too much perfume. But he must talk to her, or get Mommy to, in order to plan our party. Mommy doesn't repeat half the things Daddy tells her to say.

"Every note she sings is flat. Does she have any idea how awful she sounds? She's going to ruin everything." And it's true that Nina can't sing. She has no ear for music. And while I don't feel this unfortunate flaw is justifiable reason to force her parents to pay more than their share for the party, Daddy does. Or so he implies whenever he speaks of her.

"This is not a wedding. If she thinks we're rich, she's wrong. I want her to understand that we're already sending one daughter to college. I didn't have a party when I had my bar-mitzvah."

"Your parents couldn't afford it."

"And we can?"

"This is 1962, Nathan. Everyone has parties"

"But we're not everyone, are we, Jeannette. Just make sure this Steiner woman keeps the cost down."

Some months before my bat-mitzvah Mommy tells me we're going to Chicago.

"Chicago? Without Daddy?"

"I thought we'd visit Uncle Joe and Aunt Frances."

"Did I ever meet them?"

"No."

"And Daddy said it was okay?"

"Yes. I've already got plane tickets."

I'm going to Chicago. Jeanie's never been. I can't believe Daddy's letting us go. And alone. One whole week with Mommy. It's the best bat-mitzvah present I could ask for, even though no one has said that's what it is.

Mommy does crossword puzzles during the flight. I interrupt her with too many questions, but she doesn't mind. I love Mommy better without Daddy. I feel guilty but free.

Chicago is bigger than Boston and twice as cold. It's the middle of January and there's a hard layer of mud packed ice on the ground. We line up for a taxi at the airport. I hang on to Mommy's arm for fear I'll be blown away. There's wetness in the wind. It rips right through my woolen coat. We pull the taxi door open against it, fighting to keep it that way until we're safely inside; then we must pull hard to get it shut.

Lakeshore Drive is not at all what I've imagined. I could see to the other side of all of the lakes I've known. This water travels on and on and on.

Aunt Frances and Uncle Joe live in the glass penthouse of a skyscraper. When the taxi comes to a stop, the doorman rushes to help us, as if he's been waiting there just for this moment. He doesn't need to consult his "*Residents*" book to tell us where to find them. "The elevator is over there. Just tell George where you're going."

A pasty old white man, slumped over with sleep in his wheel chair, is pushed into the small elevator cage by a large colored woman. George, a young man with a smile painted onto a face full of pimples, is seated on a stool in full dress uniform. He's manning the buttons.

It's a long ride to the top. I notice the floor numbers skip from 12 to 14.

"Mommy, why don't they have a number 13?"

"It's bad luck," Mommy whispers. The colored woman chuckles.

The cage stops on the 15th floor. George presses the button to hold the door while the colored woman wheels the old man out of the car. Once the door is securely shut again, I ask Mommy, "Why did that woman laugh when you said it was bad luck?"

"I don't know. Maybe she thinks superstition is silly."

"Or maybe she thinks superstition ain't supposed to be *white*," George snickers.

"Mommy's superstitious and she's white." George's smile disappears. He turns back to his buttons. He's silent for the rest of the ride. He mutters "you're welcome" to our "thank you" as we step off.

Uncle Joe's been retired for years. His work history is sketchy. Aunt Frances is the president of a prestigious liquor company. Mommy says she's rich.

Aunt Frances' maid, Greta, is waiting at the door. She's a dumpling in uniform, straight out of the French farce we saw at the Falmouth

Summer Theater last year. Greta is German. The French maid raced across the stage and back, grabbing at this and dusting at that. Greta moves deliberately with a dignity more suitable to her age. She leads us from the foyer to a living room with pristine white sofas and floor-to-ceiling windows looking out onto the lake.

Aunt Frances is not at all what I expected either. I didn't know older women could look like this, tall and slender, deep gray eyes carved into a handsome face. Streaks of gray and white and black run through hair cut close to the head. She's wearing a black silk suit with a wispy black and white silk polka dot blouse and black and white polka dot pointy high-heeled shoes.

Francis's hands are soft but strong. She reaches out, explores my face like a blind person, searching me out. She whispers to herself, "What lovely eyes."

I tell her, "You're the most beautiful woman I've ever seen." I quickly tack on, "Next to Mommy, of course," but I'm lying.

She touches my hair and says, "I'm so glad you're here." Her voice is deep, unhurried.

She tells us Uncle Joe is out somewhere. He'll be back for dinner. Greta brings tea and a tray of cookies with tiny cakes and chocolates. Aunt Frances asks me about school, my friends, my bat-mitzvah, but soon she and Mommy drift off into family stories. They forget I'm there. I try not to remind them so that they won't censor themselves.

I have to use the bathroom. Aunt Frances asks Greta to show me where the guest bathroom is. Tripping over my feet, I confide to Greta, "I wish we had a guest bathroom. It would be so much nicer if Daddy didn't bring his patients into ours." She shows me into a small pink room with just a toilet and sink. I wonder where we'll take our baths, but I'm afraid to ask.

Uncle Joe is short and wiry; Aunt Frances outdistances him by at least two and a half inches in heels. He doesn't have a single hair on his head. I laugh at his jokes, but I have no idea if or why they're funny. It's irritating to have to shift. It's Aunt Frances I'm interested in.

At dinner Aunt Frances suggests that we go shopping for my bat-mitzvah dress. She likes Saks Fifth Avenue. I've never been. Whatever

Aunt Frances likes sounds good to me. Uncle Joe tells us to count him out. "Shopping is for women." We laugh, but I can't help thinking by the way Uncle Joe dresses that he must enjoy a bit of shopping. Mommy tells me when we are alone that Aunt Frances does it all for him. In the morning she chooses what he'll wear that day and lays it out on their bed. Daddy would never stand for something like this. I like to watch him match his suit, shirt, tie and socks. Sometimes he asks me what I think, but he's quite good at it and I know he doesn't need my help.

Dessert is something rich with a thick layer of chocolate icing. I eat it all to be polite, but it's only the icing I taste. My mind is on this place called Saks Fifth Avenue and the French Bistro Aunt Frances knows close by where we've planned to have our lunch. I wonder how I'll manage to sleep through the night.

Greta has placed our bags in the guest rooms. Each one has a full bed and dressers. I thought Mommy and I'd be sleeping together on a pull-out couch like we do with most relatives. In between the bedrooms is a bathroom with adjoining doors. It is large and bright red and gray with a full tub and shower. The towels are thick and soft, also red and gray. I didn't know bathrooms came in these colors. On the edge of the tub is a bottle of bubble bath.

"Your mother told your Aunt Frances that you like to take bubble baths," Greta says.

I open the bottle. It's never been used. It smells like Mommy's lilacs. I think it's too nice and maybe I should save it. I put it back. Once Greta leaves, I bounce on my bed.

Mommy runs a bath for me and adds a capful of sweet lilac bubbles. She knows I like the water so hot that when I step out I am red like a lobster. Steam covers all the mirrors, so I can't see myself as I step in. With my head propped against a blow-up bathtub pillow shaped like a seashell and held in place with plastic suction cups, I drift in and out of consciousness.

*I am standing at the podium in the synagogue. The seats are filled but there is not a single face I know. Even the rabbi and cantor are unfamiliar. The cantor signals me to begin on page 353. My prayer book doesn't* go beyond 300. I search for my sister among the faces. When I find her, she's the sister of photographs, the little blond girl with curly hair who lived eight long years before I was born.

I am standing at the podium in the synagogue. The seats are filled but there is not a single face I know. I am reciting a passage in Hebrew when I suddenly have to go to the toilet. I leave the podium without telling anyone what I am doing. I search for a toilet but all I can find are men's rooms. It is then I realize that I need a Tampon.

I am standing at the podium in the synagogue. The seats are filled but there is only one face I know. It is my grandfather's. Somehow I know he doesn't want to be there with so many people inside of a synagogue. He nods at me to begin but I have no idea where. I search the pages in my book but there doesn't seem to be any Hebrew. When I look up again, my grandfather's seat is empty. I need to find the toilet.

Mommy is tapping my shoulder. "I need a bath, too," she says. I push my way out of the lingering dream and the tepid water and begin to dry myself with the heavy red bath towel.

"Did Grandpop not like synagogues?"

"Not especially."

"Why not?"

"He and my grandfather had to get special permission to travel and work in Russia because they were Jews. Grandpop didn't believe in religion or God. It made him angry."

"Do you think Grandpop would've come to my bat-mitzvah?"

"Of course he would have."

"He wouldn't have been afraid?"

"No, of course not."

"He wouldn't have been scared that they'd lock us up in the synagogue and set it on fire?"

"That was Daddy's side of the family. And this is America. They don't do things like that here."

"They kill colored people. I know about the Klu Klux Clan. They burn churches and homes and hang colored people. They hate Jews, too."

"That's true. They do. But that doesn't happen in the North. Anyway, if your grandfather were still living, I'm sure he'd come to your bat-mitzvah. And if Bubbe weren't so sick, I'm sure she'd be there, too." I've never known Bubbe to do anything other than sit in a chair, so this is hard for me to imagine.

*I am standing at the podium in the synagogue. The seats are filled with faces from old family photographs. My father is ten, holding Uncle Larry's eight-year old hand. They are dark-skinned with deep black eyes, exotically beautiful like Romanian Gypsies. Bubbe is young, fat, wearing thick glasses. Aunt Dora is standing in the back, regal, holding a fan. My grandfather is standing next to her, handsome in his borrowed suit. Dead Russian relatives fill the pews. The air is permeated with the smell of unwashed, Orthodox men in heavy wool suits. They are davoning, their half-sung, half mumbled prayers stinking from dirty teeth, sweaty bodies, all according to the rules of the Sabbath. My father at his current age is sitting in the front row with my mother. My curly-headed blond sister of only six years is sitting behind them with my mother's father. He looks like the grandfather I knew. I begin to sing and there is silence. Then I smell smoke. Flames rush through the pews, bursting up between the people, until there is not one recognizable face, just pools of melted wax. I stand intact at the podium, wearing my sister's prom dress and her pink ballet shoes.*

I wake in the dark, drenched in sweat in strange sheets. I have to think to remember where I am. I want to knock on Mommy's door and crawl into bed with her, but I'm too old and trying to be sophisticated. I get a glass of water from the bathroom, make some noise, hoping she'll call out to me and ask how I am. But the only sound that comes from her side of the wall is a deep, steady snore. I go back to bed and wait for morning.

The morning is frosty and cold but still. Aunt Frances calls for her car. A chauffeured limousine picks us up in front of the building. Aunt Frances explains that it's her company car but that she can use it whenever she wants. It's one of the "perks." The chauffeur is called Bob. He's an elderly man, tall, straight, elegant. He wears a charcoal gray uniform with red stripes on the cuffs of his jacket and down the sides of his pants. Underneath his hat, I can guess that he has a full head of white hair. Crevices cover his face; he must have had pimples when he was a kid. I think he might also have been a fighter because his nose looks like it's been broken more than once. His hands are hidden in white gloves. He calls Aunt Frances "Mrs. Sherman." I realize I hadn't known her last name. He tells us with pride that he only drives for Mrs. Sherman. If she has nowhere to go, neither does he.

I ask Bob, "Did you know we're going shopping at Saks Fifth Avenue?"

"I do. Mrs. Sherman told me."

"I've never been to Saks Fifth Avenue." I lean forward to speak through the hole in the glass partition that separates the front seat from the back.

"Well," Bob laughs, "I think you're in for a treat."

"I've been to Lord & Taylor."

"Well, I guess you know about good shopping then." Bob winks at Aunt Frances through the rear view mirror.

"A little bit," I say, intimidated by the wink.

"Phyllis knows a lot about shopping," Mommy tells Bob. She smiles at me and I feel better. "She has a special knack for it," she adds.

"You ladies will have a good time then," Bob says.

I know I should be taking in the sights, but I've never been in a limousine before. Taxis are different. I feel I must include Bob or he'll feel left out.

"Do you have a family?" I ask him.

"I sure do, young lady. My wife and I have twenty-three grandchildren."

"Wow. From how many children?" Mommy elbows me.

"That's okay, Mrs. Mitnick. I don't mind." Bob has an uncanny way of being able to see us and drive at the same time. "We've got eight children, but only seven of them are married. My youngest is a nomad, but I expect he'll settle down one day. I have a few of their pictures with me if you'd like to see, but I don't want to intrude on your shopping time."

I don't want him to either but I say, "I'd love to see them if it's okay with Mommy and Aunt Frances." Aunt Frances looks at Mommy. I think she'll say no but then, she is the one who's taught me good manners.

"I don't see why not," she says.

"Nothing I love to show off more."

And I don't feel put out. I'm curious about people. Daddy says I ask too many questions, but I can't see what's wrong with talking to people. I sit for hours on end with Mrs. B, my friend Eleanor's housekeeper. She's an enormous colored woman from Georgia with such a soft little girl's voice that you would think she was six or seven years old if she wasn't standing right in front of you. When we're alone, she tells me anything I want to know. When Eleanor and her father are around, she's invisible. Eleanor can imitate her to a tee; I have to giggle. Afterwards I feel guilty.

Aunt Frances names the buildings we pass. She knows when they were built and who designed them. I guess that Mommy is not that interested, but she listens to Aunt Frances and nods. She wants to know about theater and music. I know Mommy better than Aunt Frances does, or that's what she'd be telling her.

Bob pulls up in front of a large, old-fashioned brick building that seems to rise forever, the top disappearing behind the clouds in a blue-grey winter sky. I strain my eyes to see where it ends. Elaborate gold letters spell *Saks Fifth Avenue* across the front. Bob reaches into the glove compartment and pulls out his wallet.

"Just a quick look," he says. "Here's what I've got with me."

I've almost forgotten. I'm glad I haven't jumped out of the car. I'm ashamed of myself for being in a hurry, but in the same thought hope it won't take too long.

The pictures aren't very good. I can hardly make out the faces. There's a little blond girl, I think she's blond, playing with a fat, fluffy dog. I ask Bob what kind of dog it is. He tells me it's a mutt. A stern looking man is his son. He doesn't look as friendly as Bob. It's disappointing. I wonder if Bob thinks so, too.

Saks Fifth Avenue in Chicago is bigger than Lord & Taylor in Boston. At least it seems so to me. The escalators are wider, the steps farther apart, so I have to pay attention getting on and off. We get off at Junior Petites, Sophisticates.

I don't try on many dresses. I never do. I know exactly what I like.

No frills, puffs, hoops or lace. Simplicity. Aunt Frances finds it in pink silk. It's perfect on me. Aunt Frances insists on buying it for me as a bat-mitzvah present. In the dressing room Mommy whispers to me, "It's very expensive."

"Is it okay, Mommy?"
"I think it makes her happy."
"Because she doesn't have any children?"
"Yes."
"Why don't they have any?
"I don't think Aunt Frances was able to have them."
"Did she want them?"
"Yes, I think so."
"I don't want any children."
"You might change your mind when you're older."
"I won't."
"Why not?"
"Everyone says I'm just like Daddy."

\* \* \*

We leave Chicago and fly to Detroit. Aunt Mary and Uncle Abe live in Pontiac, Michigan. Mommy has forgotten to mention that we'd be going there as well. She tells me I met their daughter, Shirley, in New York, but I don't remember her. I only remember a frightening drive, getting lost, a homeless man trying to wash the car windows somewhere under a bridge, and Cousin Beatrice hitting the gas pedal hard to get away.

Uncle Abe is Mommy's favorite uncle, but when I ask her why, all she can say about it is that she's his favorite niece. Like Aunt Frances and Uncle Joe, and practically everyone else on Mommy's side of the family, they lived in Grandpop's house for a while in the attic apartment where Mommy and Daddy and Gay lived before I was born. Uncle Abe was "in trouble with the law." Mommy is vague about this and warns me not to ask. As if I would. That doesn't mean I'm not dying to know.

Daddy always says, "Jews aren't alcoholics; Jews aren't drug addicts; Jews don't beat their wives; Jews don't abuse their children; Jews don't rape or steal; Jews aren't criminals." He is certain of this, even in light of the contradictory family evidence.

My cousins in Pontiac are in law school. I'm not sure if this is connected to Uncle Abe's criminal history or some separate seed sprouting on its own. Uncle Abe is a large, grouchy, white-haired man who criticizes his family in the same tone of voice he uses to scold the Detroit Tigers. He tunes in to every game on a tiny transistor radio with so much static that it's hard for me to imagine how, with two hearing aids, he always knows the score. I listen with him. For me, it's not the baseball. It's Uncle Abe's grunts and groans, his unshaven, weary face, his fingertips, brown from smoking.

Aunt Mary is short and fat. I love to sit in her kitchen and listen to her cook.

"A little more cinnamon, I think." She tastes, dips her fingers into a spice jar catching "just a pinch." She tastes and shakes her head, "No, maybe some nutmeg." This goes on until finally, with one satisfied nod, she announces that it's "okay."

Aunt Mary likes to gamble. Once her stews are simmering in their pots and her pies baking away in the oven, Aunt Mary will take off her apron and ask, "How about a game of gin?" The stakes are nickels and dimes, but there must be stakes. She always wins.

So does Cousin Frances. She is formidable in Scrabble. I can beat Mommy, queen of the crossword, but I don't stand a chance with Frances.

Mommy caves after the 11:00 news, but Frances and I are at it until 2:00 or 3:00 in the morning. Frances will never say she's tired, just that she has to work on a brief. I lose game after game, even though I use all my letters at once and gain an extra fifty points. I'm no match for her but don't mind losing too much, since I know no one else I can put in this category.

I soothe myself with leftovers and check in on the all-night movie channel I don't have in New Bedford, since Kennedy has not yet been assassinated and we don't have a television. I fall asleep from too many slices of turkey topped with cold dressing stuck in between a couple of pieces of pumpernickel before Jane Greer can dump Robert Mitchum in *Out of the Past*. I can still see the light under Frances' door when I nod off.

I wake up and feel Shayna Maydala, (Yiddish endearment for "beautiful girl"), the sassy family toy poodle, licking my feet. I know that Frances is gone. Shayna "protects" Frances until she's out of bed, yapping and growling at anyone who tries to come near. Since I'm the last one up and no one comes to wake me, she can rest her throat and jaws.

Frances doesn't appear again until dinner. She is a phantom of the night, and I begin to look and wait for her eagerly. There is little else to tell from this visit except that I have fallen in love with Cousin Frances.

\* \* \*

Several years later, Mommy asks if I would like to spend the summer in Pontiac. It's strange for Mommy and Daddy to let me out of their sight, but perhaps they don't know what else to do with me. Since I have no idea what to do with myself, I'm eager for change—anything—someone who might possibly understand me. Even Mommy has given up.

Detroit is on fire. Blacks are protesting, rioting, looting, burning down the town. Army tanks are sitting in the streets. My parents are warned about curfews, but I guess they think this might not be such a bad thing for me at this time.

The Avadenkas are glad to see me, exactly why, I'm not sure. Aunt Mary offers to give me a lunch with a few girls my age who she knows from the synagogue. She sets the table with fancy lace doilies and places tall scalloped glasses layered with different flavors of ice cream and topped with whipped cream and maraschino cherries at each setting. While she does this, she tells me as much as she knows about each of the girls and their families. Daddy would call this "gossiping."

Uncle Abe presents me with his baseball schedule. He expects me to drive him to games in his beaten up car where I can see the road by simply peering through the floorboards. Frances insists that when I go about on my own I drive her new Pontiac, the car named for the city in which we are living; the city named for the Indian Chief who succeeded in protecting his lands against the British only to be assassinated by an Indian from another tribe in a personal dispute. Frances's cousin, Alan, will drive her to work and to school when I use her car. Alan is from California and "dangerous," Aunt Mary says. He's living with them while he goes to law school. Alan and Frances work for the same firm.

When I ask Frances what Aunt Mary means by "dangerous," she tells me, "Sometimes he gets too friendly with the criminals he's supposed to be defending." Aunt Mary hasn't quite forgiven him for showing up several mornings ago with a pimp and two hookers he knows from the race track. The pimp was driving a pink and gold Cadillac. Aunt Mary put her foot down and refused to invite them in to breakfast. I peeked out the window so I could see the car.

The parfait lunch is a success. I have new friends. Judy is two years older and Sarah is a year younger. Sarah is sweet and shy and has a crush on Alan. She makes me promise not to tell him. I suspect that this is part of the reason she spends so much time with me. I don't blame her. I have a crush on him, too.

Judy is wild, loyal, demanding. She invites me to spend the day at her house so that I can meet her parents. I'm thrilled but terrified—and not of the parents. I have only just gotten my driver's license.

Judy and I are both thin, but Judy thinks we ought to go on a diet. She talks me into two weeks of eating nothing but hard-boiled eggs and because this seems to be a requirement of being her best friend, I agree. Judy announces that we'll ask each other every day if we've cheated. I don't see any reason for starving or promising that I will, and so I'm only half participating. Judy is eating six eggs a day. I eat eggs when I'm with her and whatever I please when I'm not. It doesn't seem possible for me to live in my Aunt Mary's house and eat only hard-boiled eggs. I can't see any reason for either of us to lose weight, but Twiggy is Judy's scale of comparison and she insists that the hard-boiled egg diet is the only way. It is what we are supposed to be doing.

I'm afraid that Judy will not be able to overlook my peanut butter and jelly sandwiches, Reese's Peanut Butter Cups, the spoonfuls of peanut butter I eat straight from the jar. Too much confession might not be a good thing. So it happens that I'm driving to her house for the first time to share a banquet of hard-boiled eggs.

Frances tosses me the car keys so easily that I don't tell her how frightened I am. I never told Mommy and Daddy I was taking driving lessons until I passed my test. I saved my allowance for weeks to pay for them. Daddy let me drive the Mercedes once while he was in the car, and the only other car I've ever driven is Uncle Abe's. I know I'll have to work pretty hard to inflict anymore damage to it. But Uncle Abe doesn't like his car to go anywhere without him, and Frances is afraid it will fall apart from under me in the middle of the expressway. I'd rather take the risk than to put a single dent in hers, but this does not appear to be up for discussion.

Frances has drawn what she sees as a "simple" map to Judy's house. I read maps like Mommy, not well at all. I like the kind of directions that tell you to take a left or a right at the Texaco station on the corner of Main Street and Jackson Avenue. Look out for the Golden Arches just before the Texaco. No little n's, s's, e's and w's expecting me to know which way is north, south, east or west. Frances doesn't know any of this. She thinks I'm smart. I take the map. I take the keys.

The car smells like it's never left the lot. If Frances has lit one of her Parliaments in here, she's done a good job of covering it up. I open the ash tray just to see. It's spotless. I back out of the driveway carefully and immediately head in the wrong direction. I discover this when I arrive at the first intersection and none of the street names match anything on my map. East must have been the opposite way. I turn around, pass the house again and start over. Ahhh, yes, an Indian name, but since this is east which way is south? I have to stop and mentally draw my own map. I've pulled over in the wrong direction and now must find a place to turn around again. I see a nice little residential side street with no stores with parking lots and choose the first available driveway. I turn around but now—where is that map? I have no idea which way I came or which way I'm headed. I stop the car in the middle of the street. There is no one in sight.

I curse the map, my driver's license, Judy, myself, my cousin, the City of Pontiac and the damned hard-boiled egg diet. I promise God that if He will only help me find my way out of here, I won't lie anymore about the peanut butter and jelly sandwiches or the Reese's Peanut Butter Cups. But where the hell am I anyway? I start to cry.

No good at all, I must get somewhere. I decide to back into the same driveway to get my bearings. But it's already too late to realize that a driveway is not such a good idea when I hear the scrape of the red-winged Chevy parked just in front of it. I check my watch. I've been gone exactly fifteen minutes. In this brief time, I've managed to get lost and sideswipe a car.

It's 1965. There are no cell phones. I park Frances's car just where it is, in the middle of the street. I examine the houses, trying to figure out where the owner of the Chevy might be. The house with the driveway has two window boxes with pansies and a ginger-colored cat peering out behind bleached white lace curtains. How bad can these people be? Well, they could be heroin dealers. I've been warned they live in houses just like this.

But there's nothing else to be done. I walk up to the front door and stand there. It opens before I ring the bell. A short, stubby woman in a frayed terry bathrobe and pink fuzzy slippers grabs me up in her plump outstretched arms.

"Oh, you poor thing, I've been watching you from the window. Did you hurt your car on my husband's Chevy? Oh, look, you're crying. Please come in." I let her lead me to an overused, ratty chair where the cat jumps and hisses loudly. I decide not to sit.

"Can I use your phone? My cousin's going to kill me. It's a brand new car. I'm so sorry about your husband's car. I hope he's not too mad. I'll pay for it. I can get a job."

"Honey, please, sit down. Relax. The phone is right there on the table. Do you want a cup of coffee? Get off that chair right now, Gerald!" The cat gives me another hiss and vacates the chair.

"Gerald was my late husband's name. He disliked cats and wouldn't have appreciated me naming Gerald after him. Not one bit. So you don't have to worry about Gerald complaining. Believe me he would have if he could. How about that coffee now? Cream and sugar?"

I collapse into the chair and nod yes to the coffee, to the cream and sugar. I hate to be pleased that Gerald has passed on, but I am. I stare at the phone. I'm still sitting like this when the woman returns. She hands me the coffee and takes the phone.

"Would you like me to call someone for you?" For a moment, I consider how nice that would be. But then I imagine this woman with nothing to lose, glad that I have scarred her dead husband's perfect car, bursting unannounced into Frances's day. I cannot do it.

"Thank you. I'm okay." I wish she'd go away, busy herself with dishes, pretend she isn't taking in every word I say. She stands there and waits.

Frances is in a meeting. I grit my teeth; say yes, it is important, yes, I would like the secretary to please ask her to step out.

"Phyllis? Hi."

"Fran, I had an accident. I sideswiped a car. I'm so sorry. Are you mad?"

"Are you okay?"

"Yeah, fine. I got lost."

"Where are you now?"

"In the living room of the woman whose husband's car I hit. But he's dead." The woman smiles. Frances is silent.

"I didn't kill him, Fran." I try to keep my voice low. The woman hands me her insurance card and I read the information to Frances.

"What should I do with the car?"

"What do you mean?"

"Well, I'm sure you don't want me driving it."

"Phyllis, take the car and go to Judy's. I have insurance."

"You're not mad at me?"

"Why would I be? It was an accident."

"Fran, I don't understand the map. I need lefts and rights."

"Do you have some paper and a pen? Tell me where you are and I'll tell you how to get there."

Is it possible that's all there is to it? A left on Chippewa, not a right. Two blocks down, another left. Frances doesn't tell me I'm stupid for not being able to read her map. She asks again if I'm okay, says she'll see me at dinner and goes back to her meeting. I don't understand any of this.

I leave without giving the woman Frances's insurance which I've forgotten to get. She doesn't appear to be concerned. She is only disappointed that I don't stay longer. I think she would like to tell me more.

Judy's house is several minutes away. It feels like hours. Judy and her parents inspect the car. They laugh, "It's "only a scratch, nothing to worry about." I hear a history of totaled cars, ambulance rides to the hospital, near fatal injuries, all meant to reassure me, but they only frighten me more when I think of what I now know to be the five blocks I must negotiate in order to bring the car back home. I even consider spending the night, but I don't believe I can survive on hard-boiled eggs.

"You were thrown from a horse and you got back on," Judy reminds me.

"That horse was old and cranky and didn't belong to Frances."

"What's the worst she can do? Take the car away?"

The question hangs there. It is not the worst she can do. She can not love me anymore; she can send me home; she can not sit up half the night talking with me; she can not believe in me. But I don't say any of this to Judy. She ought to know that there are much greater losses than a car.

The drive home is too easy. I'm able to think. I'm a bad person, a worse friend. I can't drive five lousy blocks without getting lost and having an accident and I pretend to be on a diet with a friend who is starving herself to death. I sit in the parked car and stare at myself through the rearview mirror. Fran's right. I do wear too much makeup. Too much hairspray. And she hates it when I wear V-necked tops like the one I'm wearing now because she thinks they make me look too thin. She says my collar bones stick out. Maybe she's right about that, too. Mommy doesn't think I can ever look too thin. It doesn't matter. I don't like what I see.

It's supper time and for once, Frances is home before me. She's in the kitchen with Aunt Mary, sampling gravy from a ladle.

"Oh, Phyllis, try this." She offers me the ladle. "You won't believe how good it is." I take the ladle, sip the sauce and burst into tears. Aunt Mary grabs the ladle.

"It's nothing to cry about," she says. "I've made better."

"Why aren't you mad at me? I don't understand. I smashed your car. My father would've murdered me by now. You haven't even asked to see it yet."

"Okay, if you like, let's go look at the car."

We stand together in front of the car. I point out the damage. Frances nods and says, "Okay, now can we go in and eat? We'll take care of it tomorrow. It's just a little paint"

*Just a little paint.* Is she punishing me in some odd way by pretending it doesn't mean anything? Will she retreat after dinner, become silent, behave as if I don't exist? Will she call my parents and tell them I'm too much to handle; that she's putting me on the first flight to Boston?

I eat roast beef for supper and promise myself that I will confess all to Judy. No one asks if the hard-boiled diet has come to an end. I know Uncle Abe would like to know; he'd like to say something about how he can't understand how anyone could lose weight and eat what I eat, but Frances gives him a look that stops him. He's already called Daddy once this summer to complain that I'm "eating them out of house and home." He asked him to send money just in case. Frances called Daddy to say they could well afford to feed me and he was not to send a single penny. Mommy asked me if I was gaining weight. After all, she warned me, they are a fat family. But right now I don't know how much trouble I'm in.

Frances tells everyone goodnight after dinner. She's behind on a brief she's been writing and says she will lock herself in her bedroom and not come out again until it's finished.

There is nothing to be done. I help Aunt Mary with the dishes. I go over the lineup of baseball games with Uncle Abe. He warns me sharply that nothing is to interfere with this, not a date with John Lennon or an Aretha concert. I might as well be good for something while I'm living here, and it's about time I learned about baseball.

Clearly my father has taught me nothing. I argue that I watch baseball with Daddy but to Uncle Abe that means very little.

"You have to be there, smell it, get some dirt in your eyes, sweat, eat a hotdog, drink some beer, yell. What do you do when you listen to the games with me? You get up to make sandwiches (he doesn't mention that I make one for him); you go to the bathroom; you play gin rummy with your aunt; you talk on the phone with your friends. This is no way to experience baseball."

I want to tell him it's a slow game, but I know what he'll say. He'll mutter something about me "being impatient," blow cigarette smoke in my face and make that guttural sound he sometimes makes just before he coughs up a gob of phlegm in a smoker's fit.

"Just when you go to the bathroom, just when you stick your head in the refrigerator, just when you answer the damn phone (unlike Daddy he doesn't say "darn"), that's when you're going to miss the play of the century. That's baseball. You have to pay attention."

We go over the calendar several times to make sure he hasn't missed a date. I let him think this is all sacrifice on my part. The baseball itself I can take or leave, but I'm guessing there's a lot to be learned from Uncle Abe. I suspect it might take away some of his pleasure if he thinks I'm a willing companion.

Just before I make my Dagwood sandwich and settle in for *Late Night at the Movies*, I knock on Frances's door.

"Come in," she says.

"It's me. I just want to say goodnight."

I wonder that the bed doesn't buckle under her, upset the barricade of books she's lying behind. Why did I think she wasn't really writing a brief but was trying to stay away from me?

Frances sighs. "Give me a hug and a break. Sit with me for a few minutes. Just a few or I'll be up all night."

I find a way to her; curl up into warm flesh.

"I wish I could have played Scrabble with you tonight. It would've been a whole lot more fun than this."

"Really?"

"Really. I like to win. I'm much more confident that I can beat you at Scrabble than I am that I can impress this judge."

"That's silly, Frances. You impress everyone."

"Too bad you're not the judge." We laugh and I let her push me off the bed.

"If I don't get back to work now——will you bring me a glass of milk and some cookies?"

"Franny, I want to be just like you."

"It'll take a few of you to be *just* like me." She traces her hands around the outline of her body.

"You're beautiful, Fran." Even in my fear of fat, I mean it.

I fall asleep in front of the television. I miss most of the movie and leave my sandwich plate next to the couch on the floor. In the morning, I can hear Uncle Abe complaining to Aunt Mary about crumbs and wasted electricity.

"Sorry," I mumble.

"He doesn't mean it," Aunt Mary says. Uncle Abe starts to cough into his handkerchief and I'm not so sure.

"Hard-boiled eggs?" Aunt Mary asks. I look at the French toast swimming in maple syrup on Uncle Abe's plate.

"No. I'll have some of that, please."

"It's about time. Are you going to tell your hard-boiled egg friend?" Uncle Abe is not about to let me slide.

"Yes, I am."

"Well, good. So now you're going to eat during the day, too?"

"Yes."

"Mary, you better go shopping or I'll have to go on her egg diet." I laugh.

"Not a bad idea," Aunt Mary tells him. "You could lose a few pounds."

"Yes, I could," he pats his belly, "but why would I want to?"

"The last time your uncle went on a diet, he was so crabby we all wanted to move out. And that diet was on doctor's orders and lasted a week."

"Good morning." Frances sits down at the table, delicately for someone of her size. I like to watch her move.

"It was terrible," Aunt Mary nods. "I was ready to let him die sooner and happier than stay on that diet. And it wasn't as bad as six hard-boiled eggs a day." In truth, Aunt Mary is not ready to let Uncle Abe go a second sooner, happy or not. When he dies of emphysema a few years from now, she will have to be restrained from jumping into the grave with him. What is this kind of devotion, this love?

"They wouldn't let me eat a damn thing that tasted good. And they wanted me to quit smoking."

"God forbid," Frances laughs. She tosses me a pack of Parliaments and a set of car keys. "At least we can all go out together."

"What's this?"

"You can't bum them from me when I'm not home. I get them by the carton. They're cheaper."

"And these?" I hold up the car keys.

"I like to ride with Alan."

"Fran, I just wrecked your car yesterday."

"You didn't wreck it. It's a scratch. You're not going to stop driving, are you? You'll have a pretty boring summer. You'll be fine."

"You're really not mad at me."

"No, but I will be if you don't ask me if I finished my brief. Doesn't anyone around here care? I was up half the night." She winks to let me know she's kidding.

"Did you finish it?"

"Not before you were asleep. I make my own midnight trips to the refrigerator."

Uncle Abe makes that coughing, grunting sound again. "Am I the only one around here who eats at mealtimes?"

After breakfast, I take a long, hot shower. I stand and stare at myself naked in front of the bathroom mirror. In spite of the steam clouding the glass, in spite of who I've been telling myself I am, perhaps for just a little while, even for one brief moment, I can see what Frances sees when she looks at me.

# [23]

# BECAUSE OF MRS. GOLDBLUM'S GARBAGE

My father cultivates grudges the way some people collect butterflies. And though his most fertile fields are with our relations in Philadelphia, he never lacks ample pickings right at home on Clinton Place.

The Goldblums are at the top of his list, and he plots how he will pin their wings to the wall. Our back porches are separated by only a ten-foot patch of poorly attended grass. We hang out our wash and charcoal broil our dinners directly under their stained glass hallway window. Sometimes I gaze up at the flowered panes and wonder if they're watching us, if they're peeking out between the cracks of dust and dirt that have accumulated there.

For me, Judge Goldblum is only a myth. He died before I could meet him, but he lives on in my father's stories of the various and sundry lawsuits brought about by his litigious wife, many of which have survived him. No one is safe from her. And when I hear my father beating his fist against my sister's bedroom door at 5:00am on a snowy morning, I know I have only a moment more to snuggle in. This vigilance about shoveling is due to the ever present threat of a slip and fall suit that just might be brought about by the calculating Mrs. Goldblum, or even by some hapless patient who may fall in sincerity but may also wish to make the best of a bad thing.

The legend goes that Mrs. Goldblum has two daughters. One has escaped through marriage. I don't remember her at all. Whether she's still married or not, I can't say, but she's never come home again. The second daughter, Gilda, is stuck like a bird in a cage.

When I'm very small, I sometimes see Gilda leaving the house early in the morning to teach at the elementary school. I even remember a nice-looking young man who comes to call. But before I can begin to worry about what it might be like to have her as a teacher, she's dismissed under a heavy cloud of scandal. For all I know, it might be some minor infraction or indiscretion. You have to weigh in the fact that it is only 1956. Nevertheless, it's whispered about and never explained clearly by anyone I could ask. Mrs. Goldblum never went out much anyway and after Gilda loses her job, she too is rarely seen, and sadly, never again with that nice-looking young man.

None of this, however, can explain such deep-seated enmity between the Goldblums and my father. He cares nothing for rumors and certainly, he's no stranger to prejudice. If they choose to hide away behind their own walls of worn gray shingles, so be it. My father believes firmly that "good fences make good neighbors." He wants no part of them. No, their offenses stoke a fire deep within his psyche and they're rendered meaningful in garbage.

Mrs. Goldblum has no wish to part with her garbage. And so once she and Gilda are no longer able to move around among the old newspapers, magazines, unanswered mail, tin cans and bottles, broken furniture, rusted appliances and clothing that is washed but never ironed, they expand onto the back porch and finally, when that too is overflowing, onto the front porch.

My father who has survived the schtetl; my father who has talked his way from the ghetto of South Philly into my grandfather's stone mansion in Roxborough; my father who has finally moved from two rooms on Dartmouth Street to what is one of the most affluent neighborhoods in New Bedford, has managed by some quirk of providence to move next door to a garbage dump. His protests are unremitting.

"Jeanette," he brandishes his arms about in frustration, "Have you looked out there recently? The last time I measured, it was four feet high. I know it's above six feet by now."

"What Nathan?"

"Mrs. Goldblum's garbage."

"Oh, well." My mother has no answer for this.

"I'm calling the Department of Health. And I'm not giving her any warning this time. The last time she cleaned it up just long enough for them to come and inspect and the next day it was back again. I have no idea what she did with it. Can you imagine the inside of that house?"

"I've seen it," I announce.

"When did you see it?" My father wants to know, as any association with the Goldblums is strictly forbidden. After all, there is a war going on.

"When Gilda mended the bird's broken foot. Remember?"

"Oh, I didn't know you went inside."

"Uh huh, they asked me in for milk and cookies. I was a little afraid to drink the milk after seeing *Arsenic and Old Lace*, but I drank some of it. The cookies came out of a box. They were nice to me. And she put the bird's foot in a splint and made him well again."

"What's the inside like?" My father momentarily forgets his anger in lieu of his curiosity.

"Like the outside. There's junk everywhere. They have this big table in the middle of the room and it's piled up with yellow newspapers—and there are stacks of old newspapers and magazines all over the place. And there are mountains of empty cans. Some of them are cat food and they smell awful. Yuck. And the cats run all over the kitchen. It stinks in there, but they're really nice, Daddy."

"They're really nuts," my father quips back at me. "I don't want you over there again. How will it look? Here I am reporting them to the Board of Health and my own flesh and blood is going over there for milk and cookies." It's painfully clear to me that my father is more concerned with compiling evidence against the Goldblums than he is with my welfare or safety. "Don't you tell them I'm calling the Board of Health. I want to make sure they catch them this time." He tiptoes – something I've never seen my father do –from the kitchen into his office, as if he fears that the Goldblums might know from the sound of his footsteps exactly what he is up to.

"They're not so bad, Mummy, are they?"

My mother hesitates. My father has talked to her recently about how they should at least appear to be united in their viewpoints to their children and to the outside world. I have overheard this discussion from my vantage point at the top of the back stairs. My mother settles on what she feels might be a neutral position.

"It was nice of Gilda to help you with the injured bird."

"She is nice, Mummy."

"Yes, nice, but perhaps not quite right in her head."

"Is she crazy like Aunt Kathie? Aunt Kathie is nice."

"Who said Aunt Kathie is crazy?"

"Daddy, I heard him."

"You might have misunderstood, honey. He was probably talking about something that Aunt Kathie did that he thought was foolish or he couldn't understand."

"But he said 'crazy,' I heard him."

"You know your father," my mother abandons "the united we stand" approach, "sometimes he says things he really doesn't mean.

"He doesn't think Aunt Kathie is crazy?"

"Well, he thinks many of the things she does are foolish, silly, and he calls them crazy. But he doesn't mean she's crazy like Mrs. Goldblum or Gilda."

I'm struggling to understand. Even my aunt has confessed to me that no one in their right mind would consider her normal. If she's not normal, and she's not crazy like Mrs. Goldblum and Gilda, what is she? How is it any different?

"How is it different, Mummy?"

Before my mother can attempt to respond, my father marches triumphantly into the kitchen. The grin on his face tells me that he he's been successful with whoever he's spoken to from the Department of Health. Often he comes in glaring and muttering something about bureaucracy, bribery, dishonesty, democracy and the future of political elections in this country.

"They're coming right over. I told them about the mouse droppings. That did it."

"What mouse droppings? Do we have mice?" I want to know if I'll get to see my mother and sister jump up onto chairs again.

The Health Department comes. The Health Department goes. Over the years, their fashions change slightly, but their official demeanor, shabby shoes, pens that always seemed to be out of ink, as well as their perceived indifference to my father's complaints are consistent. And with the passage of time, my father's calls grow less frequent, although with any reinforcement, which we all try not to give, he can work himself up in a flash and be found rifling through the phone book, digging for their number.

My father is from a family of union organizers, and he tries to utilize the talents he's acquired to rally the neighborhood in protest of the Goldblums. But my father is the only refugee, the only Russian, the only secret socialist, the only inhabitant of Clinton Place to have a father whose greatest goal was to belong to the carpenter's union. He's dismayed to discover that people don't respond with much fighting spirit to being anti-Goldblum. They're amused by and rather enjoy having a local Adams family to observe, but they're all New Englanders, and New Englanders are much too proper to confront their neighbor with odious appearances. They simply trot by as if it does not exist. No, they never put their noses up in the air. That would be snobbish.

The Goldblums to some extent cooperate with this New England stance. They make themselves practically invisible. I step outside on a cold, crisp autumn morning to see a shadow of a rake and human form disappearing around the side of their house. A basket of tell-tale leaves left sitting on the lawn is the only evidence to separate fact from hallucination. Then the basket itself disappears at some point when I'm not looking, and I'm left to wonder if I've ever really seen it at all.

"I think I saw Gilda today," I tell my mother.

"Oh, I see her sometimes, too."

"Does she ever speak to you, Mommy?"

"Mmmmm, well, if I catch her eye, I say hello."

"Does she answer?"

"Yes. She says "hello" and "how are you."

"Really." I feel inexplicable pain. I wonder if she associates my father's calls to the Board of Health with the timing of my visit to the house and the healing of the wounded bird. Maybe she thinks it's my fault. I think somehow it must be. The sick feeling in my stomach is impossible to put into words. I don't know how to say this to my mother, so I don't say anything. The moment passes.

My father is no quitter. In fact, he can often be heard in warmer weather, when the heat forces him to allow the windows to be opened, stating emphatically enough to me that he can be heard in any of the surrounding homes where vacuum cleaners are not running, "Don't be a quitter! You'll never get anywhere in this world if you give up." And so my father is never free from this fixation to reap revenge on the Goldblums.

Mrs. Goldblum likes a good fight. She has a sense of the macabre. Just two blocks away from us are the Roosevelt Apartments, an unwelcome addition to the natural decline of the town and the immediate neighborhood. They burn their trash. One cold night, well after Clinton Place has shut its lights and gone to sleep, several fire engines screech into the courtyard with their sirens blaring and lights flashing. In a fit of neighborly concern, feigned or real we can only guess, Mrs. Goldblum has reported that our house is on fire. My mother laughs about it the next day. She confides to me that the firemen refused to leave until they searched every inch of the house, basement to attic. She thinks it's funny that I've managed to sleep through the whole affair. She takes pride in my capacity not to be disturbed. My father is not amused.

In truth, no one cares much about the Goldblums but my father. He tries to elicit support from Geoffrey, an obese cigar-smoking attorney who lives across the street. Geoffrey puffs noisily on his Havana, a questionable gift from an even more questionable client. He blows smoke rings thoughtfully across his belly and up into the air. "Don't let it get to you, Nate. I don't let it bother me."

"He doesn't let anything bother him," my father mumbles as he and I head back over the pebbled courtyard. "And he has to look at it every day right across from him. You see, Phyllis, that's why he doesn't have a successful practice."

"Because of Mrs. Goldblum's garbage?" My father frowns. He often forgets that he is talking to a child, and he's never quite sure if I'm mocking him.

"No, not because of the garbage. He just doesn't care about anything. Look at him. He's a fat slob with a cigar hanging out of his mouth."

"You used to smoke cigars, Daddy," I remind him. I like Geoffrey. He's funny and he pays attention to me when I talk to him.

"And I gave them up, didn't I? My point is that you can't be successful in this world if you don't give a darn. Geoffrey is a fool."

"But he went to Harvard, Daddy. You always say people who go to Harvard are smart."

"He's smart but he's lazy. He's not a hard worker. He's always sitting around on his fat butt. I don't see him running off to his office every day. I bet he doesn't have too many clients. He probably is so lazy that he takes forever to work on their cases and things like that get around. You keep that in mind," he says, suddenly remembering I'm there. "You have to be a hard worker to get anywhere in this world."

Obviously, the fat and lazy Geoffrey is not going to help my father in his campaign against the Goldblums. Neither is my father's newest friend in the neighborhood, Jack. Years have passed and I am now visiting from college. Jack is also an attorney, but unlike Geoffrey, he is slim and according to community gossip, slick. Unlike the good-for-nothing Geoffrey, Jack is always in his office. He is busy wheeling and dealing to pay for his summer home and his boat, along with the many improvements he's made on the colonial he's recently purchased from the family of old friends who lived directly across from us for most of my childhood. My father approves of Jack. He especially likes the fact that Jack often stops by with a bottle of wine and two glasses. Jack does not smoke cigars, at least not in front of my father. But even though they have this "good old boy" relationship, Jack is no ally in the Goldblum Wars.

"C'mon Nate, what can you do? She's crazy. Just ignore it." Another one. Just ignore it. If only he could. But he can't. Time passes. My mother dies, and the Goldblums become an add-on sentence. My father has not called the Department of Health in a number of years, although he still refers to them with nostalgia. "I used to call the Department of Health," he muses, "but it never did any good." He does not qualify this statement by placing blame directly on this anonymous line of workers but only alludes to the fact that not much would have done any good. It is the closest he will come to an admission of defeat.

My father is nearing his ninetieth birthday now, and we've all gathered to throw him a party. He's delighted when he spots our cameras. His mission is on his mind. Since my husband is the newest member of the family and has not ever been engaged in actual battle with the Goldblums, he is the most likely candidate for the front lines. My father slips his arm through Arthur's and says with all the charm that he can muster, "I need your help. I want you to do something for me. I want you to take that camera, go next door and take pictures of the garbage. I'd like different angles, front and back. Get some good shots, okay?"

Arthur is too stunned to ask questions, and my father still has the capacity of making his requests feel more like commands. He has no idea what my father is up to. I don't know how I could have missed it, but I've neglected to warn him about my father and the Goldblums. I see him slipping on his coat and ask him where he's going. He hesitates.

"Well, your father just asked me to take some pictures of garbage."

"Well, I guess you're part of the family now," I laugh and grab my coat. "C'mon. I'll go with you, and when you're done taking the pictures, we'll go for a ride and I'll tell you all about the Goldblums.

# [24]

## "SUICIDE IS PAINLESS"

After his frantic return to the hospital in the middle of the night, my father is back on dialysis. My husband and I rush back to New Bedford to try to assess what arrangements will have to be made. My father is adamant about returning to his home. We're concerned that he'll continue to fire any help we find him, and he will end up alone and helpless in the middle of the night. And his mind is not as clear as it was before he stopped dialysis. He's weaker, barely able to walk.

The last time my father insisted on going home, my sister decided to have the convalescent center create an obstacle course that would replicate what Dad would have to navigate at home. My father agreed to return to the convalescent center for dialysis treatment until he could successfully accomplish this. Cooking, cleaning and walking up and down the stairs were simulated. At the end of an amazing two weeks, Dad managed to do it all, including the steps. And it was hard not to root for him. I would call daily to get his enthusiastic reports.

"Guess what I did today," he would announce proudly. "I climbed all nineteen stairs and made myself a fruit salad."

"That's great, Dad."

"And I want you to know it tasted a heck of a lot better than the crap those women who came to the house were feeding me. I don't need anybody cooking for me. I can do it myself."

"And how will you get the groceries to the house?" I hated to do this.

"Don't worry about that."

Some days I would just let it lie there. Other days I could not. I despised beating him up with reality as much as I loathed patronizing him.

In the end, we allowed him back with an agreement to have help in the house. The comings and goings of these unfortunate figures must have reminded my sister of the parade of nannies who attempted to care for me during my mother's illness. According to my father's memory, my sister was more often than not their executioner. Talented as he reported she was, they often quit before she could get them fired. Never one prone to noisy weapons, my sister was the master of the silencer. Quietly, according to my father, she would inform the innocent and earnest new kitchen intruder what she would like for breakfast.

"What will you have, dear?"

"Scrambled eggs and toast, thank you." My sister was always polite.

Not until after the eggs were being scrambled, and the new victim had just pressed her finger down to start the toaster would my sister open her mouth again.

"No, I'm sorry. I've changed my mind. I want French toast instead, please."

On occasion it would stop here. Other nannies were more sympathetic. The poor child's mother has almost died. She has a new baby sister. Poor thing gets little attention from her busy father. And one does catch more flies with honey, after all.

So the French toast would begin. And of course, Gay would smile appreciatively from where she sat patiently at the table. Just after her requested two pieces of bread had been dipped into egg, her still sweet voice would complain, "No, no. I don't really want French toast. I want to have oatmeal."

If it had not stopped yet, it generally did here. My sister would insist politely that my mother would have made her whatever she wanted. If the poor Nanny didn't have enough wits about her by now to throw off her apron and grab her coat, two scenarios could develop.

One or two of these women had the misfortune to try to discipline her themselves. These attempts were met with several swift kicks to the shins which only delayed their inevitable and final exits through our back door. My father's attempts to curtail her not so passive dismissals were to no avail since he was never there to witness them. And there is where his memory is to be challenged. My sister only remembers two nannies, both of whom she insists quit due to my father's constant complaining and difficult demands. Somewhere therein lies the truth.

My father has no great love of hired help, but naturally for very different reasons. My sister was an eight-year old child, furious at the absence of her mother. My father is now a ninety year-old man faced with the loss of his kingdom. His talent lies in his sucker's punch, which we know well, but is news to outsiders. The honeymoon with new help can sometimes last up to three weeks. During these tentative initiation periods, he sits quietly in his corner waiting for the bell to ring for round two. These well-meaning (some more than others) Florence Nightingales for the elderly are enamored by my father's attempts to teach them Shakespeare, Milton, Emerson. But somehow, before they have the time to absorb any of this, they're propelled into Dante's *Inferno*.

The most vulnerable is my namesake, Phyllis. I have a strong suspicion that bearing my name won't help her. By day three, Phyllis adores my father. Do I realize how intelligent he is? Do I appreciate what a kindly, cooperative patient and employer I have for a father? This is a piece of cake compared to the nasty old people she's used to. Do I know that my father's charming?

For several days, it even seems as if my father's cloned the "perfect" Phyllis. Nothing's too much for her. She brings him fresh fish, only his favorites, from her husband's trucking business. She overlooks the hour or so she spends here and there waiting nervously on the front porch for my father to return from driving escapades that would cause him to lose her services if discovered by Medicare. She keeps these AWOL adventures from us until her period of enchantment ends.

And how does this come to pass? Not having taken a hit in the first round, Phyllis comes out undefended in the second. "Oh, Dr. Mitnick," she gushes, "tell me more about Macbeth."

"Get me my tea," my father bellows, "you're not here to learn about Macbeth. Read it on your own time, not mine!"

"Dad's a bit edgy," she admits when I phone.

"Are you calling him that?" I ask.

"Calling him what?"

"Dad."

"Oh, no. I'm sorry. Dr. Mitnick." She misunderstands the point of my question.

"Phyllis, I don't care what you call him as long as it's okay with him. The reason I'm asking is that he's such a stickler for respect. If you slip and call him "Mister" instead of "Doctor," it could definitely make him 'edgy.' I don't know what calling him "Dad" would do."

"Oh," she sighs, relieved that she hasn't lost an ally in me. "Well," she continues, "he yells at me. He never used to. He even asked me if it was that time of month." There's a break in her voice.

"Phyllis, Phyllis, Phyllis. You're not letting him see that he's getting to you, are you?" I'm teasing, but my humor is lost on her.

"Well, I did cry."

"In front of him?"

"Yes," she whimpers, "only because he got me so upset. He told me my grammar stunk and where did I learn English anyway. I told him I didn't have no fish today because I only bring it when it's fresh." Her voice is beginning to break again. "He yelled that I couldn't say 'no fish,' and I thought he was mad cuz I didn't have the fish." She's sobbing into the telephone. I sigh. It's painfully clear that my hopes for Phyllis have been unrealistically high.

I shamelessly persuade her, flatter her, and remind her of her earlier adoration. When she still threatens to quit, I resort to what a good Jewish daughter knows best, a large dose of old-fashioned guilt. There I have her. She promises not to quit without calling me first.

The next phone call is not long in coming. She's sobbing so loudly that I have trouble understanding who it is until she mumbles, "He's impossible." I know how cruel he can be, and still I cajole, desperate not to have to break in yet another caretaker, if the agency will even consent to send him someone. Phyllis is adamant that she's leaving until I play really dirty pool and remind her of every prior patient she's described to me, starting with the Alzheimer's patient who did nothing but dribble and nod his head all day. This she now much prefers to my father and doesn't hesitate to say so. I throw another Alzheimer's patient in her face, one who would sit very quietly until she exploded suddenly, without warning, grasping at Phyllis' hair and clothing, ripping out some of each. Phyllis is quiet. She agrees to stay at least until I arrive for the weekend. I know it's pointless to even try to get her to commit to more.

We don't make it to New Bedford until after 9:00 at night. I open the front door while my husband gets our bag out of the trunk.

"Oh, my God, it's hot in here. He didn't even leave a light on."

"I hope he's okay." Arthur sets the bag down in the front entryway and I feel my way to a lamp. The light reveals the same living room, everything in its proper place.

We make our way up the stairs, afraid to turn on the hall light. The door to the television room is closed. The light is out in my father's bedroom but the door is slightly ajar. I lean in to check. He's sound asleep. I tiptoe out.

"He's out cold," I tell Arthur. "Why is this door shut?" I knock lightly on the door and it opens to my touch. A large shadow jumps up from the couch.

"Who are you?"

"I'm Candice."

"What are you doing here?"

"Taking care of your father."

"What happened to Phyllis?"

"He fired her. She wouldn't have come back even if he hadn't."

"Why is the house so hot? Why are you sitting here in the dark? Don't you want some air, some light or the TV?"

"No," Candice whispers, "please, he doesn't want it."

"What?"

"He doesn't want me to open any windows or turn on any lights. He says the television will keep him awake and I might not hear him if he needs me."

"If you have to sit here all night in the dark without air or anything to do, you're going to fall asleep and won't hear him anyway."

"I tried to tell him that—

"But he wouldn't listen."

"—but he wouldn't listen."

"You must be Phyllis and Arthur."

"Oh, yes. Sorry." We both shake her hand.

"I'll put our things away." Arthur tactfully leaves me with Candice.

"Why don't you go home and get some rest. I'll take it from here. And I'll talk to him about the air and the television. We can get him a bell to ring if he needs you."

"Oh, thank you, but I'm here until 8:00 when the morning person gets here."

"Well, then, we're going to open a window and turn on the television or a light. He's sound asleep. If he wakes up, come and get me."

"I appreciate it, but I'd rather you talk to him first."

"Let's at least open the window." I can see she's tempted.

"I don't want to make him mad."

"How about I say I opened the window. In fact, I will." I go over to the window and push. It's locked. I unlock it and push again, harder. It doesn't move.

"Help me out here, Candice." She takes a couple steps back and then sighs and joins me at the windowsill. We nudge and prod, take a break, say "one, two, three," and shove. Up it goes. A breeze immediately forces its way through the stuffy heat.

"That does feel good," Candice admits.

"I can't promise you won't get fired, but I can promise you won't die of asphyxiation."

"I do listen for him," Candice says. "The first night I was here, I heard him walking around and I came out to see if he needed anything. He was mumbling something about some medicine the doctor gave him, that it will help him when he's ready. Do you know what he's talking about?"

"No," I lie.

I join Arthur in my old bedroom. He's already opened the windows.

"He's looking for 'the vial' again."

"He's awake?"

"No, not now. Candice told me he was looking for it the other night."

"That's too bad. I thought he stopped after he talked to the doctor."

"So did I." I sit on the edge of my childhood bed. I'm in that warp of time when parent becomes child and child becomes parent.

"What can I do? I can't make him stay in a place he doesn't want to be but he can't stay alone. He won't move in with us, and he fires all the help."

"This one seems nice," Arthur offers hopefully.

"They're all nice. This isn't about them. It's about him. He wants to be in control. He's lived his whole life so he'd never have anyone telling him what to do. He's losing that and he wants out. Can you blame him?"

"I prefer to be stuffed and put over the mantelpiece."

"You'd never be this difficult."

We smile. We go to sleep. There's nothing to be done. We can only take this one minute at a time.

\* \* \*

We're all concerned that Dad wants to kill himself. He wanders around in the night searching for vials that don't exist, but there are plenty of poisons in the house if he's determined. Knowing that Dad will never listen to reason, even the doctor's visit hasn't dissuaded him, we decide to employ a tactic proposed by my sister which is actually ingenious. We call the rabbi and ask for his assistance. Since no one in town but our family has ever called this rabbi for anything, he's more than eager to comply. And it's only because we no longer live there and have no concept of who this rabbi is that we consider this possibility.

The rabbi's wife is reassuring on the phone. In a heavy accent which I guess as Israeli, she tells me not to worry, the rabbi's first concern is with his congregants, and she guarantees he'll call as soon as he returns. This is his forte, she tells me.

The rabbi calls within the hour and agrees to stop by that afternoon. I'm too distraught with my father's condition to entertain the thought that the Jewish population of New Bedford must be considerably diminished if this man has no appointments but us.

Fortunately, the rabbi arrives wearing his yarmulke. If not, I might have mistaken him for a real estate agent. While Dad is resting, my sister and I fill him in on all the details. He warms to the occasion. He's thrilled, in fact, to have been called upon in this way. He begins to share with us his frustrations with the congregation in New Bedford. They expect him to deliver more impressive sermons and to be a politician. He reminisces on his former career as a trial lawyer. By the time Dad finally descends the stairs from his nap, we've almost forgotten the purpose of the rabbi's visit. But the rabbi is inspired.

We gather around Dad. "Look who's come to visit with you.....Rabbi Glick." The rabbi wastes no time with amenities, as if expecting that the New Bedford Patrol for Wanton Rabbis is only moments away. He tunes and lowers his voice to the delicacy of the subject matter, but Dad, of course, is unable to hear him.

He repeats, "Dr. Mitnick, your daughters are very worried about you. Do you know that?"

Dad's gaze shifts from one errant daughter to the other. We've broken the "Mitnick Code of Silence" and spoken with an "outsider."

"Well, Rabbi, I don't know why they'd be worried about me."

"Well, they tell me you want to kill yourself."

"What's that?" Dad looks at me. "What's that he's saying? I can't hear him."

I silently determine that I will not serve as interpreter, especially not of this message. After all, that's why we've summoned the rabbi in the first place. I pass the ball back to Rabbi Glick.

"You'll have to speak up. He can't hear you." I wait for the rabbi to attempt to shout this message while retaining his dignity. He almost succeeds.

"YOUR DAUGHTERS TELL ME YOU WANT TO KILL YOURSELF."

Dad's eyes flash daggers, as if to say there might be others in the room who are in danger. But he confesses. "Yes, well it's true. I don't see much of a reason to hang around here anymore. I'm tired of reading, and they all have to go home. I just think it's about time, that's all."

"Dr. Mitnick, that's not your decision. And if you do something like this, they'll be left with terrible feelings of guilt."

"Why should they feel guilty? I love them."

"Do you know that your father loves you?" Rabbi Glick looks in my direction.

"Yes, I know he loves me." I wonder where this is leading.

"Do you know your father loves you?" Rabbi Glick turns to my sister.

"Yes," she's also questioning where the rabbi is going with this.

"And do you love your father? Are you going to feel terrible if he kills himself and always wonder if you couldn't have done something to stop him? And won't you have to live with that question the rest of your lives?"

We meekly nod our heads in assent. The rabbi turns to my father who seems amazed that he has been the instigator of this intrusion. But the rabbi takes no notice of this. He proceeds indifferently with his interrogation.

"Is this what you want for them? A life of guilt and recrimination? Do these two loving daughters deserve this for the rest of their lives? Do you really want this? Tell me." The rabbi is resolved.

We all sit silently awaiting my father's answer. There is a moment when we're not sure. I see him wavering between the omnipotence of lifetime guilt and the raw spot that the rabbi has tapped. He's reliving things we cannot know. He feels the weightiness of his own guilt and makes a decision. He responds softly, thoughtfully. "No, no. I don't want that."

The rabbi is on now. He zeros in on the tears forming in my father's eyes. He's emboldened by signs of moisture gathering in the cracks of skin that border his lids. My father is his, he thinks. In fact, he thinks we're all his, spellbound, waiting for his next move. He has no idea of the boundary he's crossed, the walls he's scaled, the barbed wire through which he's cut to go beyond the "no trespassing" signs so carefully positioned around the "Mitnick Zone."

"You know that suicide is against Jewish Law. How do you think your daughters will feel if you can't be buried next to your wife?" My sister and I shoot long glances at each other. Although this move was Gay's idea, the rabbi has already privately told us he would never follow it through. I wonder what Gay's thinking. I hate that we're reduced to deceit.

My father digests the cemetery information, but this is not his focus. He looks at me and studies my face for a few moments. Slowly he asks, "Would you feel guilty if I killed myself? Would you think it was because I didn't love you?" The rabbi shifts uncomfortably and I feel my husband's arm gently on mine.

"Dad, I'd know it wasn't because you didn't love me. I know you love me. And I don't want you to suffer or be in pain. None of us do. We didn't argue with you when you chose to go off dialysis. We didn't argue with you when you decided to go back on. We all agreed it was your decision and we'd support you no matter what. And we have, haven't we? But to actively kill yourself...yes, it would make us feel terrible. I would know that you loved me, but I would still feel terrible."

"You're concerned with living your life as a Jew," my husband reminds him, "and as Jews we always choose life. It's not your business to decide when and how. That's God's business. He decides. We choose life."

Dad sits back and pauses quietly. The Rabbi deflates. He doesn't like my husband stealing his moment. He starts to say something and thinks better of it. I see him looking with longing at the front door.

"This I don't want. I want you to know I love you. I don't want you to have any question. I won't do it." His mind has clearly shifted and he frowns. "What about dialysis? Is it against the Jewish Law for me to go off dialysis?"

The rabbi falters. "Do you want to go off dialysis?"

"I want to know, what is the Jewish rule here?"

In this moment I find myself wishing we'd all let him be. I know him too well. He's afraid now that he'll be doing something wrong by going off dialysis even though he has no desire to stay on. In his confusion, he doesn't see the difference between actively killing himself and removing himself from extreme measures. At this point, he's sorry he ever went back.

"Dad," I try, "dialysis is up to you. We just don't want you hurting yourself." Hurting himself. What, after all, is the difference? Ingesting poison or allowing his body to become poisonous? Rabbi Glick is silent. My father fires a well-aimed missile at him.

"So, Rabbi, I understand they won't be renewing your contract in the fall."

To his credit, the rabbi barely misses a beat. Only the slight nuances of color drained from his face give any indication that my father has hit his target.

"Yes, Dr. Mitnick, this is true. I doubt very much they'll be renewing my contract." The rabbi sits back with a sigh. My father grunts. He's not the only one dying here, and if only for a moment, that knowledge brings him some sense of satisfaction.

* * *

The Rabbi is in for a penny, in for a pound. My father is back in the convalescent center, after firing one aid after another, and Rabbi Glick visits him regularly. I wonder what they talk about since my father doesn't like him or particularly respect him.

I find out exactly what they're discussing as a result of my father's psychiatric exam. Gay and I think there's some dementia, along with depression and anxiety, and we think he'd be more comfortable with medication. We request a psychiatric evaluation. Miraculously, no one objects to this but Rabbi Glick. He calls me.

"Why do you think your father needs a psychiatrist? He's as sane as I am." I decide it's best not to comment on that. Instead I make the mistake of defending myself.

"Dad's depressed and anxious. Wouldn't you be if you were in his shoes?"

"The doc says you think he might have some dementia."

"He might."

"What makes you think so?"

"He called my clinic so often that we had to take his phone away. He kept calling collect and my secretary didn't know what to do. She kept accepting the charges and telling him I'd call him back. But he'd call back five minutes later. He had no idea he'd just called."

"Your father's a bit impatient," the rabbi offers.

"Yes, but he's not an idiot. He wouldn't call my office like that. He genuinely doesn't remember making the calls."

"Well, he certainly sounds lucid on the stock market."

"What are you talking about?"

"He gives me tips. He says, 'Rabbi, you aren't going to make any money being a rabbi. Obviously, you didn't make any as a lawyer. Let me give you some advice.' And then he tells me how to invest."

The psychiatric assessment differs from Rabbi Glick's. Dad's given a medication cocktail which does lessen his anxiety. Happily, he continues as financial advisor to the rabbi, so he is unaware of any changes. I never tell Rabbi Glick that my father can tell stories from years ago with accuracy but doesn't remember much about what he's had for lunch. If he's visiting my father for his own financial gain, he's going to get what he deserves.

Dad goes back and forth about his dialysis. One day I receive a call from the convalescent center that he's told them he doesn't want to go today. Please come tomorrow. I tell them to let him do whatever he wants. Naturally, I hear from Rabbi Glick.

"Why did you take your father off dialysis?"

"We didn't take him off. He took himself off. For all I know, he'll be back on tomorrow."

"You have to talk to him."

"What do you mean?"

"You have to insist that he stay on."

"Rabbi, it's up to him."

"You're the one saying he's not competent."

"And you're the one saying he is."

"It's against Jewish law. And you'll be killing him."

"Rabbi, no disrespect intended, but we've checked on the Jewish law. This is his decision. He only went back on it in the first place because he thought you'd refuse to bury him next to my mother. We've told him that isn't true. He's confused, but if he's telling the doctor he doesn't want dialysis—

"He told me yesterday he does."

"Because he thinks you won't bury him next to my mother. You don't understand. He gets something in his head and because of the dementia, it's hard for him to get it out."

"How can you deny your own father his life?"

At this point, I've been patient long enough. I take a deep breath.

"Rabbi Glick, you are overstepping your bounds. This is none of your business. I thank you for your concern, but you are misinformed. Good-bye."

He's still talking when I place the phone back into the receiver. I'm shaking when my husband comes to find me. It's Christmas and we're at his brother's house.

"What's wrong?"

"I just hung up on a rabbi. Is that a sin?"

"Not if it was Rabbi Glick."

"It was."

"Do you want me to call him back and talk to him?"

"It might be a good idea, before he calls the police and has me arrested for murder." Arthur laughs.

"It's not funny."

"Yes, it is."

"Maybe I'll think so in a few years."

I give Arthur the rabbi's phone number and leave him alone to make the call. As I close the door behind me, I find myself humming a tune. I laugh when I realize that it's the theme song from Mash. *Suicide is painless*—-.

# [25]

# 353 DALEY STREET

All of Philadelphia appears to be under construction, but 353 Daly Street stands exactly as it did as far back as I can remember it in 1954. The only difference I notice when I enter the house is that the large step at the bottom of the stairway where I sat with my cousins waiting for our interviews with Bubbe is gone. At first I wonder if I have remembered it differently, but my Aunt Ruthie sees my eyes wander there and hesitate.

"Yes, we had the bottom step removed to make the room bigger. Does the house look the same to you?"

"Yes, it's exactly the way I remembered it." And sadly, it is.

As soon as the door is closed behind me, all daylight is shut out along with it. Aunt Ruthie, once a great beauty, now lumbers along with her oxygen, straining for the next breath to carry her heavy frame to the couch. She walks with a four-prong cane. In the center of the room sits a commode, astonishing only in the prominence of its location.

Aunt Ruthie proves to be as sharp as ever. She sees me take in the commode as quickly as she's noted my observation of the missing stair. She has no way of knowing that the memory this is evoking is her own mother forty-five years ago. Most likely, when she looks at me, she sees her brother, Nathan, and feels him judging her.

"You know," she says, "my good friend, my neighbor, she came in here and she says to me, 'Ruth, why do have that commode in the middle of the room? Can't you move it to the side somewhere out of sight?' I told her, I said look, this is my house now, I can put my commode anywhere I want. Anyway,—" and this is addressed to me— "I don't do anything nasty in there. I do that in the back." She flicks her still regal head in the direction of the location of what I suppose to be a second commode, as the only bathroom in the house is located at the top of a narrow staircase.

"It must be hard for you to get up the stairs now." I'm having trouble picturing her being able to get up the stairs at all.

"Oh, I'm used to it," she smiles, and the twinkle in her eye and determination in her glance remind me of my father. It is a sweet memory.

"You looked so much like my Dad when you said that. I used to watch him climbing the stairs and think, what determination."

"We're tough," she admits and laughs. "Come on," she wills herself up from the couch, "first you'll eat and then I'll answer your questions. But I'm going to tell you right now, my mother never would have gone back to Russia. The terrible torture she suffered there! She had to swallow her jewelry and then get it back out of her own shit, excuse my crudeness. The stories she told. It was a horrible life, and she never would have gone back there." I've already told her on the phone that the documents we have say something different, that in fact Sophie did return to Russia, so I don't belabor the point.

Aunt Ruthie plods heavily through the narrow space leading into the dining area and the kitchen beyond. Heavy dark furniture piled high with odd assortments of bric-a-brac line the walls on either side, producing a tunnel effect. I perform a hopscotch technique behind her to avoid stepping on her oxygen cord. I fail miserably and almost break my neck tripping over it. Aunt Ruthie laughs good-naturedly.

"The damn thing is a pain in the neck, isn't it? But I get around pretty good."

"You do." And my admiration is sincere. Negotiating one's way around this house would not be easy under the best of circumstances.

Ruthie opens a huge refrigerator, and it looks like she's been cooking for a week.

"Do you like kasha vanishkas?"

"Oh, you still make it? I love it."

"And there's meat and string beans and broccoli. Make yourself a plate and stick it in the microwave." The microwave is the only indication that we are about to enter the 21st century. "We've had our lunch. Later, we'll all sit down and have dinner." Again she instantly reads my expression.

"You are staying for dinner, aren't you?"

I gulp and nod, feeling about five years old again. It's one more meal than I've planned on, and after all, it has been ten years. Aunt Ruthie does not wait too long to comment on this fact.

"So, you have to be writing a book to come and see me?"

"I've been talking about coming to see you for a long time." And that part at least is true. However, there is no denying the fact that it has taken this book to physically get me there.

"I brought you something." I pull a package out of my backpack, a hand-painted gefilte fish plate I purchased earlier that day in the Jewish Museum.

Aunt Ruthie opens it with little enthusiasm. She eyes the plate with even less. "I don't eat gefilte fish, except on the holiday."

"Oh," I sigh, defeated by time itself. "I remember that you always had gefilte fish."

"I'll use it for something." Aunt Ruthie sets it on the floor and not wanting to risk any more assaults on my gift-giving ego, I refrain from asking for what.

"What do you want to know?"

"What was Sophie like?"

"My mother?"

"Yes, what kind of person was she?"

"Oh, she was smart and funny. You know, she used to read the cards, tell the future like a gypsy. The neighbors would come around and she would help them with their problems and tell their fortunes. Oh yeah, people came from all around the neighborhood to ask her advice. The gentiles came, too. She knew a lot of people. She had a lot of friends."

"Did she speak English?"

"Yeah, she spoke English. I mean, not like you and me, but she could make herself understood. And she could write her name in English. She was so proud of that. She went to school to learn how to write her name, but my father put a stop to that."

"Why, was he jealous?" I knew that my grandfather had not been able to sign his name in English. His inability to speak English had cost him work.

"Yeah, he was jealous, jealous of all those good-looking men who went to the school. He went one time, saw all those handsome men, and he dragged her home with him. That was the end of her English lessons."

"Funny, I don't think I ever heard her utter a single word in English. When we were here, she only spoke Yiddish. Why didn't she speak in English to us?"

"Well, that was your fault."

I'm silenced by this statement in a way that I have not been silenced since my father's death. It's not possible for me to comprehend how this could have been my fault. It occurs to me once again that she is seeing my father and that the blame is directed at him. I will never know the truth about Sophie. And what would that truth be even if Sophie were alive now to tell it? A patchwork of memory, sewn together roughly, pieces repeated, overlapping, missing, torn into fragments of unfastened threads.

Now she sits framed forever in a photographic collage. My sister has taken an old photo of her and placed it in a collage with her Russian family. My great Uncle Ben has not yet been murdered in the pogrom. Then there is this Sophie I have never seen, Benevolent Sophie, who greets all her neighbors from behind her crystal ball. Lastly, there is Bubbe Sophie. She is the great enigma. This Sophie only has meaning through my father's interpretations.

"Do you remember your father?" I ask.

"Yes. I was seven when he died."

"My father took it pretty hard. He told me about coming home to find a black ribbon on the door."

"I don't know about that, but he took it hard all right. He had a nervous breakdown and had to go to the hospital."

"I did hear that from Pudgie. He also said Dad was on medication."

"He was a mess. He had to walk with a cane. Your poor Uncle Larry only had six months to go in law school. He took a job at Bud's working with dangerous electrical equipment to support the family. He never did go back."

"I always heard it was Dad who supported the family."

"He did, but he couldn't work after the breakdown. Larry was next in line. Then he got married and had kids and opened the auto parts store. It was hard on my brother, your father, that is. He didn't get along too well with my mother and she depended on him for everything. When my father died, I guess he wanted to get the hell away from all of us. And Bobby was a handful. My mother threw a fork at him once."

"What do you remember of Dora?"

"Ah, Aunt Dora, now there was a real queen. She bought your father and Uncle Larry clothes when they were kids. When your father finished medical school, she bought him a car and gave him the money to set himself up in practice. She got my parents out of Russia."

"Did your mother talk about her parents?"

"Oh, yes. She wrote to them all the time. She was always afraid we'd leave her like she left her parents. So you see, we didn't get very far." I don't comment that Ruthie's two youngest sons still live with her and haven't gotten far either.

"And the rest of the family?"

"The letters stopped coming during the war. Your Aunt Rosie tried to contact them, but everything came back 'no longer at this address,' or something like that. We never heard from any of them again. Some cousins went to South America."

"Yes, I know."

"I never knew them. I was too young."

"How did my mother fit in with your family?"

"Oh, we all loved Jeannette. She wasn't stuck up like your father. He'd come in here like he owned us. She liked coming here. When they were dating, they came for dinner every Friday night. She was good to my mother. She made her a coat."

"I never heard that story."

"We all thought she was too good for your father. He'd come in here and tell my kids what to do, how to live their lives, as if they didn't have parents. As if our lives weren't good enough for him."

I eat lunch. It's seven courses of Jewish and Russian dishes. I do my best, even though I'm full after the chicken soup. Aunt Ruthie tells me more about her life, her kids (I still can't tell them apart) and her favorite television programs. She points out various *chachkis*, where she got them or who gave them to her. My fishplate is still on the floor. It's somewhere between the Johnny Walker Red sign and the Niagara Falls pillow.

I've just finished doing the dishes for Aunt Ruthie over much protest when the two sons who are living with her come in the door. She introduces us and we shake hands like strangers which in fact we are. They sit next to each other on the couch and stare at me.

"She ain't stuck up like your Uncle Nathan," Aunt Ruthie says. If this is to relax them, it fails. I wonder if I can keep this up through dinner. I make an effort.

"I guess my Dad gave you a hard time."

"Yeah. He used to lecture us about education." One cousin answers for both. Again, I have no idea which one.

"He used to lecture me about education, too."

"Then he'd give us some money."

"I remember that. I remember Aunt Rosie telling all the cousins to say thank you to Uncle Nathan. I was embarrassed."

"He'd always tell us what to do with the money, as if five dollars was going to get us a college education."

"He probably expected you to save it. He thought he was doing a good thing."

My cousin softens. He tells me about his life, his marriage, his divorce, moving back in with his mother. My other cousin is silent.

And so it goes through dinner. They are strangers. This is my fault as much as it is theirs. Maybe more mine than theirs.

My cousin insists that I not help with the dinner dishes. I'm relieved as conversation is running short. I excuse myself to use the restroom before going to my hotel for the night. When I come downstairs, I notice that the fish plate is now in a somewhat prominent place on my aunt's sideboard. She's moved it in front of a plastic fish some relative sent her from somewhere in the Caribbean. It's leaning against a pillow her oldest son brought her back from Las Vegas. She doesn't mention the change of venue and neither do I.

I hug my cousins, the silent one, too, and hug and kiss my Aunt Ruthie goodbye. I know it is unlikely I will see her again. I thank her for sharing her stories with me and for the meals.

"Your chicken soup is better than ever."

"Better than your Aunt Rosie's, eh?" She winks at my cousins.

"If she could remember how, she'd still be challenging your soup." I smile sadly. Aunt Rosie is in a nursing home. She has Alzheimer's.

"You could put on a few pounds," she notes. Some things never change.

As I walk down the steps of 353 Daily Street for the last time, Aunt Rosie calls after me.

"Thanks for the fish plate."

# [26]

# UNVEILING

We choose mid-October for my father's unveiling. It's more than six months and just short of a year since his burial in January of 1997, well within the time allowed for this Jewish informal ceremony that places the stone and ends the official period of mourning.

Gay and Rob and Arthur and I pull into the empty parking lot of the Jewish Cemetery. The wind picks up just enough to set a kaleidoscope of leaves dancing across the lonely grounds, forming shifting bouquets in between and around the monuments. The only other sounds of life come from the gulls circling, squawking, then leaving in small groups in the hope of better breakfast pickings elsewhere.

We pull up our collars and reach for our gloves. It's not nearly as cold as the day we buried him, when one of the men from the *minyan* wrapped Gay and me in blankets from his car to fend off the blasts of the coldest day of that year. The chill of autumn is clearly here, but the sun is strong and promises a warmer afternoon.

It's easy to find their stones, side by side, the only Mitnicks buried here. They're close to the entrance. My mother's stone is naked, her unveiling over eleven years ago; my father's is covered in the veil netting we are about to remove.

I tap my sister on the shoulder. "Do you remember Mom's unveiling?"

"No," she says. "I think there were more people."

"There had to have been," Rob chimes in. "Looks like it's just the four of us."

"Dad had the rabbi, even though it wasn't necessary. But Gay, you don't remember removing the veil?"

"No. I don't remember too much about it except that the rabbi went on and on about how Mother had become religious and studied torah with him. Did you know about that?"

"No, not really. Sometimes I was surprised to see some of the books she was reading, and I knew she went to a few of his classes. I found The Jewish Book Of Why in her things and took it home. She didn't say too much about it." I felt sad that she hadn't shared that with me. Was she afraid I'd make fun of her or think her foolish? I hoped that wasn't it.

I lean into Arthur. "Do you remember it?"

He shakes his head no. "I wasn't around then."

"I didn't know what I was supposed to do. I remember Dad handing us a pair of scissors or a knife—I don't know—and I just stood there. I think I handed it to you, Gay, and then you handed it back to me. I was shocked. I'd never been to an unveiling. Then Dad and the rabbi both blurted out to cut it off. And Dad, like I was drowning in the swimming pool all over again, raised his voice, 'Cut it off. Hurry up, will you? Leave some for Gay.' It was like we were kids again, unwrapping some macabre present from weird Uncle Morris."

Gay laughs. "Fortunately for me, I never got any of those."

"Was that the uncle who sent you the dirty hairbrush?" Arthur asks.

"Yes. Everyone said he was a horrible man, but he was always kind to me."

"Should we wait and see if anyone else is coming?" Rob asks. He's the most practical among us. "Do you think Jack might show up?"

"We could wait a few more minutes," I say. "I did let him know about it."

No one says anything. Jack was a good friend to my father. In fact, he was the son my father always wished he'd had. But we have a day that the four of us have planned to remember our father, and I don't think any of us wants Jack along. It's not that we don't like him. We actually have come to like him. But we want to be alone with our own Dad stories today.

We give it another ten minutes before Rob says, "I think we should start." We nod in agreement. This time when I hand Gay the scissors, she cuts away at the material. When she is halfway through, she hands the scissors back to me to complete the job. As if we'd planned it, we both touch the stone and say, "Bye Dad."

"Oh no, we forgot to bring stones." There is only grass and pavement here and even though I know it is hopeless, I look around to find some; then I have a brainstorm. "No, let's go collect the stones from Horseneck Beach. We'll stop back here and put some on each of their graves. He'd love that."

"Great idea," Gay hugs me. "I thought we'd go there anyway."

"Oh, and we can stop at his favorite clam dig on the way back and have clams and lobster."

Arthur looks at me with a mischievous smile. "And he was on the kosher side of the family?"

"How about topping it off with Gulf Hill Farms ice cream?" My sister and I clasp our hands together.

"A perfect unveiling for Nathan," Rob smiles.

We pick up the discarded netting and head back to the car. I read the headstones of the parents of various friends and the friends of my parents as we pass by. If my sister remembers or notices them, she doesn't say. She's holding Rob's hand and smiling at him. These are not moments I ever wish to break.

We climb back into the rental car and head for Horseneck.

"Do you think there was ever a beach Dad loved more than Horseneck?" I ask.

"Not since we've known him," Gay responds.

We're quiet for the rest of the drive. I fall into memories of so many times at Horseneck. Some of these include my mother, wrapped up like a nun or a Muslim woman to protect herself from the sun. She was prone to develop skin cancers but never refused my father's wish for a family day at the beach. I guess Gay's thoughts were running along the same lines, although she could have been remembering the bits of sand that always seemed to insert themselves into our tuna fish sandwiches or the iced lemonade Mom always made.

The beach was deserted. Ours was the only car in the parking lot. We made our way slowly to the sand, not quite the way we'd run there as kids.

As if we were searching for diamonds, we sought out the best stones we could find, sifting the sand through our fingers in silence, putting them into our jacket pockets only after washing them off in the surf to make sure they were perfect, exactly the ones we wanted, the ones we imagine our parents would have preferred.

As if we have all the time in the world, we make our way back to the car and the parking lot, stopping several times to look out on the vast ocean we may not see again for some time. The ocean is different here than anywhere else in the world. We grew up on the edge of this Atlantic, as if it were our mother's milk.

Gay and I hesitate as the men get into the car. We hold hands as we have done so many times in our lives. These are the last of these particular rituals we will share, although we know there are inevitably more in store for us in our fragile lives. We hug each other tightly and stay together for a few precious moments before we release each other and head for the car.

The fried clams are as good as I remember them. The hot sauce falls short, but the tartar sauce does not. The cows are still being milked at Gulf Hill Farms. The pistachio ice cream is even better than I remembered.

We are tired and bordering on cranky when we have trouble finding the cemetery again. Rob always has to drive and I am always nauseous riding in the back seat. We stop at a gas station and ask for directions. We've made a left turn instead of a right and it takes another fifteen minutes to correct this. I wonder if Gay is reminded of riding with our father who resisted ever asking for directions while my mother poured over maps similar to the ones she used to draw prior to her aneurism but after her brain bleed had great difficulty in reading. Given the developing fatigue by everyone in the car, I don't ask.

The Jewish cemetery is as empty as it was on our earlier trip. I ask Gay, "Do you think anyone ever visits these graves?"

"Maybe," she says, "if they never escaped from New Bedford."

"It actually seems a pretty town now that I'm an adult," I comment.

"And you live in New York City," she adds, laughing. "And you're not living with our parents."

Was it really so bad, I wonder? It's hard to know. Memory. It's a bit like myopia.

We place our stones on the graves, step back and have a last look. Nathan Mitnick. Jeannette Berg Mitnick. Now only existing in our minds and in our photographs, along with their parents and their grandparents before them.

We decide to pass on dinner. The fried clams and ice cream aren't sitting so well in any of our stomachs. And there is a deep sadness in each of us. It is unlikely that we will ever be in New Bedford together again, all four of us. It is finished. There are only cold stones left standing of our lives in this place.

We drive back to the nondescript motel where we are staying, the house having been long sold to a young woman for a price that would have made my father shudder. Arthur was the only one to advise waiting. He was right. The house did triple in value over the next few years.

Even though it is only 4:00pm, we say goodnight and good-bye and go off to our separate rooms. There are no words left to say. We will drive back to New York the next day. Gay and Rob will leave for Providence very early in the morning to drop off their rental car and fly home to Denver.

Arthur and I drive by the house the next morning. The young, divorced, single mother who lives there now has painted the front door purple and there is a welcome sign with her family name. The swinging sign that has always hung from the side of the house, announcing my father's office and reading Dr. Nathan Mitnick, M.D. has never been removed. He would have liked that. He had hoped that I would live there, see my patients in his office, that not too much would have to change.

"Dad would have hated the purple door," I tell Arthur.

"And the welcome sign," Arthur smiles. "But she hasn't taken down his office sign."

"I noticed that. But she will, or someone else will one of these days. I don't think I want to come back here again. I want to remember it as it was."

And so in a funny way, I am my father's daughter, even if I do open windows and adjust the seats. Or perhaps it is just natural, human, to want to hang on to the lives we've created, to the sign that says I made it out of the shtetl. I made it from an osteopath to an MD. In reality, this was no small feat.

I adjust the seat way back in the Cadillac my father has given us when he finally stopped driving. He said he didn't want us to have to rent a car every time we came to see him. But there is more to it than that. I think he must have known that every time I would hear the sound of the windshield wipers, a very particular sound in this car, I would think of him. He would always be in this car with me, driving me somewhere in the rain.

# APPENDIX A

Guide to Family Names and Relationships*
Ukraine, (formally part of Russia) 1909—Philadelphia, 1930's

Nathan Mitnick: my father—born 1905—died 1997

Son of Zlateh (Sophie) Schulman Mitnick
Son of Yosef (Louis/Joseph) Mitnick
Brother to Lazarus (Larry) Mitnick, Rosie Mitnick Frank, Bobby Mitnick, Ruthie Mitnick Cantor
Husband of Jeannette Berg Mitnick
Father of Gay and Phyllis Mitnick

Zlateh (Sophie) Schulman Mitnick
Daughter of
Sister of Benny Schulman
Wife of Yosef (Joseph) Mitnick
Mother of Nathan and Lazarus (Larry), Rosie, Bobby and Ruthie

Benny Schulman:
Brother of Zlateh (Sophie)
Brother-in-law of Yosef (Joseph)

Yitzhak:
Brother of Yosef (Joseph) Mitnick
Dora: Sister of Yosef (Joseph)

*Customs inspectors often changed Yiddish and Russia names when immigrants entered the United States. Thus Zlateh became Sophie and Lazarus became Larry. This also happened for ease of spelling and pronunciation. There is still some confusion as to whether the original family name was Mitnick or Mednick, as both spellings appear in the original documents.

CPSIA information can be obtained
at www.ICGtesting.com
Printed in the USA
FSHW010843311019
63544FS